HOME
REPAIRS
MADE
EASY

Written by
DICK DEMSKE

Illustrated by
JAMES E. BARRY

Editor-in Chief
DONALD D. WOLF

Design, Layout
and Production
MARGOT L. WOLF

HOME REPAIRS MADE EASY

Belair PUBLISHING COMPANY

Library of Congress Catalog Card Number: 79-84283
International Standard Book Number: 0-8326-2240-0

Introduction

Welcome to the club!

It is not exactly an exclusive club. Its membership includes virtually everyone who owns a home or lives in an apartment in this country and probably in the world. All you need do to join is pick up a hammer or screwdriver or bathroom plunger and perform one of the small but essential maintenance tasks associated with modern living—repair a squeaking floor, free a stuck window, open a clogged drain, replace a worn washer or fuse. For, unless you have a full staff of servants to deal with such mundane matters, you will probably end up doing at least most of them yourself, for reasons economic, expedient, and essential.

Not everyone is able to perform all necessary home repairs himself or herself. Therefore we have attempted to compile in this book those jobs which should pose no major problems for the average do-it-yourselfer with reasonable dexterity.

Every effort has been made to ensure the accuracy, reliability, and up-to-dateness of the information and instructions in this book. We are not infallible, however—and neither are you. We cannot guarantee that there are no human or typographical errors herein, nor can we guarantee that you will not err in following our directions. We only hope that, if this happens, it will not lessen the feeling of satisfaction you receive from doing-it-yourself.

DONALD D. WOLF

Contents

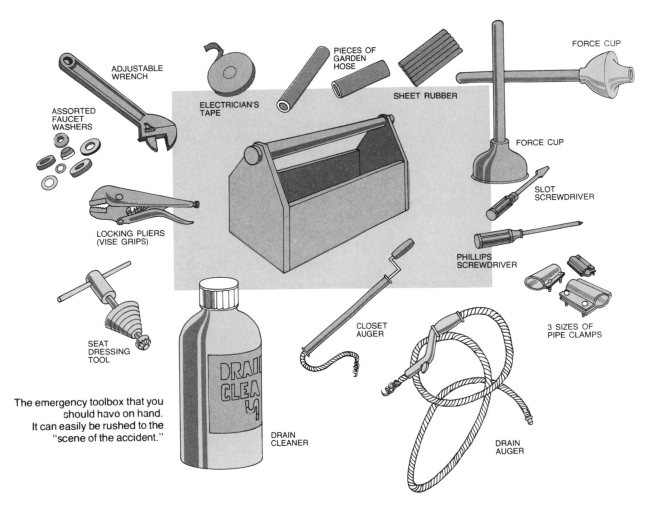

ADJUSTABLE WRENCH

ASSORTED FAUCET WASHERS

ELECTRICIAN'S TAPE

PIECES OF GARDEN HOSE

SHEET RUBBER

FORCE CUP

FORCE CUP

LOCKING PLIERS (VISE GRIPS)

SLOT SCREWDRIVER

PHILLIPS SCREWDRIVER

3 SIZES OF PIPE CLAMPS

SEAT DRESSING TOOL

CLOSET AUGER

DRAIN CLEANER

DRAIN AUGER

The emergency toolbox that you should have on hand. It can easily be rushed to the "scene of the accident."

THE EMERGENCY TOOLBOX

If you have ever tried to loosen a screw with a pocketknife, or ruined a brass nut by mangling it with pliers, you know the importance of using the right tool for the job. Plumbing, just like any other trade, requires the use of specific tools—some of them designed for only a single function. You should be familiar with these so that, when the time comes, you will know what to use where.

That does not mean that you should head for the hardware store with a blank check in your wallet. Not at all. Other than a few tools that you should have on hand for emergencies, you should buy tools only as you need them. Too many do-it-yourselfers look on the hardware store as a child looks at the candy store—they want everything in sight. As a result, their workshops become displays of seldom-if-ever-used tools that would be more suitable for plumbing an in terplanetary rocket than a household system. Resist the impulse to buy.

The wise homeowner is prepared for plumbing problems before they occur. You don't know when the sink will become clogged or the toilet will overflow, and you will want to be able to react quickly to such household crises. How you should react is detailed on pp.11-29 and 243. But you should have an emergency toolbox on hand that you can rush to the scene of the accident.

You probably already have many of the tools needed for such a toolbox. For leaky faucets, these will be screwdrivers (including Phillips-head, if your faucet handles are held on by this type of screw), an adjustable wrench, locking pliers, electrician's tape, and a supply of faucet washers in assorted sizes (you can buy such an assortment at any hardware store). You might also want to purchase a seat-dressing tool (cost: about a dollar) in case a new washer doesn't stop the leak.

To attack clogged drains, keep drain cleaner—either liquid or dry type—near the kitchen sink. If the cleaner doesn't do the job, you should have the familiar "plumber's friend" or force cup—a rubber suction cup on the end of a wood handle. One type has a flat bottom and is intended primarily for sinks. The ball-type plunger, with a rounded bottom rather than a flat opening, is especially effective for unclog-

ging toilets. On most of these the rounded bottom can be turned up for use in unclogging sinks. A drain auger or "snake"—spring steel or coiled wire with a small metal handle—will be needed to remove some particularly stubborn obstructions in drainage pipes. A closet auger is specially designed for unclogging toilets; a drain auger can also be used, but care must be taken not to damage the vitreous china finish.

You may never have occasion to use them, but it's a good idea to have a couple of pipe clamps of various sizes (⅜-inch, ½-inch, ¾-inch), along with some small pieces of sheet rubber or short lengths of garden hose. If a pipe ever springs a leak these items will let you make a quick, although temporary, repair.

With your emergency toolbox packed and ready, you should be able to handle most common plumbing problems.

As you become more familiar with your household plumbing system, you may wish to undertake projects more ambitious than simple repairs—installing new fixtures, perhaps, or even adding a bathroom. Your collection of tools will grow apace. Just remember to buy them only as you need them.

LEAKY FAUCETS—NOISY FAUCETS

The ceaseless "drip... drip... drip" of a leaky faucet is a close cousin to the ancient water torture, causing daytime aggravation and nighttime insomnia. More than that, it is water—and therefore dollars—down the drain. Your water bill doesn't distinguish between what you use for drinking, cooking, washing, laundering, and the like and that which trickles away without serving you in any way. Dripping water can also stain a sink or lavatory and eventually wear away the finish of the fixture, too. It's better to make the repair as soon as the problem is noticed.

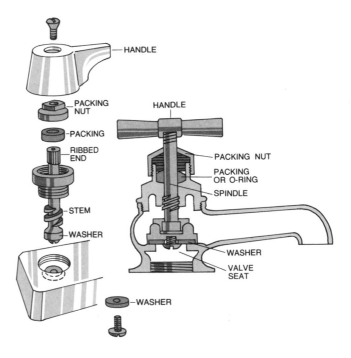

First shut off the water supply at the supply stop in the line below the faucet. If there is no supply stop, turn off the water at some point farther back in the line. If necessary, turn off the valve where the water enters your house.

On some faucets, the handle covers the packing nut. It must be removed to give access to the nut. On other faucets, the packing nut is exposed. In the latter case, wrap the nut with tape or rags to protect the chrome finish. Remove the packing nut by turning it counterclockwise with an open-end wrench or monkey wrench.

Remove the faucet stem or spindle (you may have to replace the handle to turn it out). Check the washer at its lower end. If the washer appears worn or damaged, carefully remove the screw that holds it in place and take out the washer (if necessary, apply penetrating oil to loosen the screw). Replace with a new washer of the correct size. If the rim around the stem bottom is intact, use either a Type A or a Type B washer. If the rim is damaged, file it away completely and install a Type C washer.

Shine a flashlight down inside the faucet body and check the seat to make sure it is smooth and free of nicks. If the seat is damaged or rough, grind it down with a dressing tool. There are various types of such tools (all inexpensive), and all are used in much the same way. Clamp the tool on the faucet (some types of dressing tools are held in place by the packing nut or bonnet) and turn the stem by the T-handle; a fluted grinder at the lower end of the stem reconditions the seat.

On many faucets, badly worn seats can be replaced. Remove the old one (usually an Allen wrench does the job), and screw a new one of the correct size in its place.

With the seat reconditioned and a new washer in place, reassemble the faucet. If a leak continues around the stem, remove the handle and packing nut or bonnet and examine the O-ring or packing around the stem. If it is worn away or damaged, replace with the proper new parts.

1. Remove packing nut.

2. Remove stem.

—WASHER

3. Remove old washer.

4. Replace washer.

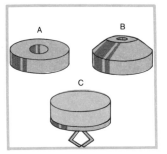

A   B

C

5. Types of washers.

6. File damaged rim.

7. Use of seat-grinder.

8. O-ring or packing replacement.

9. Recessed bath faucet removal.

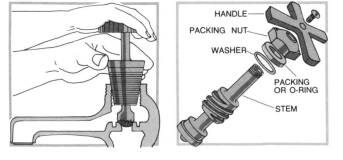

HANDLE—

PACKING NUT—

WASHER—

PACKING
OR O-RING

STEM

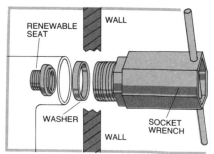

RENEWABLE
SEAT

WASHER

WALL

WALL

SOCKET
WRENCH

On some types of bath faucets, the bonnet holding the stem in place is recessed in the wall. You will need a socket wrench with an extension to remove it for repair and replacement of the washer. Otherwise, the procedure is the same as above.

The design and construction of noncompression (single-control mixer) faucets vary greatly, and so do their repair procedures. Most manufacturers of these faucets include repair instructions along with installation instructions. The best advice is to file away this repair sheet for future reference.

Most problems with noncompression faucets occur when parts wear out. Replacement of the old parts is the only real remedy.

●

A faucet that squeals or chatters when you turn it on or off is just as annoying as a leaky one. Take it apart as above, and make sure that the faucet washer is tightly screwed to the stem. If the washer is worn, replace it, even though the faucet may not be leaking. If the stem (after being screwed back into the faucet) can be moved up and down, the threads are probably worn and the stem should be replaced. Occasionally a design deficiency will cause faucets to chatter and whistle. A new faucet is the only cure.

1. Loosen packing nut.

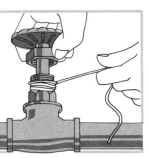

2. New packing.

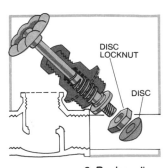

DISC
LOCKNUT

DISC

3. Replace disc.

LEAKY VALVES

The various types of valves are shown on p. 14. With gate and globe valves, the most common problem is leakage around the stem. To repair, first shut off the water at another valve between the leaking unit and the water source, or at the main house intake. With an adjustable or open-end wrench, loosen the packing nut. Hold a bucket beneath the valve to catch the water remaining in the line, then remove the packing nut. Remove the old packing and wrap new packing around the stem, then replace the packing nut.

When a gate valve does not do its job of regulating or closing off the flow of water through a line, it usually indicates either an obstruction or damage in the valve seat that prevents the valve wedge from closing properly. It may also mean wear of either the wedge or the seat. Whatever the cause, the entire valve should be replaced.

Globe valve repairs are similar to faucet repairs. After removing the packing nut, screw the stem out of the valve body. Inspect the disc or washer at the bottom of the stem. If it is worn or damaged, unscrew the locknut that holds it in place and replace it with a new one.

Ground key valves may become grooved or worn by tiny particles in the water rubbing against the metal, allowing the water

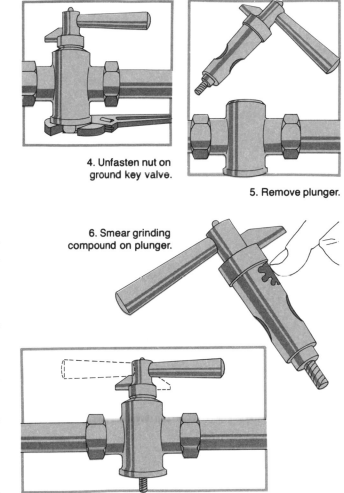

4. Unfasten nut on ground key valve.

5. Remove plunger.

6. Smear grinding compound on plunger.

7. Replace, rotate plunger back and forth.

to leak through. The surfaces must be re-polished. Shut off the water supply and unfasten the nut or screw at the bottom of the valve that holds the plunger in place. Pull out the plunger. Smear a small amount of valve-grinding compound on the sides of the plunger and replace it in its sleeve. Ro-tate the plunger back and forth to wear the two surfaces smooth, forming a leakproof joint. Remove the plunger and wipe it clean. Wipe clean the inside of the sleeve, then reassemble the valve. If the parts are too badly worn to respond to this treatment, replace the valve.

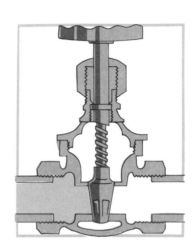

Cutaway: gate valve open.

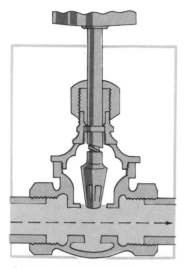

Cutaway: globe valve open.

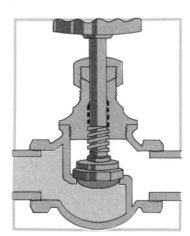

Cutaway: gate valve closed.

Cutaway: globe valve closed.

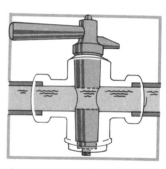

Cutaway: ground keyvalve open.

Cutaway: ground keyvalve closed.

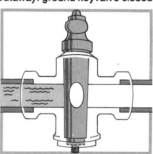

TOILET TANK TROUBLES

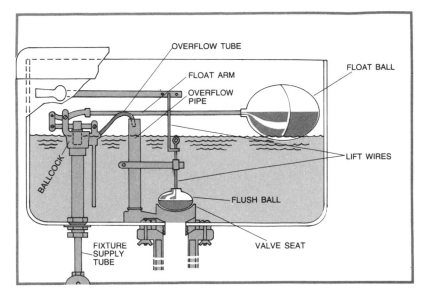

Cross section of toilet tank.

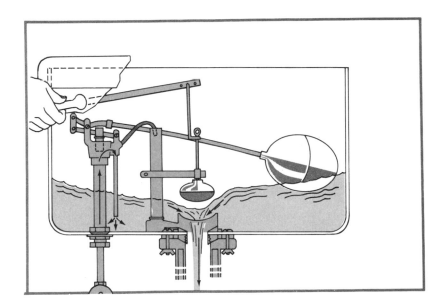

Cross section showing flushing action.

The flush mechanism inside a toilet tank may seem to the uninitiated as mysterious and complex as the workings of a space-vehicle computer, but it is really quite simple. Basically, it is made up of two assemblies: a ballcock, which regulates the filling of the tank, and a flush valve, which releases water from the tank to the toilet bowl and then shuts off this flow. Individual parts of each assembly may wear out and

Home Repairs Made Easy

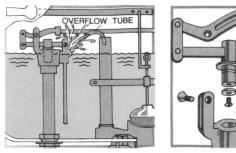

Leak at overflow tube; water spurting out.

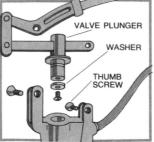

Leak at plunger stem; replace washer.

need replacement; sooner or later the entire assembly or assemblies will have to be replaced.

Sometimes when a toilet is flushed, a fine spray of water shoots up against the top of the tank, often leaking out around the cover. Check the overflow tube on the ballcock

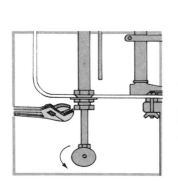

1. Remove fixture supply tube.

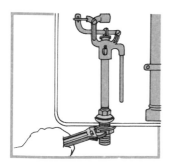

2. Remove old ballcock.

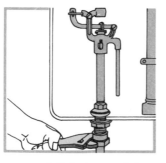

3. Install new ballcock.

4. Refasten supply line.

to see if it has a hole or is split. If so, replace the tube (usually plastic). There could also be a faulty or damaged connection between the overflow tube and the ballcock. If this is the case, correct the connection.

If the toilet tank overfills, check for a worn washer on the bottom of the ballcock plunger stem and replace if necessary. Also, check to make sure that the operating levers are moving freely. If they are frozen tight and you cannot free them, replace the entire ballcock assembly.

When the toilet will not stop running, with water going through the overflow tube, pull up on the float arm (the metal rod between the ballcock and the float ball) to see if this stops the flow. If it does, unscrew the float ball and shake it to tell if there is water inside. If water is present, the float ball has sprung a leak and should be replaced. If the float ball checks out, bend the float arm down slightly to lower the ball. This should stop the water from running. If the flow still persists, turn off the water supply, remove the valve plunger, and replace the washer. If that doesn't stop the leak, the ballcock should be replaced.

Replacing a ballcock is no more difficult than replacing any of its parts, except possibly the float and float rod. First empty the water from the toilet tank. Shut off the water at the supply stop, at some other valve in the line, or at the main house inlet, and then flush the toilet. Place a pail or basin under the supply connection to catch the water that remains in the tank. Unscrew the fixture supply tube and the locknut from the ballcock shank and remove the old assembly.

Remove the locknut from the new ballcock and place the shank through the opening in the tank, with the large rubber washer inside the tank. Tighten the locknut over the shank, then fasten the supply line. Connect the overflow tube in the ballcock and place the other end into the overflow pipe

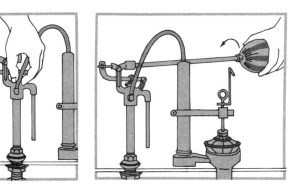

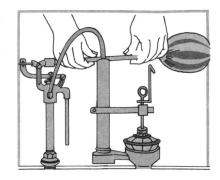

5. Connect
overflow tube.

6. Fasten
float ball.

7. Bend arm
if necessary.

of the flush valve assembly. Screw the float arm into the ballcock assembly and fasten the float ball at the end of the arm. Check to make sure that all connections are tight, then turn on the water, allowing the tank to fill. It may be necessary to adjust the float arm by bending it slightly to permit the tank to fill properly and to keep the arm clear of the overflow pipe and other parts of the mechanism. Be careful, and use both hands when bending the arm; do not damage the threads at either the ballcock end or the float ball end.

Another type of ballcock eliminates the need for the float ball and float arm, thus also eliminating the sources of a lot of toilet troubles. This device works on a different principle than conventional ballcocks (fluid energy), filling the tank faster with less noise. Installation of the floatless ballcock is similar to the installation of the conventional unit (less float arm and float ball).

If the toilet continues to run because the tank fails to refill, the problem is with the flush valve. Check the stopper guide on the overflow pipe to make sure it is aligned correctly so that the stopper ball drops into the center of the valve seat; adjust the guide if necessary. If the stopper ball still does not seat properly, it may be damaged; inspect and replace if necessary. Also check the valve seat, cleaning the surface with very

fine steel wool. If it is nicked or otherwise damaged, replace it.

To replace the flush valve, first shut off the water and empty the tank as above. Remove the old flush valve, lift wires or chain, washer and locknut holding the valve seat in place. Insert the discharge tube of the new valve assembly through the tank bottom. With the overflow pipe positioned, tighten the locknut to lock the discharge tube in place. Center the guide arm on the overflow pipe over the valve seat and tighten it in place. Install lift wires through the guide and the trip arm and screw the flush ball onto the lower lift wire, aligning it to

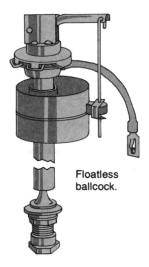

Floatless
ballcock.

1. Replace stopper ball.

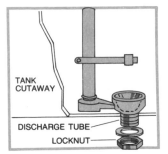

2. Insert discharge tube.

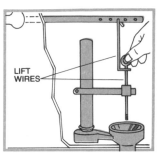

3. Install lift wires.

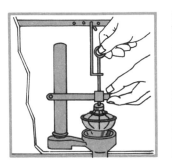

4. Install flush ball.

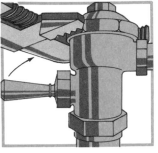

5. Remove cap from flush mechanism.

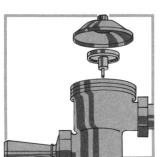

6. Lift out inside cover and valve.

7. Unscrew disc ring.

drop into the exact center of the flush valve seat. (Some flush valves use a chain in place of the lower lift wire; no guide is needed with this type.)

The toilet tank serves as a reservoir for the large amount of water needed for flushing action — more than could be delivered quickly through the ½-inch or even ¾-inch water lines normally used in residential plumbing systems. In some commercial and public buildings and apartment houses, where toilets are located near a main water supply line, such a reservoir is not needed. The much greater capacity of the pipe can deliver enough water directly. Here, a different type of flush valve, usually lever-actuated, is used to regulate the flow. When problems arise, such as continual running of water into the toilet bowl, the fault is somewhere within the flush valve.

The construction and operation of flush valves vary greatly, depending on the manufacturer, but most have certain similari-

8. Insert new washer.

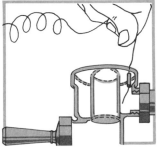

9. Run wire through bypass.

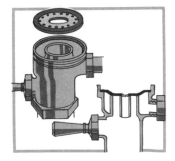

10. Insert new diaphragm.

ties. When troubleshooting such a valve, first shut off the water supply. Some types have a cutoff on the valve body — usually a large screw. Otherwise, close a stop valve in the supply line.

Wrap tape around the cap at the top of the valve to protect the finish, and remove the cap with an open-end or adjustable wrench—do not use a pipe wrench! Lift out the inside cover and valve. Inspect the washer on the valve for signs of wear or damage. If it needs replacement, unscrew the disc ring that holds it in place and pry out the old washer. Insert a new washer and replace the disc ring, screwing it down firmly, but not too tightly.

With the inside cover and valve out, run a fine wire through the bypass hole in the flush valve body. If this is clogged, the water flow into the bowl will not shut off.

Clean the surface of the seat on which the washer rests. Sediment that has collected on the seat may prevent the valve from closing tightly. If the seat is worn or damaged, it should be reground or replaced (see Leaky Faucets, pp. 11-12).

If leakage persists, the rubber diaphragm inside the valve body may be worn or damaged. Unscrew the disc to remove the old diaphragm and replace it, making sure to insert the new diaphragm with the cup down. Screw the disc back in place.

●

A cross-connection is a physical link between the fresh water in your supply system and any waste water. Cross-connections are not always obvious and may exist without your being aware of them. Some examples are a faucet spout that would be under water should the drain stop; a connected water hose left in a bucket, tub, or pool; or a toilet overflow pipe below the water level in the tank. When you spot a potential cross-connection, correct it as soon as possible.

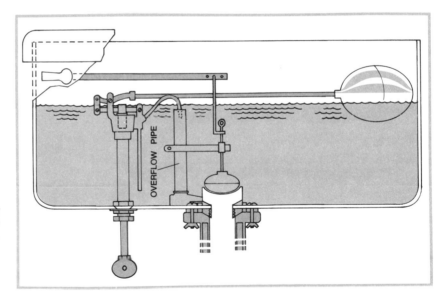

Cross-connection: toilet overflow pipe below the water level in the tank.

OVERFLOW PIPE

CLOGGED TOILETS

When you flush the toilet and the water level in the bowl rises rather than recedes, head for the emergency toolbox fast! The plumber's friend is your first line of defense. Place the plunger over the discharge opening in the toilet bowl and work it vigorously up and down. This should clear the stoppage.

If the plumber's friend doesn't do the job, try the snake, or auger. A closet auger, designed to get the auger wire right down to the blockage, is preferred. You can use a drain auger if that's all you have on hand, but be careful not to scratch the inside of the toilet bowl.

Work the snake into the trap and crank it in one direction until it becomes tight. Pull it back; often it will bring the obstruction up with it. If it doesn't, try again, cranking the snake until it pushes through and clears the stoppage.

If all else fails, remove the toilet from the floor, turn it upside down (placing it on old newspaper), and work the obstruction out through the discharge opening. If it has already passed into the waste line and is stuck there, work it out with the snake.

To remove and reposition the toilet follow the instructions for installing a new toilet (below).

As with all other fixture replacement projects, turn off the water supply before removing an old toilet, either at the fixture supply stop valve or at some other valve in the supply piping. Then flush the toilet, holding down the handle until most of the water drains from the tank. Lift off the tank top and sop up the small amount of water remaining in the tank with rags or a sponge.

Disconnect the supply line at the bottom of the tank (first wrapping the nut with tape to avoid damage if you intend to use the same supply line to the new toilet). If the tank is a separate piece, remove the bolts that hold it to the bowl and lift it off. Some tanks are mounted on wall brackets or screwed to the wall; in that case, disconnect the tank first from the bowl, then from the wall and lift it off.

Toilet bowls are usually held to the floor by two or four bolts, which are concealed

Use of plunger (left) and working auger into trap (right).

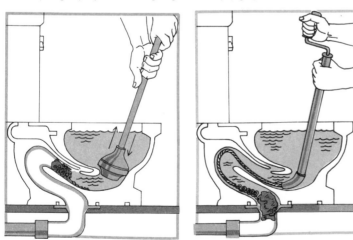

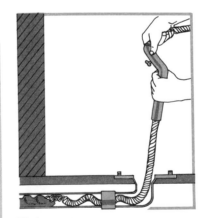

Work auger into drain
or waste line
and get the obstruction out.

Home Repairs Made Easy

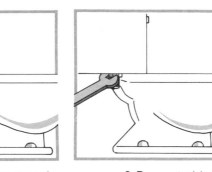

1. Disconnect supply.

2. Remove tank bolts.

3. Pry off caps and remove nuts.

beneath caps of ceramic or plastic material. Pry off the caps with a putty knife and remove the nuts, using a wrench. Twist the bowl slightly to free it from its seal, then lift it straight up (do not tilt the bowl, since there is likely to be some water remaining in the trapway that might spill out).

There is no obvious use for a discarded toilet tank. However, you can still find old toilet bowls recycled to serve as planters on the lawns of homes and in front of some plumbing supply shops. If your esthetic senses move you in that flowery direction, so be it. Otherwise, junk your old toilet. (If it is in good operating condition and not badly cracked, you may even be able to sell it for a few dollars.)

Remove the hold-down bolts from the floor flange around the drain opening. With a putty knife, scrape the old wax gasket or other material from the flange, then wipe it clean. Insert two new hold-down bolts in the flange slots.

If the old flange appears damaged, or if it is a new installation (rather than a replacement), fit a new floor flange into the waste-pipe opening. Screw the flange to the floor, first making sure that the slots for the hold-down bolts are aligned with the holes in the bowl base. Insert hold down bolts in the flange slots.

Some toilets are secured by only these two bolts; others require two more toward the front. Mark the location of the front

4. Twist and lift bowl.

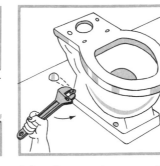

5. Remove bolts from flange.

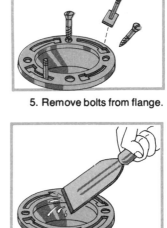

6. Scrape flange clean.

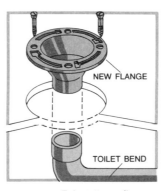

NEW FLANGE

TOILET BEND

7. Install new flange.

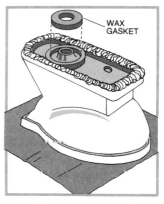

WAX GASKET

9. Putty the bottom of bowl.

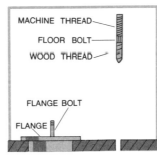

MACHINE THREAD

FLOOR BOLT

WOOD THREAD

FLANGE BOLT

FLANGE

8. Install floor bolts.

Home Repairs Made Easy • Clogged Toilets

1. Set bowl.

2. Twist to set.

3. Check that it is level.

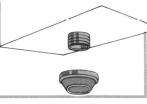

4. Place washer on tank outlet.

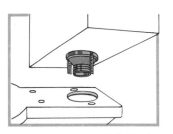

5. Set tank.

6. Tighten floor flange nuts.

7. Set bolt caps.

8. Install seat.

bolts, using the bowl itself as a guide. Drive hanger bolts (one end has a wood thread, the other a machine thread to accept a nut) into the floor at these locations, making sure that they are perfectly vertical.

Set the new bowl upside down on pads or a blanket on the floor. Place a new wax gasket around the outlet, and apply a bead of plumber's putty completely around the base rim. Lift the bowl and align it over the bolts, then lower it gently and as straight as possible into position, with the discharge opening over the floor flange opening. Press down on top center of the bowl and twist it very slightly to settle the ring of putty into the floor. Use a carpenter's level to check that the bowl is perfectly level, and shim with wood wedges if necessary (but be sure you don't lift the bowl too much and break the putty seal, or the seal around the discharge opening).

If the toilet is a two-piece unit with a separate tank, place a large rubber washer on the tank outlet. Carefully set the tank atop the bowl. Tighten the nuts that hold the tank to the bowl, taking a few turns on one nut, then the other, and alternating this way so that it is tightened evenly — but not overtightened. Using the tank as a guide, align the bowl with the wall (do the same if the toilet is a one-piece unit). Place washers over the flange and floor bolts and tighten with a wrench — again, do not overtighten. Place a small amount of putty inside the bolt caps and place them over the exposed bolt ends.

Install flush mechanism in tank as instructed on pp. 15-19. Connect the fixture supply line the same way as it was when you disconnected it (see illustrations p. 21). Install a new toilet seat, inserting the hinge bolts through the holes in the bowl, slipping washers over the bolts and tightening (once again, not too tight) the nuts. Place the tank top on the tank and turn on the water to complete the installation.

CLOGGED SINK DRAINS

This is another annoyance that you often bring on yourself (or other members of the family do) by removing the outlet strainer and allowing food wastes, grease, and other "indigestible" matter to run into the sink drain.

If the drain is not completely clogged, try running scalding water into it for several minutes. That may clear the stoppage. If it doesn't, try a dry or liquid chemical drain cleaner, following the manufacturer's instructions. (Do not use pure lye.) If this clears the drain, flush it with hot water for several minutes.

If the chemical doesn't work or if the drain is completely clogged, try using the plumber's friend. Remove the strainer from the drain and make sure there is enough water in the sink to cover the plunger, providing a good seal. Work the plunger up and down until the drain is cleared and water runs out normally.

Some plumbers prefer a force pump rather than the plumber's friend or plunger for unclogging sink drains. The force pump must be positioned squarely over the drain and covered with enough water to make a firm seal. Then pump the handle to clear away the obstruction by air pressure. If a plumber's friend or force pump doesn't do the job, check the trap below the sink. If there is a cleanout plug, place a pail below it to catch the water, then remove the plug. Try to clear away the obstruction. If that doesn't work, or if there is no cleanout plug, loosen the slip nuts and remove the trap. If the stoppage is in the trap, remove it. If not, use the drain auger, feeding it into the drain line. Rotate the auger, then work it in some more. Rotate it again and repeat the procedure until the obstruction is cleared. Reassemble the trap, then run scalding water down the drain for several minutes.

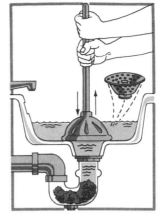
Use of plunger.

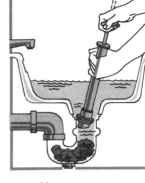
Use of force pump.

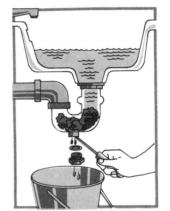
Remove cleanout plug.

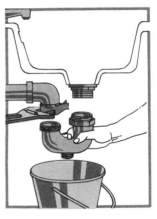
Remove trap.

Use auger in drain line,
rotate it, and work it in some more.

Home Repairs Made Easy

CLOGGED LAVATORIES

When a lavatory with a pop-up drain stopper becomes clogged, first twist the stopper to disengage it, then lift it out. Often, accumulated hair, grease, and the like are caught on the stopper, causing clogging. Clean it off. With the stopper out, use a length of wire with one end bent into a hook to fish out debris that may be stuck between the discharge outlet and the trap.

If clogging persists, follow the measures prescribed for sink drains on the preceding page. Plug up the overflow outlet with rags before using the plumber's friend; otherwise it cannot make an airtight seal and will not work effectively.

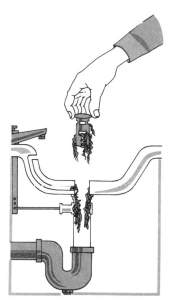

Remove stopper.

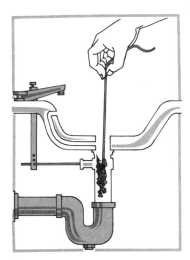

Use wire to fish out debris.

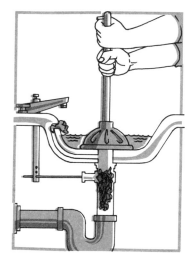

Plug up overflow and use plunger.

CLOGGED BATHTUBS

If scalding water, chemicals, and the plumber's friend (remember to plug the tub overflow with a wet cloth or rags) don't work, you will have to get at the obstruction by removing the trap. If the bathroom is on the first floor, the tub may have a P or S trap that is accessible from the basement or crawl space. In this case, loosen the slip nuts, take off the trap and clear the line with an auger, as under Clogged Sink Drains on p. 23.

Many second-floor and some first-floor bathtubs are fitted with drum traps, usually located near the bathtub drain with an access cover flush with the floor. If the tub is recessed into a wall niche, the trap may be on the other side of the wall — in a closet, perhaps, or beneath a kitchen cabinet. Or it might be within the wall itself; builders often leave an access panel in the wall next to a recessed bathtub, which is easily removed to service all the tub plumbing.

Make sure the tub is empty before opening the drum trap; bail the water out if necessary. Use an open-end wrench (never a pipe wrench) to remove the drum trap access cover. Work the drain auger in the line between the tub and the trap — the obstruction may be found there. If not, work the auger in the outflow line from the trap until the stoppage is cleared. Check the rubber gasket before replacing the trap cover; if it is in poor condition, install a new one. Then replace the cover on the trap. Run hot water into the drain for several minutes.

Some plumbing systems, particularly those in older installations, do not include a bathtub trap, or have it placed beneath the floor where it is inaccessible. If you can't find a trap, and the clogging resists all your efforts to work it loose, you are probably

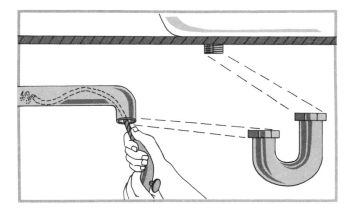
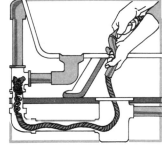

Remove debris through trap in basement.

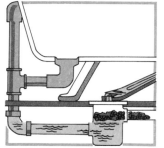

Remove drum-trap cover.

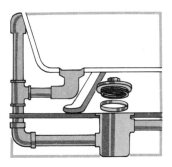

Work auger toward tub.

Work auger in drain line.

Replace rubber gasket.

best off calling in a professional. It will likely be less painful than ripping up the floors in search of the problem.

CLOGGED SEWERS

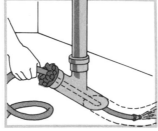

1. Loosen drain plug.

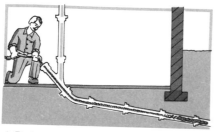

2. Work garden hose to obstruction.

3. Plug opening with rags and turn on hose.

4. Drain auger at work.

5. Electric auger at work.

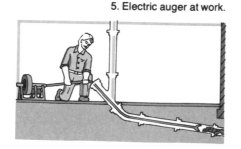

When drainage problems are noted at several or all fixtures in the house, the obstruction is most likely in the main sewer line, rather than at individual fixtures. Blockage in a sewer line may be caused by collected waste or foreign matter at some point in the underground pipe or by surrounding tree roots that have taken over. Roots will enter fine cracks in certain pipe materials and continue to grow inside the pipe until they form an almost solid mass. This can take place at a single point, or along a great length of an older pipe.

Start at the basement cleanout plug, placing a bucket below the plug. Use a wrench to loosen the plug, just enough to allow water to flow out into the bucket. When all has drained out remove the plug.

Remove the nozzle from your garden hose. Without turning on the water, work the hose into the cleanout opening until it reaches the obstruction. Stuff rags into the opening around the hose so that it is tightly sealed. Have a helper slowly turn on the water as you hold the hose tightly against the stoppage. As the obstruction begins to give way, increase the water pressure until it clears. If there is no movement, turn off the water and remove the hose.

Try turning a drain auger into the drain opening until it hits the obstruction; turn the handle and work the auger back and forth until the blockage is cleared. Run the hose into the drain to wash away the debris.

If the problem persists, it is likely that tree roots have penetrated the sewer line. You may want to call in professionals to handle the problem. Or you can rent an electric auger fitted with sharp blades for cutting through roots. Follow dealer's instructions for use of such a machine. When the stoppage has been cleared, use the hose to rinse out the drain before replacing the cleanout plug.

SWEATING PIPES

Exposed pipes that "sweat" during hot weather can be cured of this affliction by wrapping them with insulation. You can use asbestos or fiberglass insulation or a special thick insulating tape made for this purpose. Make sure to insulate the pipes before you finish off a basement. Sweating pipes will cause unsightly damage to the ceiling, which will be costly and time-consuming later.

FROZEN WATER PIPES

In cold weather, water may freeze in underground pipes laid above the frostline or in pipes in unheated buildings, in open crawl spaces, or in outside walls.

When water freezes it expands. Unless a pipe can also expand, it may rupture when the water freezes. Iron pipe and steel pipe do not expand appreciably. Copper pipe stretches some, but does not resume its original dimensions when thawed; repeated freezings will cause it to fail eventually. Flexible plastic tubing may stand repeated freezings, but it is good practice to prevent it from freezing.

Pipes may be insulated to prevent freezing, but this is not a completely dependable method. Insulation does not stop the loss of heat from the pipe—it merely slows it down —and the water may freeze if it stands in the pipe long enough at below-freezing temperature. Also, if insulation becomes wet, it loses its effectiveness.

Electric heating cable can supply the continual heat needed to prevent freezing of pipes in areas of intense cold. The nable should be wrapped around the pipe and covered with insulation.

Use of electric heating cable is the best method of thawing frozen pipe, because the entire length of pipe is thawed at one time. Thawing pipe with a blowtorch or propane torch can be dangerous. The water may get so hot at the point where the torch is applied as to generate sufficient steam under

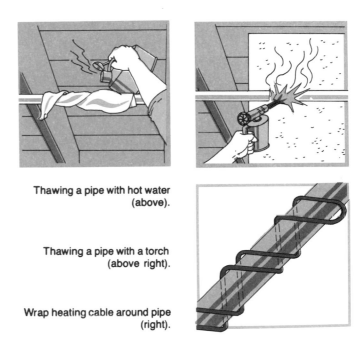

Thawing a pipe with hot water
(above).

Thawing a pipe with a torch
(above right).

Wrap heating cable around pipe
(right).

pressure to rupture the pipe. Steam from the break could severely scald you.

Thawing pipe with hot water is safer than thawing with a blowtorch. One method is to cover the pipe with rags and then pour the hot water over the rags.

When thawing pipe with a torch, hot water, or similar methods, open a faucet and start thawing at that point, thus reducing the chance of the buildup of dangerous pressure. Do not allow the steam to condense and refreeze before it reaches the faucet.

LEAKING PIPES

When a pipe springs a leak, the first thing to do is turn off the water — fast! If there is not a shutoff nearby, turn off the main intake valve. If it is impossible to shut off the water because of a worn or damaged valve or for some other reason, you can stop water from flowing through a copper pipe by

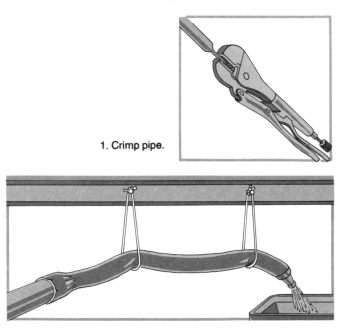

1. Crimp pipe.

2. Use hose to divert flow.

crimping the pipe below the leak or break; a vise-grip pliers is the best tool for this. Of course, you will have to replace this section of pipe later, but at least your house won't float away before you can make permanent repairs. If a pipe breaks or a connection comes loose and water is pouring out the end of a pipe, you can also place a garden hose over the end of the pipe to direct water flow into a bathtub, stationary tub, or even out a window until you can stanch the flow.

For a temporary repair of a damaged pipe, wrap a piece of sheet rubber firmly around the leaky section and clamp it tight-

ly (special clamps for this are available in various pipe sizes). Or you can cut a section of garden hose, slit it, and place it over the leak, holding it there with a C-clamp. If the pipe is actually broken, you can rejoin the two sections with a short piece of garden hose, securing it with hose clamps on each end.

To make a permanent repair, cut out the damaged section of pipe with a cutter or hacksaw. Fit a coupling to one of the remaining ends, cut a short piece of pipe to fit the cutout section, and attach it to the other end with a union.

When a leaky pipe is inside a wall, you have to break through the wall to repair it or, which is much easier, you have to disconnect it from the supply line and the fixture it serves and run a new line through the wall next to the old one.

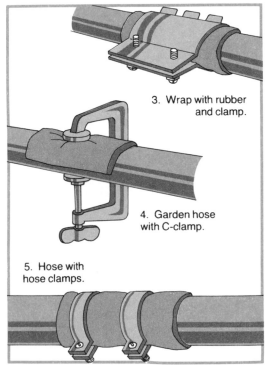

3. Wrap with rubber and clamp.

4. Garden hose with C-clamp.

5. Hose with hose clamps.

DRAINING AND FILLING THE PLUMBING SYSTEM

It may be necessary to drain the plumbing system when making certain repairs. Or you might want to drain it when leaving the home for an extended period, particularly during cold weather.

First turn off electricity or gas to water or steam heating units. Close the main shutoff valve. Starting at the highest floor and working down, open all hot- and cold-water faucets, including outdoor faucets. Flush all toilets. Open all drain valves on water-treatment equipment and the hot water heater (place buckets beneath them first). If you are draining the system to prevent freezing, pour antifreeze into all toilet bowls and drains.

To refill the system, close drain valves on water-treatment equipment and the hot water heater. Open the main shutoff valve. Close all hot- and cold-water faucets, including all outdoor faucets. Turn on electricity or gas to the hot water heater and any other heating units.

Shutting down the system:
1. Turn off electricity or gas to heating units.
2. Close main valve.
3. Open faucets, flush toilets on top floor.
4. Open faucets, flush toilets on lower floors.
5. Open drain valves on heaters, etc.
6. Pour antifreeze into toilets, drains.

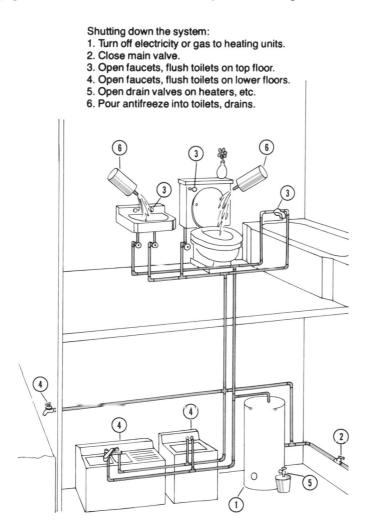

Home Repairs Made Easy

THE ELECTRICIAN'S TOOLBOX

No matter how well installed your electrical system is, things will in time go wrong. Receptacles wear out (you would, too, if people were always plugging cords into you), wiring becomes damaged or insulation frayed by an overload situation or just old age, switches fail to work. Other problems crop up that have little to do with the health of the system itself. Lamp cords need replacement, overloads cause blown fuses, and doorbells become corroded by exposure to the elements.

Most home handymen take pride in their prowess when working with wood. Wire is quite a different matter. The mystique of electricity frightens off many otherwise perfectly competent craftspersons. Yet a healthy respect, rather than fear, is the attitude with which professional and amateur alike should approach electrical projects.

True, there are some people who probably shouldn't attempt any electrical work. If you are confounded by the fine tuner on your TV or recoil in petrified terror at the prospect of replacing a blown-out light bulb, it would obviously be a mistake (perhaps a fatal one) to attempt the wiring of an addition to your house. But few home handymen feel such qualms. It is more often a matter of venturing into an unknown area.

The handyman who wants to do some simple electrical work probably already has most of the basic tools. A screwdriver, a common pliers, and a penknife are all that you need for many operations. As you get into bigger and more complex jobs, however, you will have to add to your tool collection. Some items are essential, some are optional but helpful.

For anything beyond adding an outlet or repairing a lamp or appliance, you should increase your toolbox contents with the following, as needed.

A 16-ounce claw hammer is handy for driving staples, nailing outlet boxes in place, fastening hangers, and many other purposes.

A regular screwdriver is fine for occasional work, but a special electrician's screwdriver is better for extensive projects. This tool has a long, slender blade with the tip the same diameter as the shank. The blade fits snugly into the screwheads of most electrical connections, and the shape makes it easy to work with in deep-set and difficult spots. It should have an insulated handle.

A wire stripper simplifies stripping insulation off the end of wire. A jackknife can accomplish the same thing, but the stripper has settings for each wire size so that it cuts the insulation without danger of damaging the wire. It is also much quicker.

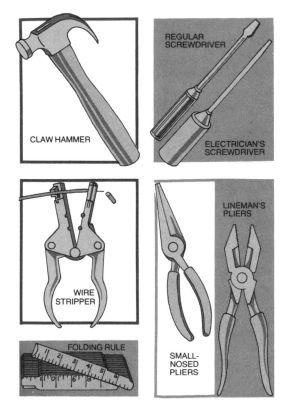

CLAW HAMMER

REGULAR SCREWDRIVER

ELECTRICIAN'S SCREWDRIVER

WIRE STRIPPER

LINEMAN'S PLIERS

SMALL-NOSED PLIERS

FOLDING RULE

A 6-foot folding rule is the best device for measuring wire runs, wall openings for boxes, and the like.

Small-nosed pliers (sometimes called needle-nose pliers) have narrow, tapered jaws to make it easy to bend wire into loops around terminals and to reach into such tight quarters as switch and outlet boxes. The better ones have insulated handles to help protect against shock.

Lineman's pliers are heavy-duty pliers used for firmly gripping cable, connectors, and the like. They also have side jaws that are used for cutting wire.

There are several varieties of multipurpose electrician's pliers. All have as their purpose the combining of as many operations as possible into one tool. The tool usually operates as a pliers, stripper, crimper, and cutter. It may also do other jobs, depending on the model.

If you already have electricity at the work site, an electric drill makes the job go faster and easier. It's not much good, though, until service is installed. In that case, a brace and bit must be used for boring holes for wires. In either case, a ⅝-inch drill bit is the most useful, although you may have occasion for using other sizes. Extension bits are particularly useful for drilling in old work.

A keyhole saw is the preferred tool for cutting out box locations in paneling and gypsum wallboard, and for any type of sawing in tight spots.

A wood chisel is useful for cutting notches in wall studs, lath, and other building materials.

A hacksaw is used for cutting the sheathing of armored cable and, where necessary, metal lath.

Metal snips (preferably "aviation" type)

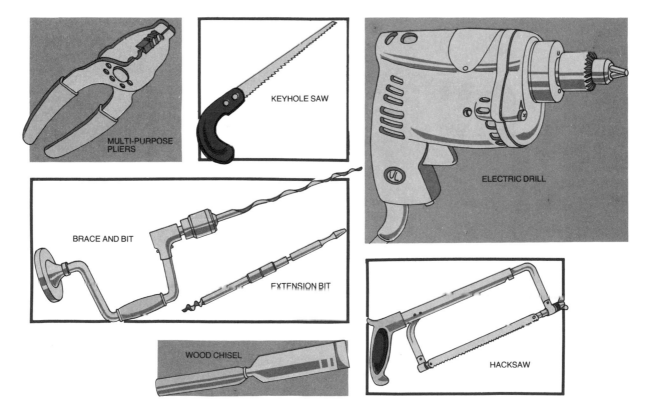

MULTI-PURPOSE PLIERS

KEYHOLE SAW

ELECTRIC DRILL

BRACE AND BIT

EXTENSION BIT

WOOD CHISEL

HACKSAW

Home Repairs Made Easy • The Electrician's Toolbox

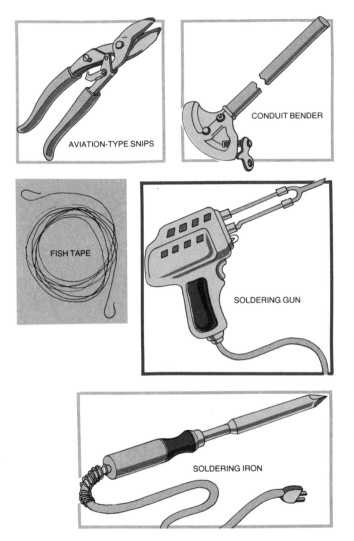

AVIATION-TYPE SNIPS

CONDUIT BENDER

FISH TAPE

SOLDERING GUN

SOLDERING IRON

can be used instead of a hacksaw for cutting the sheathing on lighter gauges of armored cable. You can develop a "feel" for cutting the metal without cutting into the wire inside.

Some splices and connections require soldering; this is especially so in appliance repairs. A soldering gun or iron is required. For most applications, a soldering gun is more useful than an iron. Rosin-core wire-type solder is usually used, along with a nonacid rosin flux.

Plastic electrician's tape is used to insulate soldered joints and splices.

Fish tape is a necessity for working in construction where existing wire must be pulled through walls and ceilings, and for conduit work.

A conduit bender or "hickey" is the best tool for bending conduit around corners and obstructions.

One of the most useful tools for electrical work is a simple, inexpensive device with a name that describes it perfectly: tester. There are large and somewhat complex versions, but in its simplest form the tester is a pair of insulated wires with bare prongs on one end of each and a small light between the prongs.

This tool has many applications, but basically it does one thing — it establishes whether current is flowing between two points. And it performs that function with complete safety for the user, an important consideration. It is also quick and easy to use and to interpret: when the light glows, current is passing through.

For example, if you are changing a light fixture that is controlled by a three-way switch and are not sure whether the current is on or off, put the tester between the two wires of the fixture and see if it glows. If an outlet doesn't seem to be working, place one prong of the tester into each slot; if it glows, your problem is elsewhere. Or if there is trouble somewhere in a circuit and you don't know what it is, check it out from end to end with the tester until you locate the faulty switch or outlet. For the money (a dollar or so), you can't find a better buy.

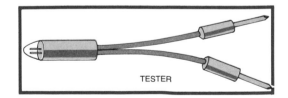

TESTER

ELECTRICAL MATERIALS

Each electrical project requires the use of specific materials. Many of these can be found at your hardware store. Others will have to be purchased at an electrical-supply shop.

Think of electricity and you think of wire, because that is what brings the power into your house and carries it to wherever it is used. The size of the wires in the system depends on the requirements of the National Electrical Code, local codes, and the end use intended, such as lighting, heating, or air conditioning.

Copper wires are almost universally used in home wiring. Aluminum wires enjoyed a brief popularity because of a shortage of copper, but aluminum is coming into disrepute because of its tendency to overheat under some conditions, and many local electrical codes have banned its use. Check your code before installing aluminum wire. Better yet, avoid using it.

Wire sizes are based upon the American Wire Gauge (AWG) system. Gauge (also expressed as Number or #) is determined by wire diameter; the larger the diameter, the smaller the gauge. Common sizes used for home wiring range from #0 to #18, although #00 (2/0) and #000 (3/0) may be required for service entry lines for 150- and 200-amp service. Most circuits range from #10 to #14, with #12 perhaps the most commonly used. Heavier circuits require larger wires; #16 and #18 are used for doorbell and intercom wiring.

The wire gauge is based on the total diameter, whether the wire is composed of a single large strand or many small strands twisted together. The trend is to make the larger wires multistrand, since the large single strand is too stiff for easy handling. Multistrand is required by the National Electrical Code for wire sizes #8 and larger (that is, #6, #4, #2 and so on).

Wire is insulated with a variety of coverings. Rubber was once the most common; but it has largely been replaced by plastic, which is less likely to corrode, dry, and crack. The types of insulation most frequently used for house wiring include R (rubber, for general use, no longer manufactured, but you may find it in existing circuits); RH (heat-resistant rubber); RU (latex rubber, for general use); RW (moisture-resistant rubber, for wet locations); RHW (moisture- and heat-resistant rubber); T (thermoplastic, for general use); TW (moisture-resistant thermoplastic), and THW (moisture- and heat-resistant thermoplastic). The wire size and insulation type are usually printed on the insulation.

Cable is often, but inaccurately, referred to as wire. Actually, the wires are *inside* the cable. Cable can more properly be called the wiring, since it constitutes the greater part of any wiring system.

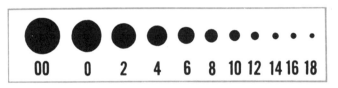

Wire sizes.

Single wire, twisted strand.

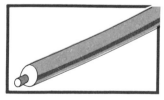

Insulated wire.

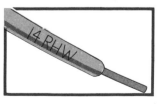

Marking on insulation.

Home Repairs Made Easy

Cable consists of two or more wires, each of which is covered with insulation, which are encased in a variety of materials depending on the type of use, size, and other variables. The wires are the actual electrical conductors; the rest is merely protection from the elements and other potential damage, as well as protection against accidental contact with the conductors.

In two-wire cable, one wire is covered with black insulation, the other with white. This color coding identifies the wires for installation—black connects to black, white to white (there are exceptions to this rule when you have to work with three-wire cable). The black wire is referred to as "hot," and the white as "neutral." If there are three current-carrying wires in the cable, the third is red. Don't be misled by "neutral." In alternating current, all wires carry a charge, and none is to be tampered with as long as there is "juice" to the line. New wiring also normally includes another wire, green-insulated or bare, designated "with ground" on the cable. The ground wire does not carry current, but is, as the name states, for grounding.

Cable has been classified for different uses by the National Electrical Code; the code designations are given below. Cable is stamped or otherwise marked with its code designation and the size and number of wires inside (and usually the brand name as well). *Type NM 14/3,* for example, is nonmetallic, sheathed (see below), and has

#	Capacity (amps)	Use
14	15	General purpose, lighting circuits
12	20	Kitchen circuits, lower-wattage appliances, almost any household circuit
10	30	Subpanel connections, high-wattage appliances
8	40	Service wiring, electric ranges
6	55	Service wiring

WHAT SIZE WIRE TO USE
(armored or nonmetallic cable)

Larger sizes—up to 3/0—are not normally used in household electrical systems except for main service into the house, which is not the domain of the do-it-yourselfer. Smaller sizes (#16, #18) are used for lamp cords and appliance cords.

three #14 wires inside. The number of volts and the UL approval seal (hopefully) are noted also.

Type AC flexible armored cable is made by several companies. It is often called "BX," but this is a brand name. The insulated wires are covered with a tough wrapping paper, and outside that with spiral-wrapped galvanized steel for flexibility. It can be used in any dry, interior work and is the best choice for installations where there is a potential for damage from tools after installation. Some codes require its use for all installations. Armored cable is more difficult to work with than nonmetallic sheathed cable.

Type NM nonmetallic sheathed cable is often called "Romex," another brand name. The insulated wires are covered by fabric, rubber, or plastic. The cable is flat or oval-shaped and is for use indoors in dry, nonvulnerable locations. The easiest of the cables to work with, it is generally preferred by do-it-yourselfers (unless the code forbids its use). A similar cable, *Type NMC,* is waterproof and can be used in damp or wet locations.

Marking on cable.

Type USE (underground service entrance) or *UF* (underground fused) cable is usually sheathed with plastic and is primarily used outdoors. It can be run through concrete, brick walls, or other similar materials. When buying cable for this purpose, make sure its designation starts with "U" (for underground).

Type SE, service entrance cable, is used mostly for wiring up to the service and is not normally used by the average homeowner. If you do have occasion to purchase any for this use, make sure it is rated with RHW or THW insulation (rubber or thermoplastic, moisture- and heat-resistant). Type SE cable can be used for wiring 220-240 appliances, such as dryers and ranges, if allowed by local codes.

Metal conduit is not cable, but a shell through which wires are pulled. Like flexible armored cable, it provides protection for the wires. Because of its higher cost, it is not used in home wiring unless called for by codes.

Thin-wall conduit, also called electrical metallic tubing *(EMT),* may be required for outdoor installations; it can also be used indoors. It is a hollow metal tube through which wires are pulled with fish tape. This type of conduit can be bent up to 90 degrees by means of a "hickey" (see section on Tools on pp. 30–32). Thin-wall conduit comes in 10-foot lengths. It is relatively expensive and requires special connectors. Wires, usually Type TW for outdoor use, are pulled through it after installation. These wires are insulated but not encased in any type of cable.

Electrical boxes come in various sizes, shapes, and materials. Shallow square or octagonal boxes are used for ceiling fixtures and junctions, deeper boxes (usually rectangular) for outlet receptacles and switches. They are usually made of steel, but Bakelite or other nonmetallic substances are often used in damp locations.

Type AC flexible armored cable.

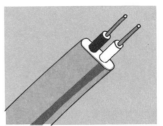

Underground cable.

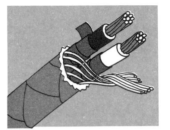

Service entrance cable.

EMT thin-wall conduit.

Type NM nonmetallic sheathed cable.

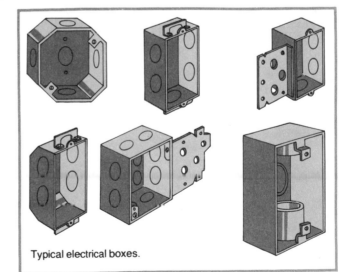

Typical electrical boxes.

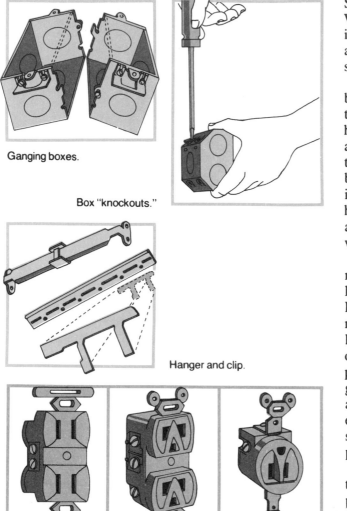

Ganging boxes.

Box "knockouts."

Hanger and clip.

Receptables for 2-pronged and 3-pronged plugs.

Shallow boxes are used for thin partitions. Wall boxes have removable sides for ganging two or more. Special waterproof boxes and connectors are needed for outside installations.

Steel boxes have "knockouts" that can be tapped or twisted out with a screwdriver tip to admit the cable. Nonmetallic boxes have integral entry holes, and most codes allow their use only in certain specific locations. Many boxes come with built-in brackets or mounting "ears" for easy nailing to framing. Other devices, such as hangers and special clips for existing walls, are used to attach boxes to ceilings and to wallboard.

Receptacles and switches are the elements that finish off the wiring system, delivering the electricity where it will be used. Receptacles provide a place to plug lamps, radios, or whatever into the system. Usually, each receptacle provides at least two outlets, accommodating plugs with two prongs or two prongs plus a third, round grounding prong. The 220-240 receptacles are larger than the 110-120 and have slanted, L-shaped or other uniquely formed slots so that only 220-240 appliances can be plugged in.

Switches control the flow of current, turning it on and off to a fixture or other power user. Three-way switches allow control from two separate locations, whereas four-way switches make it possible to control the flow of current from three or more

Receptables for 220-240 appliances.

separate locations. By far the most common type of switch for residential use is the toggle (flip up, flip down), although push-buttons may be found in some older homes. When these wear, they are easily replaced with toggles. Variations of switches include mercury, or silent, switches (no "click" when turned on or off) and dimmer switches, which allow a light fixture to be illuminated through a complete range from full bright to off. Switches, as well as receptacles, can be in one box, ganged in two or more boxes, or combined in two or more boxes.

Connection devices are used to secure the cable to the boxes so that it can't slip out. Each type of cable has its own connectors. When using flexible armored cable (type AC), fiber bushings as well as connectors are needed.

Solderless connectors are often called "wire nuts." They are plastic caps with threads inside to grip the ends of stripped wires and join them without splicing or taping. When screwed on properly, the connectors hold the wires tightly together with no bare wire exposed.

Cable is often supported by notching or drilling through the framing. Where this isn't feasible, staples, straps, or hangers are needed to hold the cable in place. See illustrations p. 38.

Surface wiring is insulated and then encased in a hard plastic housing. It is used with compatible surface-mounted outlets,

Dimmer switch.

Solderless wire connectors.

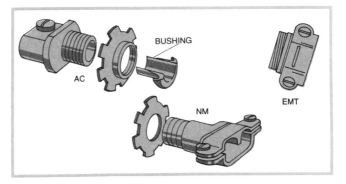

Connectors for AC, NM, and EMT cables.

Cable installed through framing.

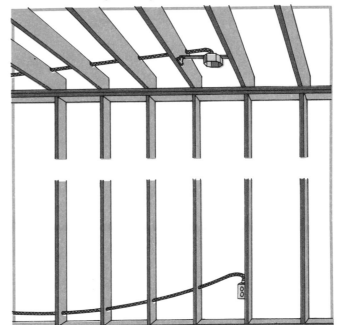

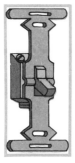

Toggle switch.

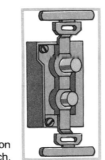

Push-button switch.

Home Repairs Made Easy • Electrical Materials

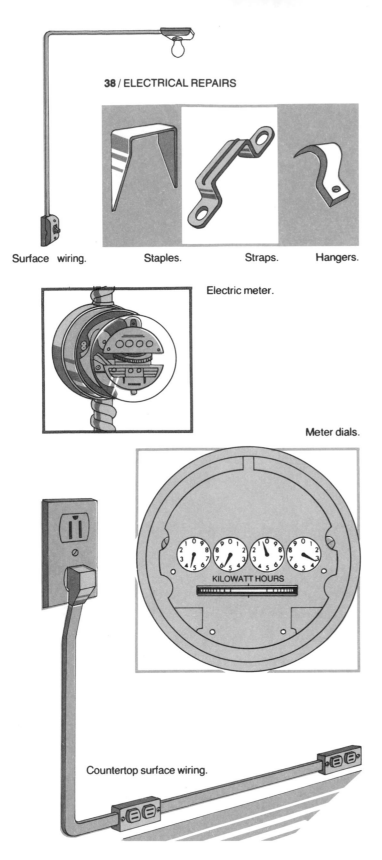

Surface wiring.   Staples.   Straps.   Hangers.

Electric meter.

Meter dials.

KILOWATT HOURS

Countertop surface wiring.

switches, and other devices on the *outside* of the walls and ceilings. It is simple to install, but rather unsightly in the main rooms of the house. It is sometimes used on kitchen counters to provide outlets wherever needed. It is also used in workshops, garages, utility rooms, and the like. But surface wiring is prohibited by many local electrical codes.

The electric meter isn't really the do-it-yourselfer's territory, and hooking one up or tampering with it is neither wise nor allowed by codes. You should, however, know what the meter looks like and how it is read. In many ways it is similar to the automobile odometer. The dials record kilowatt hours in tens, hundreds, thousands, and so on. As soon as ten hours are clocked on the first dial, it registers on the next one—and so on. To determine how many KWH have been used since your last reading, subtract the total from the previous total as noted on your electric bill. Meters are usually installed by the power company in meter boxes hooked up by an electrician.

The breaker box or fuse box (more correctly called the "entrance panel") is where the current from the power company—after going through the meter—is routed to the various circuits of the house. The current first goes to a main fuse or breaker, then is channeled to the individual circuits. Each circuit is protected by its own fuse or breaker, which "blows" when overloaded.

Fuses come in a variety of sizes and types. A larger size must never be substituted for a smaller one. Fuses are specially designed to be the weakest link in the electrical circuit—when something goes wrong, the fuse should blow. If you put in a larger (stronger) fuse, you run the risk of melting the wiring and causing a fire, because the circuit can become overloaded and the safety factor (the fuse) has been compromised.

Plug-type fuses are the commonly seen

variety, with a threaded or "Edison" base (like a light bulb). The code prohibits use of this type of fuse in new homes because of the possibility of replacing lower-amp fuses with larger ones, as noted above. But where they are already installed, they are legal.

To change a plug-type fuse, simply unscrew it and screw in a new one (again, of the same amperage). It is a good idea to turn off the main switch before doing this; but at night this can be an overprecaution, putting the area where you are working in darkness and making it more hazardous than necessary. You can replace a fuse safely without turning off the main switch if you're careful. *Don't touch* any wires, metal, water, or any other potential ground with any part of your body. Make sure your feet are dry, and stand on a board to be doubly safe.

Time-delay fuses are similar to regular plug-type fuses except that a springlike metal strip inside allows the fuse to accept brief, temporary overloads, such as occur when starting a large motor, without blowing. This is not as unsafe as it may sound, because the circuit can take a temporary surge without danger. After the motor is running, it uses much less power and poses no danger.

A short in the circuit blows a time-delay fuse in the same way as any other fuse, and any overload more than momentary in duration will also blow the fuse. These fuses, too, are rated in amperes and must be replaced only by similarly rated fuses.

Screw-in breakers are not really fuses at all, but breakers (see below) that are screwed into a fuse box. Instead of replacing these when they blow, you simply press a reset button (or, on some types, flip a switch). A screw-in breaker is often substituted for a conventional fuse when a temporary overload frequently occurs, such as that from large power tools. The

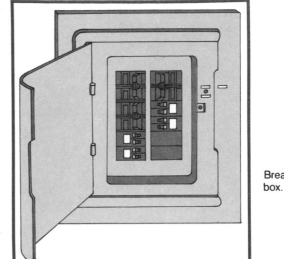

Breaker box.

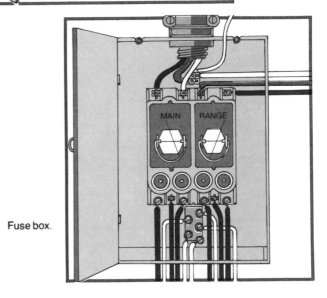

Fuse box.

Plug-type fuse.

Time-delay fuse.

breaker, should, of course, be the same amperage as the fuse it replaces.

Nontamperable fuses are designed to prevent replacement of a smaller-rated fuse with a larger one. They are permitted by the code and designated "Type S." There are two parts to such a fuse: the fuse itself, which is replaceable and much like a regular fuse, and an adapter. The adapter is screwed into the standard fuse box, then the fuse is screwed into the adapter.

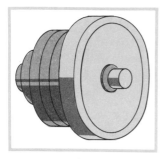

Screw-in breaker.

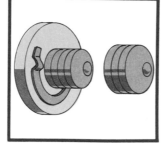

Nontamperable fuse.

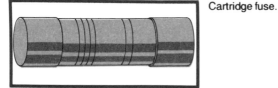

Cartridge fuse.

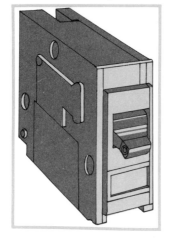

Connected breaker switches.

Circuit breaker.

The difference between this and a plug-type fuse is that the adapter is rated in amps the same way the fuse is. If you remove a 15-amp fuse from a 15-amp adapter, it cannot be replaced with any other size of fuse. And once the adapter is installed, it becomes a permanent part of the fuse box and cannot be removed. (When installing a nontamperable fuse, make sure to turn it in all the way. A spring under the shoulder will not make full contact unless it is pressed very tightly against the adapter.)

Cartridge fuses are long, cylindrical fuses, similar to those used in automobiles. In residential applications, they are most frequently used in the larger sizes, such as in the main switch. When they blow, call your utility company; the problem is likely to be major.

Most new homes and older homes with new wiring utilize circuit breakers instead of fuses. They are safer in all ways and easier to "fix" when something goes wrong. An overload or short will trip the breaker the same way it blows a fuse.

Most circuit breakers are like any toggle switch. Some, however, are buttons instead of switches. To reset a toggle breaker, flick it from "off" to "on" like any other switch. With a button type, simply press. You may find that two switches are installed in one opening in the breaker box; this means that two circuits are in that opening. Only one will be tripped (hopefully) at a time, so reset that one. For 220-240 appliance circuits, two lines are joined together. Press the connector that joins the two switches to "on" to reset. The main switch is often ganged in the same way.

AVOID HAZARDS

Make no mistake — working with electricity *can* be hazardous to your health. It is not like other do-it-yourself jobs. If you mess up while working on the plumbing, you may end up with a faucet that is leaking more than when you started to repair it; at worst you may flood the basement or even the house. But you are not likely to drown. There is not that margin for error with electricity. If you mess up here, it could result in fire, serious injury, or worse.

Always exercise a healthy respect when doing electrical work. Never "play around" with electricity. It's a potentially deadly game, and you must know exactly what you are doing. If you don't know, don't do it. Seek qualified advice and/or professional help.

Although there are times when you have to do electrical work in potentially dangerous situations, most of the time you can work in complete safety. The obvious but often overlooked condition is when there isn't any "juice" or current present. For example, you would never work on an appliance that was plugged in. Or would you? As obvious a precaution as it may seem, there are still people who go poking around inside an electrical gadget with the plug attached and, therefore, the power on. It seems so foolhardy that it doesn't bear warning against — but it is so basic to electrical safety that it must be said, as strongly as possible: *Pull out the plug!*

Another type of electrical work that can be performed in complete safety is wiring that is done before being connected to the current. This does not mean that you can't do it incorrectly, but you can work without fear — at least until you hook it up. Even when you connect new work to the system, the worst that usually happens is a blown fuse or breaker. You then leave the breaker

off and check out the system until you find the flaw. There is nothing to fear from any electrical component that is not connected to the power source. If you have doubts, call an electrician.

Even when you must work with the current on, there is nothing to fear if you are careful to take the proper precautions. Keep in mind that alternating current (as in your house) flows back and forth, and that any wire can be "hot" — and therefore off limits to your touch or any contact. If it is necessary to work around "hot" materials, keep your hands and feet dry, and never work in anything wet. It is a good extra measure of safety to stand on a wooden board whenever there is a chance of striking a live connection. Also, use insulated tools (see p. 30). It is possible to slip and touch a hot wire and not be hurt as long as your body does not form a "ground."

Disconnect appliance first.

Never work on an appliance that is plugged in...

WHEN THE LIGHTS GO OUT...

Unfortunately, when trouble occurs, the immediate reaction is often panic—or at least *over*reaction. When the lights go out, you may think that a wire has snapped. If a lamp won't work, you conclude that it's time to throw it out.

Knowledge and preparation will help you avoid the panic button. In case the lights go out, it's a good idea to have candles (don't forget matches) and flashlights handy. A battery-operated radio is another excellent panic-soother. Those who had them during the famous Northeast blackout of the 1960's at least knew what was going on (and that, in fact, the Martians were *not* coming). Portable radios work even when the power in the house is off (but they don't help much when the radio station is also without power, which is why many stations have their own auxiliary generators). It also pays to have plenty of extra light bulbs around, as well as extra fuses, flashlight batteries, light plugs, extension cords, and even spare receptacles and switches for emergencies.

What do you do when the entire house is plunged into darkness? First find your way to the candles and flashlights (which should be conveniently stored in a place known to all members of the family). Once you can find your way around without groping, check the lights in your neighbors' houses. If they are out too, there is undoubtedly a general power failure. A line is down somewhere, or something has happened at the power plant. If you can't see your neighbor's house, give him a call. (The phone works even when the power is off.) If there *is* a power failure, it will probably be futile to call the power company, because their lines will be jammed by similar callers.

If only the power to your house is off, it could be the main fuse, but it is more likely to be some problem with the service. It could even be downed service wires, a common occurrence during heavy storms. If that is the case, keep your distance! If a wire is down across a street or sidewalk, post a large sign on both sides, warning pedestrians and passing cars. Whatever the case, call the power company or an electrician to have it fixed. A blown main fuse could indicate a serious problem that should be investigated by a professional. A downed wire is nothing for an amateur to fool with.

Ordinarily, though, only a portion of your electrical system will be off at one time. This most likely indicates a blown fuse or a tripped breaker. It could be an indication of some problem in the line, but not necessarily. The first step is to check your entrance panel.

It is relatively simple to replace a fuse, and it is even simpler to flip a breaker switch (see pp. 38-40). But fuses blow for a reason, and the trouble should be corrected before the fuse is replaced or the switch flipped.

Fuses are rated in amperes, and it is a dangerous—and unfortunately too common—practice to replace a smaller fuse with a larger one. If, for example, you find that a 15-amp fuse has blown, you may be able to restore the current by installing a 20-amp fuse. Don't do it! When an overload or short circuit exists, the fuse is *supposed* to blow. If it doesn't, and the circuit is "overfused," the wiring may melt and cause a fire. And don't ever resort to the old penny-in-the-box substitute for a fuse. True, it may get the power flowing again. It may also burn down your house. Who says you can't do anything with 1¢ these days? Certainly not your fire department!

Often, you may replace a blown fuse with another of the same amperage (or reset a breaker) and have no further problem.

The temporary aberration may have been caused by a sudden (and unusual) power surge, such as a power saw being plugged into a general-purpose circuit when you are paneling your living room. If you have obvious reason to suspect such a cause, just replace the fuse and make sure you sin no more in that regard.

But if the cause of a blown fuse or tripped breaker is a mystery, do a little detective work. Look for loose wiring on the line, or frayed insulation, or some other problem. Often, these clues will show up in the basement or other exposed area (an overload that causes insulation damage may be manifested in the exposed wiring near the entrance panel). If a thorough inspection doesn't turn up the problem, replace the fuse or flip the breaker anyway. If it doesn't blow again for some time, you probably have nothing to worry about—chalk it up as "unsolved." But if it blows again, trouble is obvious. If you can't find it yourself, call in a professional. In an older home, it may simply be a sign that you need more housepower.

With a plug-type fuse, the condition of the blown fuse is often a clue to the cause of the blow. If the copper strip in the center of the fuse is broken (actually, melted apart), the cause is most likely overload. If the glass window of the fuse is darkened—perhaps so much that you can't even see the copper strip—a short circuit is the prime suspect.

Why the Fuse Blows

In most cases, a blown fuse or breaker is caused by overload. If the stoppage occurred just after you turned on a toaster or other high-wattage appliance, you can be almost sure of it. You can verify this by computing the total wattage on the line at the time the fuse blew. (A 15-amp, 120-volt circuit has a 1,800-watt capacity; a 20-amp, 120-volt circuit has a 2,400-watt capacity.) The cure for the condition is obvious: rearrange appliances or add new circuits.

When the overload is strictly temporary, as in the case of several appliances or motors being turned on at the same time and drawing an unusually high surge of power, a time-delay fuse is a convenient and safe solution (see p. 39). But don't delude yourself by assuming that every overload is temporary. Make sure of the cause before deciding on a cure.

Short circuits, as noted above, blacken a fuse window. But a short is harder to determine if you have circuit breakers in your home's entrance panel. You can assume that a short is the problem if the breaker keeps tripping and your inspection and calculations make you reasonably sure there is no overload. In either case (fuses or breakers), you must find the cause of the short before restoring the power to the circuit.

If the short occurs only when a certain tool or appliance is used or when a certain lamp is turned on, your detective chore is simple. You can assume that the fault is with the tool, appliance, or lamp rather than with the circuit; and the solution, obviously, is not to use that device until it has been repaired.

If that is not the case, you should inspect the entire circuit to find the cause. Start by

Reading a fuse; overload, at left; short circuit, at right.

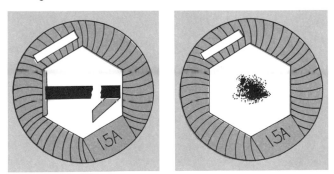

examining each receptacle and fixture on the circuit. Remove the plate and look inside. Are there any loose or frayed wires, or any bare wires touching other than those inside the connectors? You may have to pull the switch or receptacle out of the box to make that determination. (Remember, of course, to leave the power off.)

If, after examining all the fixtures on the line, you cannot find any crossed or loose wires, a more distressing problem may exist. In this case, it is probably best to call in a licensed electrician. You can, of course, find the problem yourself, but by the time you've torn down your walls and wiring, a professional probably would have the short located and fixed (and at a lesser overall price).

Power Consumed by Appliances

	WATTS
Air conditioner, room type	800–1500
Blanket, electric	150–200
Blender, food	200–400
Broiler, rotisserie	1200–1650
Can opener	100–250
Clock, electric	2–3
Coffee percolator	500–1000
Dishwasher	600–1000
Dryer, clothes	4000–5000
Fan, portable	50–200
Freezer	300–500
Fryer, deep-fat	1200–1650
Frying pan	1000–1200
Garbage disposer	500–1000
Heater, portable	1000–1500
Heater, wall-type, permanent	1000–2300
Heat lamp (infra-red)	250–300
Heat pad	50–75
Hot plate (per burner)	600–1000
Iron, hand	660–1200
Ironer	1500–2000
Lamp, fluorescent	15–60
Lamp, incandescent	10 up

	WATTS
Mixer, food	120–250
Motor: ¼ hp	300–400
½ hp	450–600
per hp over ½	950–1000
Oven, built-in	4000–5000
Radio	40–150
Range, separate	4000–6000
Range (all burners and oven on)	8000–14000
Razor	8–12
Refrigerator	150–300
Roaster	1200–1650
Sewing machine	60–90
Stereo hi-fi	200–400
Sun lamp (ultraviolet)	275–400
Television	200–400
Toaster	500–1200
Trash compactor	500–1000
Vacuum cleaner	250–800
Waffle iron	600–1000
Washer, automatic	600–800
Washer, electric, manual	350–550
Water heater	2000–5000

REPLACING DEFECTIVE RECEPTACLES AND SWITCHES

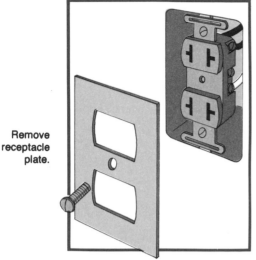

Remove receptacle plate.

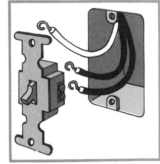

Check for loose, touching wires.

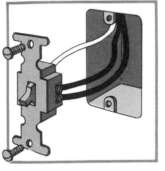

Remove screws holding receptacle or switch.

Remove wires.

Tighten wires on new receptacle or switch.

Fasten cover.

When, by inspection or testing, you determine that an outlet device is defective, replacement is required. To replace a switch or receptacle, turn off the power to the line by tripping the breaker or pulling the fuse. (The power may already be off because of a short circuit—but make sure.) Take off the cover plate, then remove the screws holding the receptacle or switch to the box. Pull the device out all the way, and take note of all connections. If the wiring is standard as described in previous chapters, you can proceed; but if it is a complicated arrangement such as a three-way or four-way switch, make a diagram of the connections before you take them apart.

Once you have noted how the device is wired, loosen the terminal screws and remove the wires. Then install a similar device, wiring it in the same manner as the old one. Make sure you loop the wire around the terminals in a clockwise direction so that the loop is tightened as you tighten the terminals screws. Fasten the device to the box. When the new switch or receptacle is in place, fasten the cover plate. Then restore the power. If your diagnosis was cor-

rect, the problem should be solved. If not, try another tack, looking for another faulty receptacle or switch. If that fails, you must suspect an in-wall problem, which is probably best left to a pro.

CEILING AND WALL FIXTURES

Wiring is built into most ceiling and wall fixtures and is connected to the feed wires inside the box (rather than the feed wires being connected directly to the device, as is normally the case with switches and receptacles). Solderless connectors are usually used. The fixtures are attached to the box in a variety of ways—some with screws or nuts, some by means of central nipples, studs, and/or straps.

When you suspect a problem in a fixture (or if you want to replace it with a new one for cosmetic reasons), first make sure that the power to the fixture circuit is off. Remove the knurled nut, screws, or hex nuts that hold the fixture to the box. Carefully pull down the fixture and inspect it. Check for loose wiring and, if that is the problem, tighten the connections.

If the wiring checks out, you can usually suspect the socket. Many fixtures have removable sockets. In that case, detach the wires and remove the socket (how this is done depends on how it is attached to the fixture, which should be obvious). Take it to the hardware or electrical-supply store and purchase a new one of the same type. Install it the same as the old one.

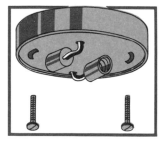

Remove nuts holding fixture.

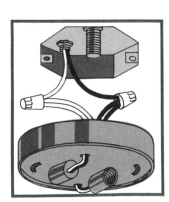

Pull down and inspect fixture.

If the socket is an integral part of the fixture, replace the entire fixture.

To replace a fixture with one just like it, remove the wire nuts and untwist the wires. Assemble the new wires and feed wires with wire nuts, black to black, white to white; if it is a complicated switch arrangement, note carefully how the wires were connected, then attach the new fixture to the box in the same way the old fixture was attached.

If you are installing a different size or type of fixture, you may need a new strap or an extension "hickey" (not to be confused with the conduit-bending tool of the same name) to fasten a new nipple to the old one in the box, in order to accommodate the new fixture. Check this out before you leave the electrical-supply house; these parts may be included with the fixture, or you may have to buy them separately. Whatever the situation, there is a way (and a fitting) that will allow you to attach the new fixture. If in doubt, describe your problem to the electrical-supply dealer and seek his advice.

Bear in mind that if the ceiling plate of the new fixture is smaller than that of the old one, you will probably have to repaint the ceiling. The now-exposed area around the fixture is unlikely to be the same color as the surrounding ceiling because of fading and rising dirt and dust; this is especially true in a kitchen.

If, after you have installed a new socket or a new fixture, the ceiling or wall light still doesn't work, the problem is in the line itself. If wiring is visible from above (as in an attic), check it out for signs of damage. If you can't find anything amiss, it is probably an in-wall problem, and you had best seek professional help.

If pull-chain fixtures are used (usually in basements and garages), the chain itself is

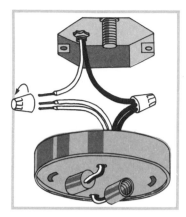

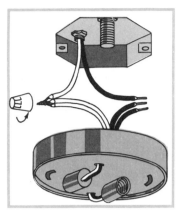

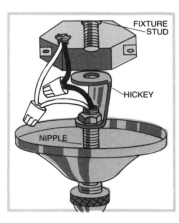

Remove wire nuts, untwist wires.

Attach wires of new fixture.

Using a hickey.

the switch, and wires are connected in the usual way—black to black and white to white. Often, this type of fixture is not pre-wired, so the cable wires are connected directly to the fixture.

Porcelain pull-chain fixture, prewired (right) and direct connection (far right).

PLUG AND CORD REPLACEMENT

Thinner and more flexible than their heftier cousins hidden inside sturdy cable, lamp and appliance cords are subjected to a lot of abuse. They get stepped on, run over, tied in knots and (although everybody knows that a cord should be gently pulled out of its wall connection by the plug) yanked about mercilessly. Small wonder that repairs and replacements are sometimes required.

A most common problem—the direct result of the type of abuse mentioned—is a cord broken at the plug. The repair is simple; just cut off the plug, bare the wires at the end of the cord, and reinstall the plug. Net loss: a few inches of cord.

But this can't always be done. Many plugs—especially on lamps and small appliances—are molded to the cord. If the wire breaks just above the plug, there is no way to rewire the plug. In this case, or if the plug itself is worn or damaged, replacement is required.

On common lamp cord (#16 or #18, two-wire) this is quick and easy—in fact, it is literally a snap. Just snip off the cord above the old plug (or above the break) and snap on a replacement—no baring of wires or tightening of screws. There are several types of such plugs. Some are slipped over the cord and a lever is pressed down, forcing pins through the insulation to make contact with the wires (all inside the plug, of course). On others, the prongs are squeezed together to make the contact in a similar fashion. But warn off the cord-jerkers; this type of connection is not intended for tugs-of-war.

Appliances (except for low-wattage ones) usually have heavier cords, and snap-on plugs will not fit. If a molded plug on such a cord must be replaced, cut the cord above the plug (or the break). Separate the wires at the end of the cord, and strip off

about ⅝ inch of insulation from each. A wire stripper is the best tool for the job; if you use a knife, be careful not to cut into the wire. If the plug is not a molded type, remove the fiber insulating cover from the prongs (you can pry it loose at the edge with a screwdriver if it is a snug ift) to ex-

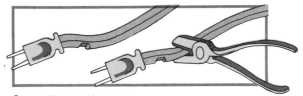

Cut cord beyond break.

Bare ends of wire and reinstrall plug.

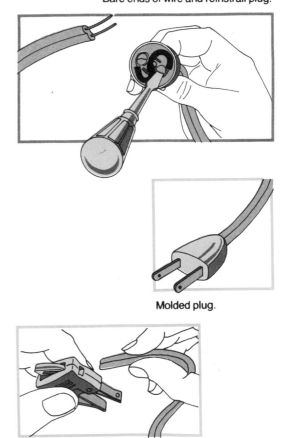

Molded plug.

Lever-type snap-on plug.

pose the wires. Loosen the terminal screws to release the wires, then pull off the plug. If an Underwriters' knot was tied within the plug (as it should have been), you may have difficulty pulling it off. Rather than cutting off the cord, untie the knot. That way you won't have to strip new wire (thereby shortening the cord even more), and you can retie the knot properly by following the old bends (see p.50).

(see p.50).

Slip the new plug over the cord. Whether or not an Underwriters' knot was originally there, tie one inside the new plug. Separate about 3 inches of wire. Loop the black wire

2. Squeeze prongs together.

1. Squeeze-type plug—
slip body over cord.

3. Pull body over prongs.

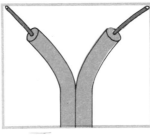

2. Separate, strip wires.

1. Cut cord above break.

3. Remove fiber insulating cover.

Home Repairs Made Easy • Plug and Cord Replacement

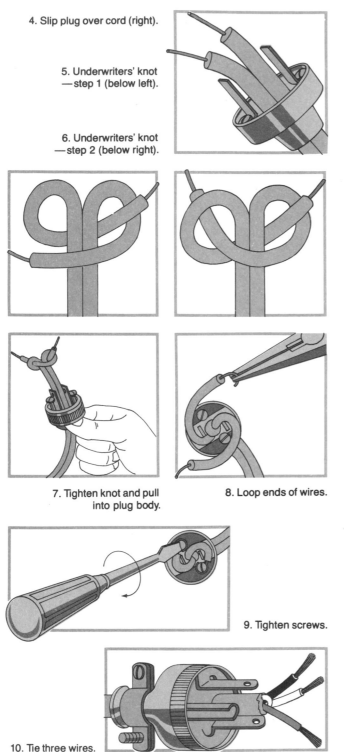

4. Slip plug over cord (right).

5. Underwriters' knot —step 1 (below left).

6. Underwriters' knot —step 2 (below right).

7. Tighten knot and pull into plug body.

8. Loop ends of wires.

9. Tighten screws.

10. Tie three wires.

behind itself and the white wire. Loop the white wire over the end of the black, and bring it up through the black loop. Tighten the knot and pull it down snugly into the plug body. This will provide a strong degree of protection against cord-jerkers.

Use a small-nosed pliers to bend loops in the ends of the bared wires. Fit the wires inside the plug and place the loops clockwise around the terminal screws—black to brass, white to chrome. Tighten the screws, then place the fiber insulator over the prongs of the plug.

Replacement of a three-prong plug is similar. Tie all three wires together in a tight knot, and pull the cord until the knot is snug against the plug. Loop the green wire around the green or dark-colored screw, and fasten the other wires as above.

Many appliances have separate cords, with a wall plug on on one end and an appliance plug on the other. Wall plug replacement is as above. If the appliance plug (or the cord at the appliance plug) is damaged or worn, it too can be replaced.

Most new appliance plugs are riveted together and are removed by cutting the cord. If your appliance has a removable appliance plug (held together by screws or bolts) and the problem is with the cord rather than the plug, you can simply cut back the cord and reinstall the old plug. Otherwise replace it.

11. Connect wires to terminals.

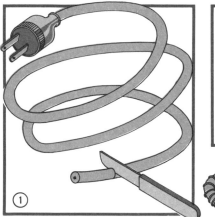

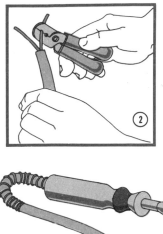

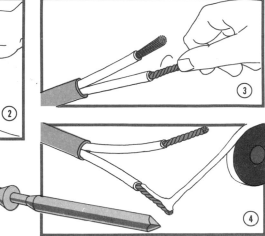

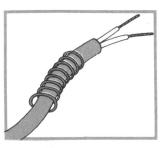

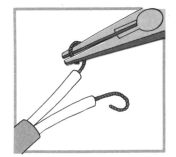

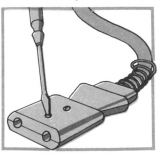

To install a new plug:
1. Remove outer insulation from cord.
2. Strip insulation from wires.
3. Twist stranded wires.
4. Heat, apply solder.

To install a new plug, first use a knife to carefully remove about 2½ inches of outer insulation from the cord end. Strip off about ¾ inch of insulation from each wire, taking care not to damage the wire. Twist each stranded wire tightly, then heat with a soldering gun or iron and apply a small amount of solder to each. This will make it easier to attach the wires.

Remove the screws holding the appliance plug casing together. Insert the cord through the spring guard. Bend the wire ends into loops. Place the loops under the terminal screws so that tightening the screws (clockwise) will close the loops. Tighten the screws. Place the spring guard into one half of the casing. Attach the other half of the casing with screws or bolts.

Sometimes the fault is with the cord itself. If it is damaged so far from the end that it will be shortened too much by repair, throw it away. If insulation is badly frayed, scrap it. Sometimes an extension cord is damaged by overload, if too many appliances are run off it. The wires become hot, and insulation melts. It is beyond repair.

Cord damage may not always be obvi-

Home Repairs Made Easy • Plug and Cord Replacement

Remove appliance
plug casing screws.

Insert cord through
spring guard.

Bend wires.

Tighten terminal screws.

Place spring guard into casing.

Assemble casing.

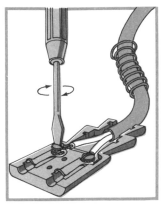

ous; broken wires may be hidden by the insulation. One almost sure sign of this condition is when the lamp or appliance goes on and off as you move the cord, making temporary contact between broken wires. Replace the cord.

When a cord is to be replaced, always

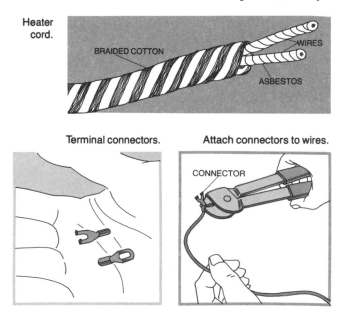

Heater cord.

BRAIDED COTTON
WIRES
ASBESTOS

Terminal connectors.

Attach connectors to wires.

CONNECTOR

buy the same type and size as the original. Lamp cord is not up to the high-wattage demands of such heat-producing appliances as toasters and irons, which should be fitted with "heater" cord wrapped with asbestos layers inside a braided cotton or nylon jacket. If you are in doubt, take along the old cord when buying new at the hardware or electrical-supply store.

Plugs are attached to new cords as above. At the other end, it depends on what the cord is attached to. On a lamp, for example, the cord wires are fastened to terminals in the socket (see p.54). On appliances, the situation varies, depending on the type and the manufacturer. Many appliance cords have round connectors at the ends of the wires for fastening to terminal screws. You may be able to buy a new cord with these fittings at an electrical-supply store or from the manufacturer of the appliance. If not, you should be able to find the connectors themselves at an electrical-supply house. Attach them to the bared ends of the wires by soldering and/or crimping them on with an all-purpose tool or pliers.

LAMP REPAIRS

When a bulb breaks, it can be difficult and dangerous to remove it from the socket for replacement. Make sure the plug is pulled out before you attempt it. Wad up newspaper or a paper bag and press it down firmly on the broken bulb, then turn it counter-clockwise until the bulb base is removed. If that doesn't work because the glass is broken off right down to the base, try turning it out with a needle-nose pliers (again, make sure that the plug is out). If it still won't come out, wedge a screwdriver inside the base, pressing it against the sides and turning until the base is removed.

When a lamp does not go on or flickers on and off, the obvious first thing to check is the bulb. Is it screwed all the way into the socket? Does it work in another lamp socket?

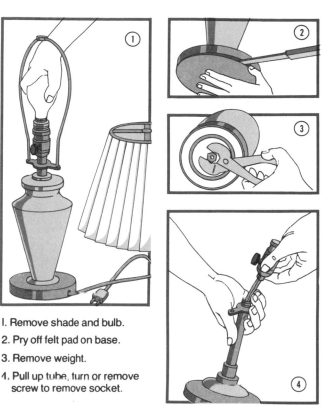

1. Remove shade and bulb.
2. Pry off felt pad on base.
3. Remove weight.
4. Pull up tube, turn or remove screw to remove socket.

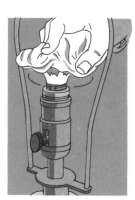

Wad newspapers to remove broken bulb.

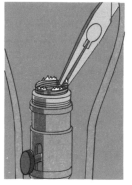

Use pliers to remove broken bulb.

Wedge screwdriver in base and turn.

If the bulb checks out all right, make sure the lamp cord is plugged all the way into the wall outlet.

Next, remove the plug and inspect the cord for signs of damage. Make repairs or replacements as detailed on pp. 48-50. If the cord and plug are all right, the problem is in the switch or socket. In either case, the fitting should be replaced.

Lamp design and construction vary greatly, but the wiring is basically the same. To replace the socket on a typical lamp, first remove the lamp shade and the bulb. With a knife, carefully pry off the protective felt pad on the bottom of the lamp base. If there is a weight there, remove the nut holding it in place and remove the weight. Lift the tube that runs through the lamp body about 6 inches out of the top. Turn the tube counterclockwise or

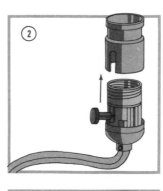

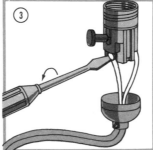

1. Press in at button of socket, remove outer shell.

2. Remove socket inner shell.

3. Remove wires.

4. Pull out old cord.

5. Attach new cord.

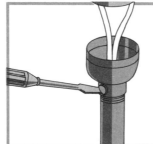

4. Pull out old cord.

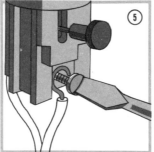

5. Attach new cord.

loosen the setscrew (or both, depending on the installation) to remove the tube from the lamp socket.

Press in at the bottom of the socket's metal outer shell and lift it straight up. Remove the insulated inner shell to expose the wiring. Loosen the terminal screws and remove the wires. (If you are simply replacing the cord, pull the old cord out the bottom of the lamp, thread new cord though the tube, strip the ends of the wires and attach to the terminals on the socket, and reassemble. If you are replacing the socket, read on.)

Take the old socket with you when you buy a replacement, and get one of the same type. Remove the outer shell and insulated shell from the new socket and loosen the terminal screws. Fit the cord through the socket cap, and install wires on the screws, looping around so that, as the screws are tightened, the ends of the wires are tightened around them.

Install the socket cap on the tube, threading it on and/or tightening the setscrew. Pull the wire through the lamp bottom until the socket sits firmly in the cap. Place the insulated shell over the socket. Position the outer shell at a slight angle, then press the bottom into the cap—it should snap securely in place. Reassemble the lamp, install bulb and shade, and let there be light!

Disassemble new socket; fit cord through cap; attach wires.

Fasten socket cap to tube.

Seat socket in cap.

Place shell over socket.

Snap outer shell in place.

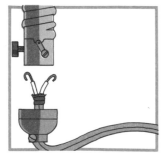

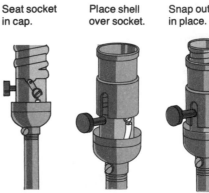

FLUORESCENT FIXTURES

Fluorescent lights give several times more illumination per watt consumed than incandescent lights. They also produce less heat, and the tubes last five to ten times longer. Because of this long life expectancy, problems that arise are often likely to be other than a burned-out tube.

Inside the fixture is a starter, a switch that opens automatically after current has flowed through it for a moment (accounting for the brief delay between the time the fixture is turned on and the time it actually lights up) and remains open. Some starters are replaceable, others (called rapid start) are built into the ballast. The ballast—wire wound around a steel core—momentarily delivers a higher voltage when the fixture is turned on, sending an arc through the gases in the tube that produce the light. It also limits the total power that can flow through it, stabilizing the light. When something goes wrong, the tube, the ballast, and especially the starter, must be suspect.

If the tube does not light, check the fuse or circuit breaker, and the outlet, plug, and cord if the fixture is a lamp; take corrective action if indicated. If those check out, replace the starter, tube, and ballast in that order until the light works properly (below).

When a fluorescent light blinks on and

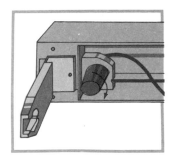

Remove starter.   Install new starter.

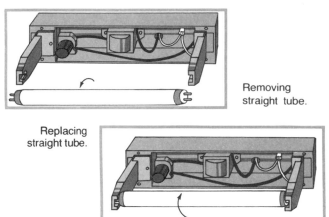

Types of fluorescent tubes.

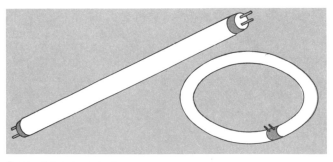

Removing straight tube.

Replacing straight tube.

off, check to make sure the tube is seated properly in the socket (see below). If the blinking persists, remove the tube and lightly sand the contacts on the tube and in the socket; then reinstall. If it still blinks, restrain the temptation to smash the offend-

Check ballast connections.

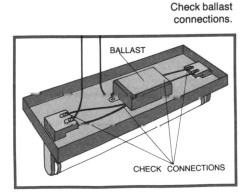

BALLAST

CHECK CONNECTIONS

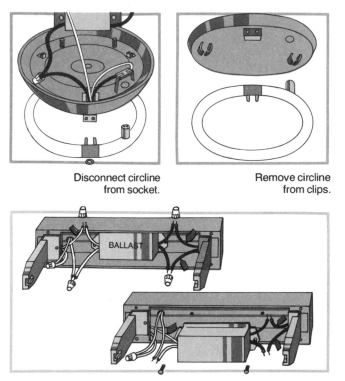

Disconnect circline from socket.

Remove circline from clips.

Disconnect ballast wires and remove ballast mounting screws.

the tube is discolored on one side only, remove it and turn it over. If discolored on one end only, remove the tube and reverse the ends.

To replace a tube, starter, or ballast, unplug the lamp or turn off the power at the entrance panel to the fixture circuit. If there is a cover plate, remove it (on lamps, the starter and ballast may be in the lamp base). To remove a replaceable starter (a small metal cylinder), give it a quarter-turn counterclockwise and pull it out. Insert a new one and turn it clockwise to lock.

Tubes are of two types: straight and circline. To remove a straight type, give it a quarter-turn and lift it out of its sockets. To reinstall or install a new one, place it in the slots and turn it to lock securely. To remove a circline tube, carefully disconnect it from the socket, then pull it out of the retaining clips on the fixture. Connect the new tube to the sockets, then press it into the retaining clips.

To replace the ballast, first remove the tube (or tubes). Label all ballast wires with coded tape to insure proper installation of the new unit. Disconnect the ballast wires from the fixture wires by removing wire nuts or loosening screws. Hold the ballast (it is relatively heavy) and remove the mounting screws or nuts; then remove the ballast.

Hold the new ballast in position and install mounting screws or nuts. Tighten. Connect all ballast wires to the fixture with wire nuts or by tightening screws (see pp. 46-47 for use of wire nuts), making sure you match up the wires according to your coded tape. Remove the tape and install the tube.

After all repairs and replacements are made, reinstall the cover plate if there is one. Then plug in the lamp or restore power to the circuit at the service panel.

ing bulb against a brick wall and, instead, replace the starter and, if necessary, the ballast of the fixture.

Sometimes the light flickers and swirls around inside a new tube. This condition is normal, and the light will become steady with use. If the problem continues, install a new starter.

A humming or buzzing noise indicates a ballast problem. Check to make sure that all ballast wire connections are tight (after first unplugging the lamp or turning off power to the fixture). If the noise persists, the ballast is worn and should be replaced.

Mild discoloration of the tube is a normal condition. If the tube becomes dark or black, it should be replaced. If a new tube becomes blackened, replace the starter. If

DOORBELLS AND CHIMES

Doorbells and chimes operate on low voltage, usually 10 volts for bells and up to 16 volts for chimes. A transformer is wired to the service entry to reduce the 110-120 voltage to the low level required. If you are replacing a transformer, make sure the new one is the proper size for your system (voltage should be listed on the bell or chime unit). You can work on the low-voltage side of the transformer without any danger, but the other side (between the transformer and the entry panel) is hot, and the fuse should be removed or breaker turned off when you are working there or on the transformer.

When the doorbell or chimes fail to work, first check the noise mechanism. Re-move the cover and inspect for loose con-nections. Tighten the screws, and clean off the contacts with a cotton swab dipped in alcohol. Replace the cover.

If the bell or chimes still don't work, go to the transformer (usually in the basement either at or near the entry panel) and listen while a helper presses the push button at the door. If it hums, the problem is not there. If it is silent and the bell is also, re-place the transformer with one of the same type (make sure the power is off first).

If the transformer checks out, try the push button. Remove the cover plate and check the contacts, which may become cor-roded by exposure to the elements. Clean

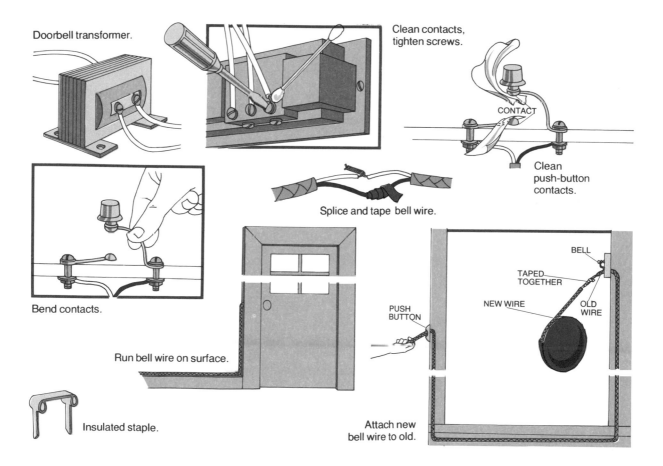

Doorbell transformer.

Clean contacts, tighten screws.

CONTACT

Clean push-button contacts.

Splice and tape bell wire.

Bend contacts.

Run bell wire on surface.

Insulated staple.

PUSH BUTTON

BELL

TAPED TOGETHER

NEW WIRE

OLD WIRE

Attach new bell wire to old.

the contacts with sandpaper or emery cloth, rubbing them lightly. Make sure the button touches the contacts when it is pushed in; if it doesn't, gently bend the contacts to correct the situation. Contacts that are badly bent or broken mean that a new push button is needed. They are inexpensive and easy to install; just take the wires off of the old and attach to the new.

If all else seems in order, check out the wiring. Bell wire (usually #18) is thin and easily damaged. For example, if you have recently installed ceiling tile in the basement, you may have inadvertently put a staple through the bell wire. Or your hammer may have gone astray while you were hanging a new ceiling outlet box and smashed through the bell wire without your knowing it. Any breaks in the bell wire can be spliced and covered with plastic tape.

If you suspect a problem within the walls, it is usually easier to replace the wire from the transformer to the push button or noise mechanism, or between the push button and the noise mechanism, than to try to locate the break. Attach the end of the new wire securely to the end of the old, twisting and taping them together; then pull the new wire through the wall with the old—and hope that the wires don't break. If necessary, run the bell wire along the top of a baseboard and up and around door jambs to where it must go, securing it at frequent intervals with insulated staples. The small wire is relatively unobstrusive.

If none of these corrective measures puts the sound of music back into your bell or chimes, the noise mechanism is probably defective. The best repair is replacement. Follow manufacturer's instructions for hooking up the new unit.

MORE TIPS FOR TOOLS

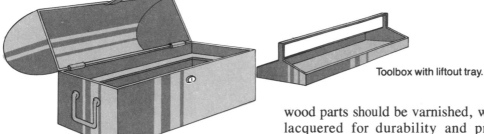

Toolbox with liftout tray.

Most of the tools you'll need for working on your home's exterior or interior are the basics with which you are probably familiar. You may already have some or all of them, and some were already mentioned previously. But if all you have in your toolbox are a cheap hammer and screwdriver, be prepared to accumulate a few more instruments —and good ones, this time.

When you inhabit a furnished room or an apartment, your tool needs are few. But when you (and the bank) own your home, you will find that you need a small arsenal of basic tools to take care of the place. You should start picking up some of them as soon as you sign on the dotted line, as all the how-to talent in the world won't help you if you don't have proper tools. Don't make the mistake of investing a small or large fortune in whatever the local hardware store has in stock, but—if you are new to the repairs game—have on hand a few basic items. You can buy others as the need arises.

Never bargain-shop for tools. Don't settle for a lesser type or smaller size than you really need. And don't skimp on quality. A penny saved can mean dollars lost —or worse. Whatever the tool, look for a sturdy body and smooth finish. Metal surfaces should be coated for rust prevention;

wood parts should be varnished, waxed, or lacquered for durability and protection against splinters.

Tool Storage

You're going to need a place to keep all those shiny new tools. The kitchen "junk" drawer might be okay to start with, but you'll soon find that the screwdriver is hopelessly entangled with string when you want it most. One of the first things you should do in your new home is to make some sort of plan for tool storage. It may be only a toolbox—at first, anyway—but it should be separate, so that you know where the tools are when you need them quickly.

A good start toward tool storage is a piece of perforated hardboard (popularly known

Hanging tools on perforated hardboard.

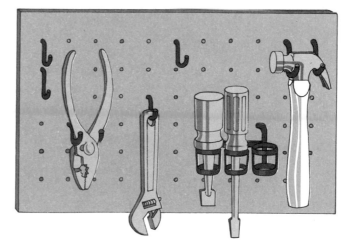

as Pegboard, a trade name). When you buy the board, get one of the kits that contain hardware for attaching it to the wall, as well as the hooks, hangers, and assorted accessories for accommodating various tools. Hang it in the basement or garage. Later on, you'll probably want a workbench, so make sure there is room for one underneath your storage wall.

Buying Tools

Does a devoted fisherman buy a cheap rod and reel? Does a dentist buy a bargain-basement drill? Of course not. The same attitude should apply to any tool. The dollar you save on a supermarket or drugstore tool can cost you many times that in time and trouble, so don't buy it. Cheap tools also often chip, break, or collapse, causing expensive damage and even injury.

Always buy quality merchandise. A good hammer is precisely tooled, properly weighted, and has maximum strength so that it will drive a nail straight, true, and fast. A cheap hammer will slip off the nail, drive it crookedly, and require more strokes. Often, the head is poorly attached so that it might fly off at a crucial time and possibly even become a lethal missile. It just isn't worth it. The same applies to all tools.

When you shop, look for tools that are stamped with the manufacturer's name or symbol. Many reputable manufacturers have generous warranties, some for life! Pick up the tool and simulate its use. Does it have a tough and sturdy feel? Is the metal smooth and polished? Anything that gets rugged duty, such as a wrench or hammer-head, should be drop-forged. If there are moving parts, do they work freely and easily without wiggle or play?

Claw Hammer

There are many kinds of hammers: ball peen for metalwork, tack for upholstery, mason's for brickwork, to name just a few. What most laymen mean by a "hammer" is the common claw, or nail, hammer. The claw hammer is the basic hammer for jobs like whacking wood into place, but it is designed primarily for driving in or pulling out nails. The best claw hammer for general use has a 16-ounce head that is firmly attached to a wood handle, either with a solid wedge and/or glue on top, or forged in a single piece with the handle which is then covered with rubber, plastic, or leather for a firm grip. A good one costs about $8.

To use a hammer correctly, grip it at or near the end of the handle and swing it from your shoulder. You may miss the nail at first, but keep trying (on scrap wood) until you get the "swing" of it. It's well worth the practice. An experienced carpenter can drive in large spikes this way with just a couple of blows.

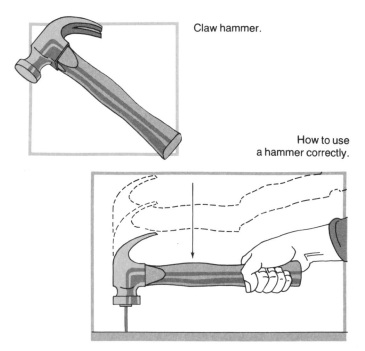

Claw hammer.

How to use
a hammer correctly.

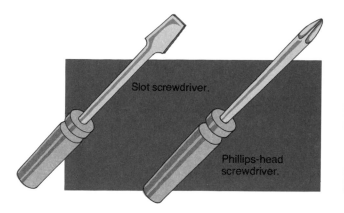

Slot screwdriver.

Phillips-head screwdriver.

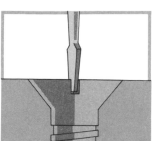

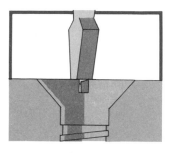

Screwdrivers

One screwdriver is not really enough for the do-it-yourselfer's toolbox. To start with, you should have the most common one, with a flat-tipped, wedge-shaped blade ¼ inch wide and about 6 inches long. This model fits the most frequently used sizes of slotted screws, but you shouldn't use it for larger or very tiny sizes. Either the blade will be too small and slip around, or it will be too big and won't fit into the slot. Sometimes the blade will fit the slot but be wider than the screw and damage the surrounding surface. So it's best to have one with a narrow blade. For heavier work, use a screwdriver with a longer shank.

A Phillips screwdriver has an X-shaped end and is used for cross-slotted screws. One of these will do for a start, the most useful being the #2, which has a shank about 4 inches long. Buy others as needed.

A good screwdriver has a tough, tempered-steel blade and a fluted handle, usually plastic. The handle should be smooth and gently rounded at the hand. The tip of the blade is usually polished, but not necessarily the shank.

A screwdriver is simple to use once the screw is started. Many novices try to use the screwdriver without starting the hole first. This may sometimes work in soft wood but is virtually impossible in hard wood. Use an awl, a nail, or a tool specifically designed for starting screws. Many old-timers start the screw by banging it in

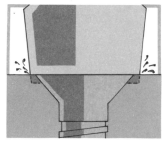

Wrong-size screwdrivers:

Blade too thin for slot (above)

Blade too thick for slot (above right)

Blade too wide for slot (right).

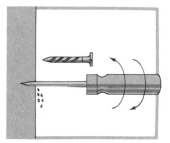

How to make a starter hole with an awl.

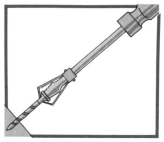

Screwdriver with clip to hold screws.

Use two hands on screwdriver.

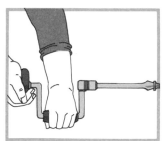

Screwdriver bit in brace.

with a hammer, but this often results in damaged and hard-to-work screw slots. It is helpful to hold the blade and screw head together in the beginning. This is not always possible, however, and some screwdrivers have metal clips over the blade that hold the screw head to the blade for use in hard-to-reach areas. Firm pressure should be applied against the screw during driving to keep the blade in place. When the wood is very hard, it is wise to predrill the entire hole (use a wood-screw pilot bit; see electric drill, p. 66). Special drill bits are available for this purpose, matching screw sizes. It sometimes helps to use both hands once the screw is started, one turning the handle, and the other held flat against the end of it to apply more pressure.

It is easy to remove screws once you get them loosened. The trouble, again, is getting them started, or "broken." Don't forget that screws are driven in clockwise, and removed counterclockwise. If a screw won't budge, give it a quick twist in both directions. For larger stubborn screws, a screwdriver bit in a brace provides extra leverage.

Quality screwdrivers cost from about $1.50 for small ones to about $4 for large ones. They are often available in sets, which is fine if the set is priced less than the total of the tools inside. Check first, because this isn't always the case.

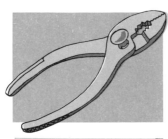

Slip-joint pliers (left).

Slip-joint pliers gripping small objects (below left).

Slip-joint pliers gripping large objects (below).

Pliers

There are numerous types of pliers, most of them used by specialists such as electricians and electronics workers. The kind the homeowner uses most often is the slip-joint pliers. It performs numerous holding tasks—and is often the wrong tool for the job. Pliers are not relaly designed for tightening and loosening nuts—wrenches are. Yet this is a common household use, and it will do if you don't have the right wrench in your toolbox.

A slip-joint pliers *is* the right tool for grasping, turning, bending, or pulling bolts, wires, broken glass, and sharp or small objects. The term "slip-joint" is applied because the tool has two slots in which the center fastener pin can be located. In one slot, the pliers grip small objects, with the forward jaws tight and parallel. When the pin is in the other slot, the concave inner jaws can go around larger objects. Some pliers have cutting jaws just inside the curved portion. These are for cutting wires, small nails, etc.

When shopping for pliers, choose ones that have been drop-forged and have either a polished surface or a bluish-black sheen. The pin should be solidly fastened so that you can't remove it. The outer parallel jaws should have fine grooves or cross-hatching, the inner ones sharp rugged teeth. Handles should be scored or tooled so that you can grip them firmly. A good pair costs $2 to $3. Special-purpose types may be more.

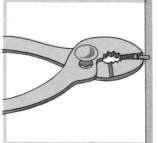
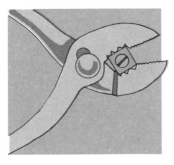

Slip-joint pliers cutting wire.

Hand Saws

Saws, too, come in a wide variety of sizes and types. The homeowner should purchase an 8- or 10-point crosscut saw for all-around work. The "8-point" means that there are eight teeth per inch. "Crosscut" means that the teeth are beveled slightly outward and knife-shaped, designed for cutting across the grain of the wood—the most common type of cut.

A ripsaw has squarish, chisellike teeth, and it cuts with the grain. Most do-it-yourselfers have little need for a ripsaw. If you must do a lot of ripping, a power saw of some kind is preferred.

A hacksaw is used for cutting metals and some plastics. It has a wide U-shaped frame with devices on each end for holding the removable, fine-toothed saw blade. A thumbscrew draws the blade taut.

A coping saw is somewhat similar in design to a hacksaw, except that the blade is much thinner and has larger teeth. A coping-saw blade can be turned to various angles for making curving cuts in wood.

Keyhole and compass saws are similar, with the keyhole blade being thinner and finer. Both are used to make curving cuts and small cuts when only one side of the work is accessible, such as in paneling, wallboard, and similar materials that are already nailed up.

When buying a saw, look for a tempered steel or chrome-nickel blade. Handles should be removable hardwood or high-

Crosscut saw.

Ripsaw.

Keyhole, compass saw.

Hacksaw.

impact plastic. Better saws have taper-ground blades, and some have a Teflon coating for rust-resistance and less binding.

Crosscut saws—good ones—cost about $10, a hacksaw about half that. Coping saws cost a little less, as do keyhole and compass saws.

Measuring Instruments

A 6-foot folding rule with extension is a good all-around measuring device. The readings are large and easily read, and some have red markings every 16 inches

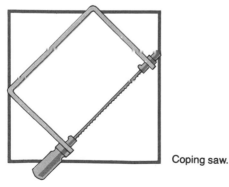

Coping saw.

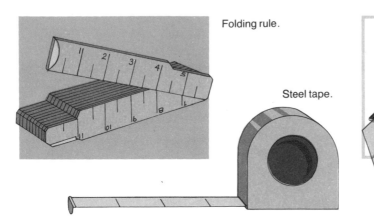

Folding rule.

Steel tape.

Utility knife.

Putty knife.

(the standard "centering" for framing). The extension is an extra 5-inch section that slides out and allows you to take inside measurements when working in closets, cabinets, etc.

A steel tape is flexible enough to wind up inside a small case, yet rigid enough when extended to stay in place. A small hook on the end holds it in place when you are measuring a long piece. The case usually is exactly 2 or 3 inches long, so that you can measure inside dimensions accurately by adding on the 2 or 3 inches. Some have friction locks to hold the tape open and spring returns to retract it quickly.

A good folding rule with extension costs about $5; a steel tape ½ inch wide by 10 feet costs a dollar or so less.

Utility Knife

This is an inexpensive tool that has a multitude of uses. It utilizes a razor blade, or a special blade that looks like one, to cut such things as gypsum wallboard, wallcoverings, thin woods, carpeting, rope, and string. It is also handy for opening boxes and cartons.

A good utility knife has a handle shaped to fit your palm, with space inside to store extra blades. Look for one that has a re-

tractable blade that you can withdraw for safety's sake when not in use. The retracting device also lets you extend it to various lengths to adjust for the thickness of whatever you are cutting. The knife costs about $2 to $3.

Putty Knife

This tool is used for applying and smoothing soft materials such as putty and wood filler. Those with stiffer blades can also be used as scrapers.

A good putty knife has a blade that extends well into the handle and is attached by rivets. The blade should be of hardened, tempered steel with a blunt end and no sharp edges. You will pay about $1.50 for a 1½-inch-wide putty knife, and up to $3 for a 3-inch model.

Chisels

A wood chisel consists of a steel blade usually fitted with a wooden or plastic handle. It has a single beveled cutting edge on the end of the blade. According to construction, chisels are divided into two general classes: tang chisels, in which part of the chisel enters the handle, and socket

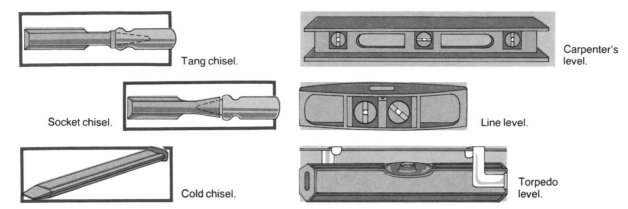

Tang chisel.

Socket chisel.

Cold chisel.

Carpenter's level.

Line level.

Torpedo level.

chisels, in which the handle enters into a part of the chisel. A socket chisel is designed for striking with a wooden mallet (never a steel hammer), whereas a tang chisel is designed for hand use only.

Wood chisels are also divided into types, depending upon their weight and thickness, the shape or design of the blade, and the work they are intended to do. For general household use, a ½-inch or ¾-inch paring chisel is probably best. It has a relatively thin blade and is beveled along the sides. The cost is $3 to $4.

Another type of chisel for your home repair toolbox is the cold chisel. This is made of hardened, tempered alloy steel and is used for striking steel, concrete, stone, and other hard materials. A cold chisel is struck with a ball peen or other heavy hammer. It costs a little less than a wood chisel of the same size.

Levels

The carpenter's level is a tool designed to determine whether a plane or surface is true horizontal or true vertical. It is a simple instrument consisting of a liquid, such as alcohol or chloroform, partially filling a glass vial or tube so that a bubble remains. The vial is mounted in a frame of alumi-

num, magnesium, or wood. Levels are usually equipped with two or more vials. One vial is built into the frame at right angles to another. The vial is slightly curved, causing the bubble always to seek the highest point in the tube. On the outside of the vial are two sets of gradation lines separated by a space. Leveling is established when the air bubble is centered between the gradation lines.

There are several other types of levels. A torpedo level is useful in tight places. It has a top-reading vial so that you can place it on a low or deep surface and tell whether it's level without bending way down to look at it. A line level hooks onto a piece of twine or string and is useful when working with concrete forms, brick, and similar jobs where lines are used.

Wrenches

There are probably more types of wrenches than of any other tool. There are open-end and box wrenches, some with a combination of each, and some with half-boxes. (A box wrench completely encloses the nut.) There are ratchet wrenches that are turned like a crank, pipe wrenches, chain wrenches, and countless others.

Your first wrench acquisition should be

Adjustable wrench.

an adjustable wrench. These come in various sizes, but one about 8 inches long, with jaw capacity up to an inch, is a good starter. This wrench has one fixed jaw, and another that is moved away from or toward the fixed jaw by means of a knurled knob.

Look for a drop-forged, alloy steel wrench with a chrome-polished or blue-black sheen. The jaws should be exactly parallel and not loose (check that by wiggling the movable jaw). Some have a locking device that holds the adjustable jaw in a constant position. A quality adjustable wrench of the recommended size costs about $5.

Electric Drill

An electric drill can do so many jobs that it is almost a must in the do-it-yourselfer's toolbox. With it you can make holes in almost any material. By using accessories and attachments you can sand, polish, grind, buff, stir paint, and drive screws.

Depending on quality, size, gearing, and special features, a drill for home use costs from $10 to $50 or more. Your best choice will be a model with the work capacity and special features you will regularly use. The work capacity of a drill depends on its chuck size and rated revolutions per minute (RPM).

The chuck size is the diameter of the largest bit shank the drill can hold. Home-use sizes are ¼, ⅜, and ½ inch. Usually, the larger the chuck, the wider and deeper the holes the drill can bore.

The RPM rating is an indication of the number of gear sets in a model, its speed, and the type of work for which it is best suited. For example, a ¼-inch drill rated about 2,000 RPM usually has one gear set and is appropriate for rapid drilling in wood and use with sanding and polishing accessories. A model with more gears would have a lower RPM rating and work more slowly but could make bigger holes in hard metals or masonry without stalling or overheating.

For most jobs around a home, a single-speed drill is adequate. However, a two-speed or variable-speed model would be more suitable if you intend to drill material (such as glass) that requires a slow speed or if you want to use many accessories. A drill with both variable speed and reverse is effective for driving and removing screws.

The trigger switch, which starts the drill, is on the pistol-grip handle, and many models include a switch lock for continuous operation. You activate the lock by pressing a button; the lock instantly releases if you tighten your squeeze on the trigger switch.

Variable-speed drills have trigger switches that allow you to vary bit speed from almost zero up to maximum RPM by trigger-finger pressure. Some have controls for presetting the maximum RPM.

Drills with reverse have separate reverse controls in different positions depending on the brand. To protect the motor, allow the drill to come to a full stop before reversing.

The front of the drill, where bits and other accessories are inserted and removed, is called the chuck. The three-jaw gear type is the most common. Its collar is first hand-closed on the shank of a bit. Then a key is inserted into the chuck body and turned to tighten the three jaws simultaneously and with considerable force. Some models have a holder to make key loss less likely.

Some bargain drills have chucks that are hand-tightened by means of knurled collars. They may either offer a poor hold on bits and accessories or be difficult to loosen when work is finished. Examine chuck placement as well as quality. The higher the chuck on the front of the housing, the easier the drill will be to use in corners.

Manufacturers' catalogs contain information on the accessories available for particular drill brands and models. The com-

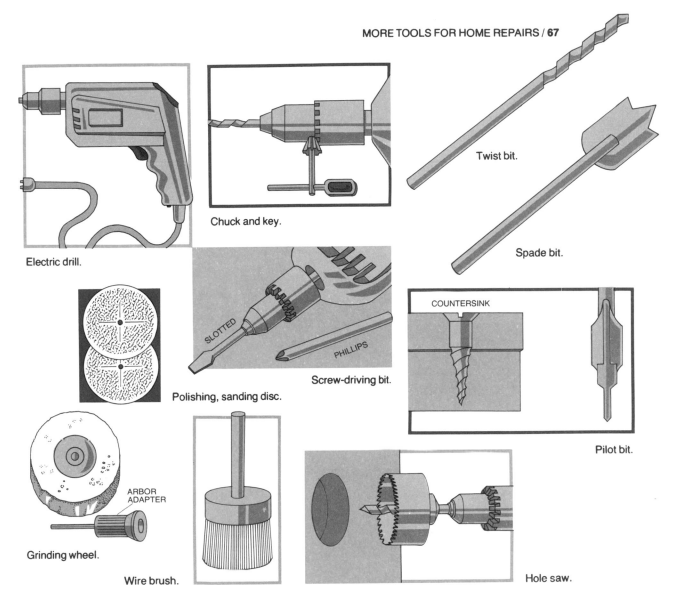

Electric drill.

Chuck and key.

Twist bit.

Spade bit.

Polishing, sanding disc.

SLOTTED

PHILLIPS

Screw-driving bit.

COUNTERSINK

Pilot bit.

ARBOR ADAPTER

Grinding wheel.

Wire brush.

Hole saw.

mon accessories that enable you to use a drill for various jobs are described here.

A drill bit has a working end that makes holes and a smooth shank that is grasped by the jaws of a chuck. Although bits can be bought individually, they cost less if purchased in sets.

The twist bit, the most commonly used, cuts cylindrical holes. It has a sharp point and two spiral-shaped cutting edges that lift chips out of the hole as the bit turns. Carbon steel twist bits are suited to drilling wood and soft metals; high-speed steel bits cut wood, soft metals, and mild steel; tungsten carbide or carbide-tipped bits cut hard metals and masonry. Cutting diameters commonly available range from $1/16$ inch to $1/2$ inch.

The spade bit cuts large cylindrical holes in wood. It has a flat, spade-shaped driving end with a pointed tip. Common cutting diameters range from $3/8$ inch to 1 inch.

The wood-screw pilot bit has three widths of cutting edge. The narrowest drills a hole to give screw threads solid anchorage. The next makes a shaft for the unthreaded screw shank. The widest makes a hole, or countersink, for flat-headed screws. A detachable stop can make shallow or deep countersinks.

The screw-driving bit attaches to drills with variable speed and reverse to drive and remove slotted and Phillips-head screws. On single- or two-speed drills, the bit must be used with a special screw-driving attachment.

Polishing and sanding discs, grinding wheels, wire-brush discs, and hole saws are usually secured to a drill by an arbor that goes through the center hole of the wheel or disc and is fastened by a washer and nut or by a screw and washer. A flange keeps the wheel from slipping down the shank that fits into the drill chuck. Some discs and wire brushes have built-in shanks that fit the drill spindle when the chuck is removed.

Discs are used either with abrasive paper for sanding or a soft bonnet for polishing. Grinding wheels are for sharpening tools or smoothing metal. Wire brushes remove paint, rust, and dirt from wood and metal. Hole saws cut round holes through boards or sheet materials by means of a rim saw blade and a centered pilot bit. Common diameters range from ½ inch to 4 inches.

Saber saw.

Circular saw.

Electric sander.

Power Tools

There are literally hundreds of specialized tools that you may use for specific tasks. Buy these as the need arises, as your skills increase, and as you undertake more detailed work around the house—especially if you begin making improvements as well as routine repairs. Power tools will make your work easier and the results better. The ones you will probably buy are: a saber saw, for fast cutting of curved and straight lines in wood and other materials; a circular saw, for extensive cutting of straight lines and invaluable for major jobs such as installing wood siding; and an electric sander, for smooth, speedy removal of wood, paint, or anything else removable by regular sandpaper.

SQUEAKY FLOORS

Why live with a floor that complains all the time? Elimination of squeaks and creaks can be managed with relatively little effort, the means depending on the floor's construction and whether the subflooring is accessible from below.

Most wood floors consist of two layers: a subfloor of boards or plywood and the finished floor of narrower boards—usually hardwood—tongued and grooved together and nailed into place. The subflooring is supported from underneath by wood joists normally spaced on 16-inch centers. A squeak is usually the result of a board or boards having separated from what is beneath. The finish floor may have pulled away from the subfloor, or the subfloor may have warped or sagged and pulled away from the joists.

It is best to make your inspection and repairs from under the floor, if this is not concealed by a ceiling or other barrier. Have someone walk around overhead so that you can pinpoint the problem. Inspect the area around the squeak. Make sure joists are level, and check between joists and subflooring for signs of warping or lifting of the floorboards.

If a squeak is detected directly over a joist, an effective method of quieting it is to drive thin wood shims between the joist and subflooring. Pieces of shingle are ideal for this. Hammer them into place over one or more joists, as necessary. Larger wedges of wood can be used if needed.

When the squeak originates between joists, first install a header of 2 x 4 or 2 x 6 lumber to act as a base for the shimming. Cut the header so that it fits snugly between two joists. Tap it up firmly against the subfloor, narrow edge up, and toenail it securely in place. Now work in shims as needed between header and subfloor. This should eliminate the noise.

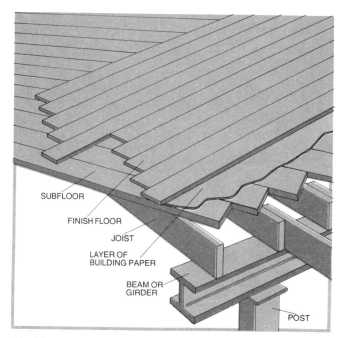

SUBFLOOR
FINISH FLOOR
JOIST
LAYER OF BUILDING PAPER
BEAM OR GIRDER
POST

Wood floor construction.

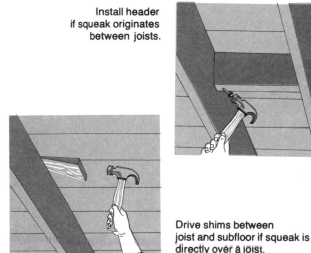

Install header if squeak originates between joists.

Drive shims between joist and subfloor if squeak is directly over a joist.

Another approach is to drive a screw up through the subfloor and into the finish floor where the squeak is found. Use a wood screw about 1 inch long for this operation—

Home Repairs Made Easy

Drill pilot
hole through
subfloor.

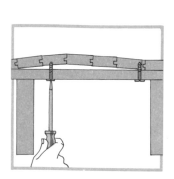

Drive screw
up into
finish floor.

Drive them in pairs, as required, along or across the board. The nails should be driven at an angle, each pair forming a V, with the points meeting under the subfloor. Drill pilot holes to avoid splitting the hardwood. Use a nailset to recess nailheads. The holes can be filled with putty or plugged with wax patching crayon. If you are doing this kind of work on a floor that is covered with linoleum or tile, about the only thing you can do is nail right through the floor covering. A lot of guesswork is involved here because the boards are unseen, so prod around with your foot to try to pinpoint the squeak as closely as possible. This will avoid having to drive too many nails. The holes in the covering can be plugged with wax crayon.

enough to penetrate the subfloor but not the finish floor — and have someone stand on the floor overhead. It is best to drill a pilot hole to help start the screw and to avoid splitting the hardwood floor. Again, be careful not to penetrate the finish floor. Maintain the weight overhead as you drive the screw so that subfloor and finish floor will be brought together.

These methods cannot be used if the understructure is inaccessible. In that case, you will have to make the repairs from topside. You can often silence a squeak by working some talcum powder or powdered stainless lubricant into the cracks between floorboards, but this is only a temporary treatment. The best way is to nail the noisy board.

Use long finishing nails for this job.

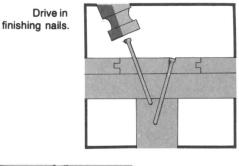

Drive in
finishing nails.

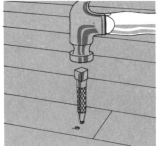

Set, fill holes
with putty.

CRACKED AND SPLIT FLOORING

Floorboards become damaged for a variety of reasons, the most common of which are shrinkage and expansion because of exposure to water. When wet, the boards expand against their joints. As they dry, they return to their former size, causing cracks to appear either between the joints or along the grain of the board. New floors laid with green or wet wood also produce cracks.

You should make it a rule never to wash a wood floor with water. Rather, treat the wood with an application of any of the floor sealers available, then give it a good waxing for an easy-to-maintain protective finish. If you use a polyurethane finish on the floor, waxing is not recommended. This durable finish is maintained by simply wiping it clean with a cloth or mop.

Cracks can be filled with a variety of compounds. You can use a mixture of glue and sawdust, a wood-fiber putty, or plastic wood. The compound is pressed into the crack and then sanded and stained to the proper color. You can also fashion small wedges of hardwood to fill the crack, hammering them in tightly, then planing the excess and sanding smooth.

Splits along the grain of a board should be filled with a mixture of glue and sawdust to prevent the board from splitting further.

A warped board can sometimes be evened off with a good sanding or by planing. First make sure all nailheads have been recessed. If the board is a wide one, you can also try to flatten it by soaking it with water, then nailing it flat. Otherwise it will have to be replaced with a new board.

To remove a badly worn or damaged sec-

1. Drill holes in corners of damaged board.

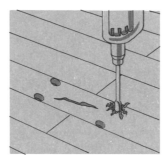

2. Chisel out damaged section across and along its grain.

3. Remove damaged section of board.

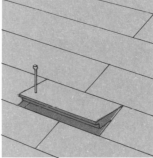

4. Nail new piece in place and countersink the nails.

tion of board, first drill large holes at each end of the damaged section. The holes should not extend through the subfloor below. Drill close to the edges of the board, then carefully chisel out the damaged section across and along its grain, taking care not to harm the tongue and groove sides of the adjoining boards. Cut the replacement piece to size. Using a chisel, remove the bottom half of the groove on the replacement piece. You can now slip the new board into place, nail it down, countersink the nailheads, and plane it flush if necessary.

Fill cracks.

Drive wedges into cracks.

Nail warped board flat.

SAGGING FLOORS

When a floor sags at any point or feels bouncy when you walk over it, part of the understructure is probably weak. This presents a potentially dangerous condition that should be corrected without delay. Because the condition usually is found on the lower floors of the house, thereby providing you with ready access to the understructure, you can often make the necessary repairs and adjustments yourself.

The cause of the sagging may be that the joists are spaced too far apart to provide rigid support for weakened subflooring. One or more joists may have warped or sagged. The beam that supports the joists may not be making contact all the way across.

Use a long straightedge and level as you inspect the subflooring, joists, and supporting beams. If a joist has warped or sagged but is otherwise sound, you can raise the

floor by driving hardwood wedges between the joist and subflooring. Additional support is gained by toenailing a sturdy crosspiece between the joists under the floor.

Check to see that all joists are resting on the main beam. It often happens that a beam sags at the center—particularly if it is made of wood. Support posts may be spaced too far apart, or they may have buckled or rotted or sunk into the concrete floor. Or they may be absent altogether, in which case you will have to add one or more new posts.

Adjustable metal posts that have a screw-type jack at the end can be used to raise the beam into position. These can be left in place as permanent supports, if needed. The base of the jack must rest on a solid cement footing. If the cement floor is less than 4 inches thick or shows signs of deterioration, you must put in a new footing.

Because of potential damage to the frame and walls of the house, you must never attempt to raise the beam more than a slight amount at a time. Put the jack post into position under the beam so that it just touches. Make sure the jack is perfectly vertical, then give the screw a half turn and stop. Wait several days to a week, then give it another half turn. Do not be in a hurry— chances are it took quite a while for the beam to sag that much, so it can wait to be straightened out. Continue a little at a time until the floor overhead is level, then either insert a chock between the existing post and the beam or leave the jack post in position permanently.

You can check the level of the floor with a long straightedge as you go along. Or you can tack a string from wall to wall across the floor above the sag. If the string is kept taut, you will be able to observe the distance between it and the floor as this distance gradually diminishes.

Use wedge to raise subfloor.

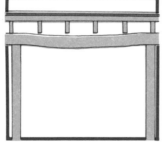

Sagging beam.

Check floor level with long straightedge.

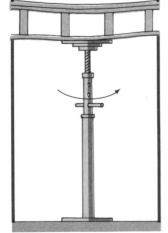

Give jack a half-turn at a time.

Home Repairs Made Easy

TILE AND SHEET FLOORING

Resilient floor coverings laid over wood and concrete are cemented in place with an adhesive such as mastic. Kept waxed and clean, they wear well, but after a time it will become necessary to replace one or more damaged tiles or deal with worn or broken sheet flooring. A seam may also come unstuck, in which case a recementing job is needed.

Finding a replacement floor tile that matches the rest is not always easy. Manufacturers of tile recommend that extra pieces be purchased with the original floor, not only to allow for wastage during installation, but to provide for just this contingency. If you are really stuck with a floor pattern, style, or color that is not available, a possible solution would be to remove several good tiles and install new ones that will create a limited pattern or decorative path encompassing the damaged area. Of course, you should first check with your dealer to see whether the tile might be available through the manufacturer. Take along a sample.

Tiles are laid butted tightly against each other, and removal of one, if not carefully done, can cause damage to others. To make the job easier, the cement and the tile can first be softened by heat. The professionals have special "hot plates" for this purpose, but you can do the job almost as effectively with a household electric iron. Set it to its hottest and put a damp cloth between it and the tile. A propane torch played over the center of the tile is a faster method, but the flame should not come in direct contact with the tile.

While the tile is still hot, work the tip of a putty knife under a raised corner or seam and carefully pry it loose. If it does not come easily—or if you are unable to use heat because of the tile's composition—you may have to cut out the tile in pieces with a

1. Loosening tile with electric iron or with torch.

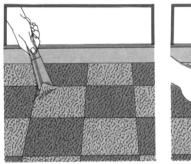

2. Prying up the tile.   3. Cut around tile edges.

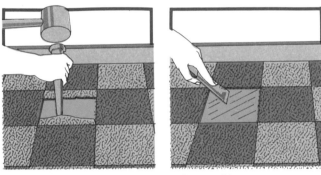

4. Chisel tile.   5. Scrape old cement.

hammer and chisel, taking care not to gouge the subfloor. Begin this operation by first cutting into the seam around the tile with a sharp knife. As you remove the tile with the chisel, work from the center out to the edges; this minimizes the possibility of damage to surrounding tiles.

Install
new tile.

Apply adhesive
under seam.

Slit "bubble."

Work adhesive
under lifted area.

Sometimes, if the damaged tile is removed in one piece by the heating method, the cement is tacky enough so that you can simply press a new tile in place. Otherwise, the old cement should be scraped off to provide a smooth base, then new cement put down. Apply it evenly and sparingly to avoid its squeezing up around the edges of the tile.

On linoleum and sheet vinyl, a seam may lift because the cement was not applied properly or has been weakened by water. This can be corrected by applying fresh cement to the area beneath the flooring material and placing a heavy object on top until it dries. Work the cement in with a flexible blade, taking care not to tear the material. Wipe off the excess and allow plenty of time for drying. If there is a bubble or raised spot remote from a seam, slit the raised portion along its length with a razor or sharp knife and work the cement under the lifted areas.

You can renew worn or grubby-looking linoleum, if it is otherwise intact, by giving it a few coats of floor enamel in a color of your choice. First prepare the floor by removing all traces of wax or grease; steel wool and alcohol will help here. When it is clean and dry, apply a first coat of paint. When that is dry, give it a finish coat. You can add more colors to provide a stipple effect or to create a pattern laid out with masking tape. The floor should then be waxed to protect the enamel.

Broken linoleum can be repaired with a patch of new material. Lay the new linoleum over the damaged surface and cut through both new and old linoleum with a sharp knife. A straightedge will help guide the cut. The material is more flexible and lies flat better if it is warm. Remove the old piece and check the fit of the cut patch. Trim the surrounding linoleum so that there is a $1/16$-inch gap all around—this will fill in later when the new piece swells naturally. Apply cement and press the patch in place. The seams can be tapped flush with a mallet or a hammer and a block of wood.

Sheet flooring and tile can be applied over any wood or concrete floor (above grade) that is in good condition. Several types are also suitable for below-grade installation. In tile you have a choice of vinyl, cork, linoleum, rubber, vinyl asbestos, or asphalt, the last two being preferred for concrete that comes in direct contact with the ground.

Before tile can be put down, any irregularities in the floor must be corrected. Make sure nailheads do not protrude. Sand or plane smooth any raised surfaces and eliminate any existing squeaks. If it is a concrete floor, fill any cracks or gouges.

Keep in mind that resilient tiles of any composition will conform to the shape of the surface they cover. If the floor is uneven, broken, badly scarred, or pitted, you will have to lay in a hard, flat foundation for the tiles. This layer can be of hardboard or plywood, and it is fastened directly to the existing flooring. If a concrete floor is subject to persistent dampness, condensation, or leakage, correct this before proceeding any further, either by laying a waterproof barrier or pouring a new topping.

Tile can be applied successfully by the do-it-yourselfer, but the directions supplied by the manufacturer must be followed to the letter. Otherwise the results can be disappointing. Your dealer can advise you as to the number of tiles you will need to cover a given area and also give specific recom-

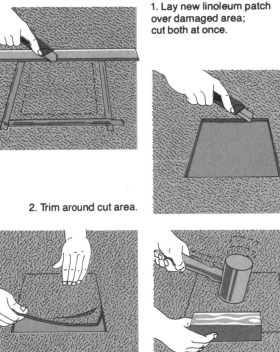

1. Lay new linoleum patch over damaged area; cut both at once.

2. Trim around cut area.

3. Press patch in place.

4. Tap seams flush.

mendations for the make or type of tile. When laying sheet flooring, first make a pattern of taped-together newspaper or heavy wrapping paper, using small pieces to fit around corners and obstructions. Use this to trace an outline for cutting on the sheet (remembering to turn the pattern over). It is a quick, simple step that can prevent a lot of irritation.

Fill, smooth cracks in concrete floor.

Make a pattern for sheet flooring (at right).

Trace onto sheet material (far right).

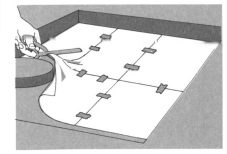

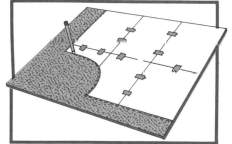

STAIR REPAIRS

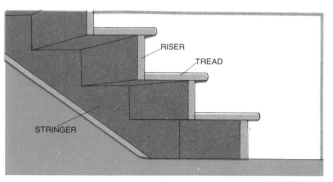

Stair construction: treads rest on a riser in simple butt joint.

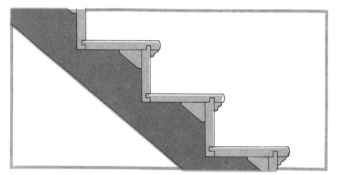

Stair construction: tread is rabbeted and dadoed.

Most stairs consist of three sections: tread, riser, and stringer. On some stairs the tread rests on the riser in a simple butt joint of glue and nails; in others a dado-and-rabbet joint or simple dado is used. The stringers or side pieces serve to support the treads.

When squeaks occur, it is because the tread or riser has worked loose at some point. If the treads are attached by butt joints (you can check this by prying off a part of the molding under the nose of the tread), you can tighten the tread by renailing it to the top of the riser. Have someone stand on the tread during the operation. Drive finishing nails at angles through the top of the tread into the center of the riser top. The holes can be filled with wood putty. If the tread is made of hardwood, you can avoid splits and bent nails by first drilling pilot holes.

On a dadoed or dado-and-rabbet setup, you can avoid nailing by removing the molding and working small glued wedges into the side of the tread slot. If the underside of the stairway is accessible, apply the wedges from behind. While under there, check for any loose wedges between the tread and stringer. Tighten these or replace them, as necessary.

Replacement of a damaged or broken tread is a job that usually calls for the services of a carpenter. However, if the wall end of the tread butts against the stringer, rather than being recessed into it, the job is considerably easier and you may wish to tackle it yourself.

Renail tread to riser to eliminate squeak.

Working wedges into rabbet, avoiding nailing.

Wedging from behind stair.

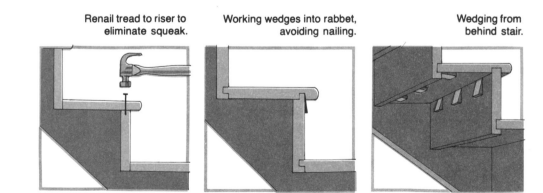

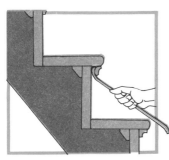

1. Remove molding from under the tread nosing.

2. Use hacksaw to loosen bottom of baluster.

3. Twist loose top of baluster from the anchor.

First remove all molding from under the tread nosing. The feet of the balusters may be toenailed to the top of the tread or glued into slots. In such cases, use a hacksaw blade to sever the balusters as close to the tread as possible, exercising care to limit damage while cutting. The tops of the balusters are usually held in place with glue and can be separated from the anchor by twisting.

Hammer carefully under the nosing of the tread until there is a gap between the tread and riser. A pry bar may help here. Depending on the construction of the stair, you can continue prying until the tread can be worked loose by hand, or you can cut the nails that hold it with a hacksaw. The tread can now be used as a pattern for the new step. Or, if wear is the only problem, it may be possible to turn the tread over and use the other side. Fasten the tread with glue and nails; fill the nail holes with wood putty and sand smooth.

4. Loosen tread from riser by prying under the nosing.

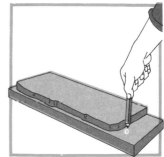

5. Use old tread as pattern for new step.

Flip tread over to other side if wear is the only problem.

STICKING DOORS

A door swells when it is damp, and then becomes difficult to open and close. Before you attempt to plane off the door rails (top and bottom) or stiles (sides), it is wise to remember that the wood will shrink as the air dries out. Think twice before planing if you suspect that this is only a seasonal problem.

The first thing to check is the condition of the hinges. Position yourself on the side of

A gap betwen door and frame is an indication of loose hinges.

Support door while tightening screws.

Knock out hinge pins.

Fill screw holes.   Deepen mortise.

the door opposite the stops (so that it closes away from you). With the door closed, examine the spaces between the door and frame. You can run a sheet of paper around the edges to observe the hang of the door; where it binds, the door is too tight. If there is a space at the top, latch side of the rail and a corresponding space at the bottom, hinge side, it means that the upper hinge is probably loose, and perhaps the lower one as well.

Open the door to expose the hinges. Relieve pressure on the top hinge by having someone lightly support the door by its handle, or by slipping a wedge of some sort under the bottom rail. Use a broad-bladed screwdriver to tighten all the screws. If a screw does not appear to have any purchase, the wood around the screw has deteriorated. This can be corrected.

Remove the door by knocking out first the lower, then the upper hinge pin. Use a screwdriver angled so that the head of the pin is driven up and out. Should the pin be "frozen" or stuck, remove the hinge at the jamb. Inspect the mortise and the condition of the wood. If the holes look pulpy or rotted, hammer in a small wooden plug coated with glue or stuff the spaces with toothpicks or wooden matches dipped in glue, or fill them with plastic wood. Trim, then replace the hinge and screw, using longer screws if possible.

The difficulty may be that the hinge plate is not recessed deeply enough in the mortise, in which case you will have to chisel the mortise deeper. Or it may be possible, if spacing at the latch stile permits, to build up the lower hinge and thus shift the door to the vertical. The shim can be any piece of cardboard of the correct thickness (a matchbook cover serves well) and it should fill the mortise completely.

When the door binds along the entire

length of the latch stile, you will have to cut the mortises deeper, as required. If necessary, you can deepen the mortises on both the jamb and the door.

Shimming will help if the door tends to spring open when you try to close it. In this case, place a strip of cardboard only behind half the width of the hinge leaf. You do not have to remove the hinge for this operation. Loosen the screws so that when the door is partially closed, the hinge leaf comes away from the mortise. Slip the shim into this space and tighten the screws. Shimming at this point serves to change the angle of the door so it leans toward the outside stop.

If the hinge stile is catching or binding along the stop, you can reposition the hinge leaf in its mortise to pull the door away a bit, thus curing the problem.

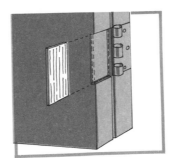

Build up beneath lower hinge with a cardboard shim.

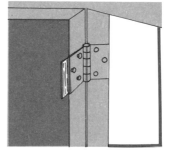

Insert shim behind half of hinge leaf.

FITTING A DOOR

Often a door binds at several points at once because it or the frame has been warped out of shape. (Cracks or stress marks on the plaster around the frame are signs that the frame is at fault.) In either case, adjusting the fit of the hinges will not do the job completely. You will have to plane or sand the door as well.

Your inspection will show where excess material has to be removed. Usually only a part of a side has to be touched up, rather than the entire length of a stile or rail. Mark off the sticking areas while the door is closed, so that you will know how much has to be cut. Remove the door and prop it on its side against some solid support. Work the plane in smooth strokes, and do not bite too deeply at any one time. If the binding exists at the latch area of the door, it may prove simpler to plane the hinge side instead. Hinge leaves are easier to remove than the lock assembly.

When the door rubs at the top or bottom, you will have to plane one or both rails, either partially or fully. Keep in mind that you will be cutting across the grain, and if you work too roughly or use a dull tool it is easy to splinter the wood. If the amount to be removed is fractional, try a sanding

Plane sticking areas.

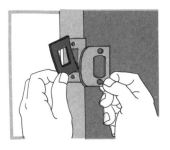

Shim behind striker plate.

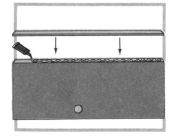

Build up door width.

Mortise for hinges.

Crayon on striker plate locates problem area.

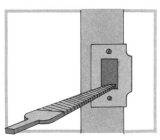

File striker plate receptacle.

Move plate, fill gaps.

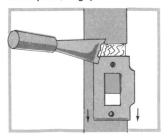

block instead, but take care not to bevel the door edges.

A door sometimes becomes too narrow because of shrinkage, with the result that the latch is not able to reach the striker plate to engage it. If the distance is small, you can correct this by removing the striker plate and bringing it closer to the door with a wood or cardboard shim.

When the space to be filled is much wider, however, the best solution is to build up the width of the door by cementing and nailing a strip of wood along the hinge stile. The strip should be wide enough to close the gap and as thick as the stile. Measure to determine where the hinge leaves should be set, and chisel new mortises to receive them. The strip can be finished to match the finish on the door.

These adjustments to the door may cre-ate a problem: the door now swings freely but the latch is unable to engage the striker plate in the frame, with the result that the plate must be repositioned. To tell how much and in what direction, rub some cray-on over the face of the striker plate and close the door. The resultant mark on the plate will indicate what has to be done.

If the latch is centered but falls short of the receptacle in the plate, you might try filing the metal to bring the hole closer. Trim wood from the mortise, if required. If the entire plate has to be moved, fill the original screw holes with plugs before at-tempting to screw the plate in a new posi-tion. Gaps between the plate and the mor-tise can be filled with wood putty and touched up with paint. These same instruc-tions apply when the plate must be moved up or down to meet the latch.

WINDOW PROBLEMS

Tap gently along window
to free it.

Insert chisel between
sash and stop.

Pry from outside.

Scrape off paint, sand smooth.

When a wood window sash sticks or binds, it is usually because paint has worked into the sash molding or because the sash or frame has become swollen. Paint-stuck windows can sometimes be freed by tapping along both sides of the sash with a hammer and block of wood. If this does not free the window, insert the blade of a paint scraper or a broad, thin chisel between the sash and the stop molding. Tap the blade in with a hammer, then

Tap block in channel.   Repeat below raised window.

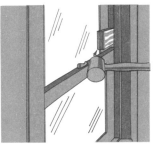

rock the tool back and forth gently to force the sash back from the molding. Repeat this at several points at each side of the sash until it can move freely. Never use a screwdriver for this job, as it will only gouge the wood.

If the sticking is severe, or if a seal forms at the bottom edge of the sash after a new paint job, the window can be pried loose from the outside without damage to the finish. A hatchet is a good tool for this, or any broad, hard metal wedge. Hammer the tool along the bottom of the sash, and pry as you go along. Once the window is free, scrape off any crusts of paint at the back face of the stop molding. Sand the molding lightly and touch up the window track.

If paint sticking is not the problem, it may be that the window has swollen permanently out of shape. Try the following method first: Cut a block of wood that will fit snugly into the channel between the inside and outside window stops above or below the sash. Give the block several smart raps with a hammer at both sides of the window. This should free the sash so that it can be raised (or lowered) at least partially. Repeat the procedure at the exposed channels at the bottom or top. A lubricant such as paraffin or candle wax may then be applied to the channels.

If this method fails, the sash will have to be removed from the frame to make the necessary adjustments. (In order to remove the top sash the bottom one must be taken out first.) Most modern windows are equipped with metal tension strips fastened to the channels. With this kind it may be possible to remove the sash simply by pressing it sideways into a channel and lifting it free.

On windows that have sash cords the stop molding must be removed first. Insert a broad chisel behind the molding and twist so that the strip comes away only partially at any one point. Work carefully to avoid damaging or breaking the molding. With the strip removed, disengage the sash cord at both sides. Fasten a nail or strip of wood to the ends of the cords so that they will not slip past the pulley. Lower the weight gently and observe the action of the pulley. If it is stiff, apply a few drops of oil to the pins.

If the window has tension strips, try adjusting these first by turning their mounting screws. If this does not work, or if no mechanical adjustment is possible, wood can be sanded or planed from the sides of the sash to make it fit. Do not remove too much material at any one time. It is a good idea first to clean and lubricate the channels and then check the sash fit as you plane or sand. It should fit snugly without binding.

When a wood window rattles, it is because there is too much space between the sash and its stop molding. An easy way to alleviate this problem is to run a strip of metal or felt weatherstripping into the space. To make a permanent repair, remove the molding and nail it back closer to the sash.

Aluminum casement and sliding windows bind when dirt collects in the tracks. Sometimes the metal becomes pitted, impeding the window's smooth operation. Usually this can be corrected with a cleanup and rubbing with fine steel wool. The tracks should then be lubricated periodically with paraffin or wax. Never try to pry the window with a sharp tool, as this will distort the tracks.

When steel casement windows stick or bind, check to see that the hinges are free of rust or accumulated paint. Look for loose hinge screws or binding in the crank mechanism. Steel wool and lubricating oil will take care of the hinges. It may be necessary to open the handle assembly for cleaning and oiling.

1. Remove window from tension strips.

2. Remove stop molding on windows with sash cords.

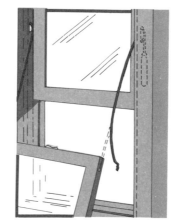

3. Disengage sash cord at both sides.

4. Keep sash from slipping past pulley.

5. Lubricate pulley.

6. Adjust tension strips.

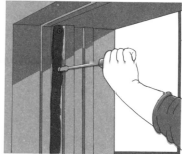

INSTALLING GLASS

Replacing cracked or broken window glass is not difficult, but it requires some care. You will need a sharp glass cutter, prepared putty or glazing compound (more flexible than putty), and a putty knife.

Installation of the glass is normally done from the outside, so if you are repairing a second-floor window it is best to remove the sash, if that is possible. Wear heavy work gloves when removing the broken pieces of glass from the frame. Heat from a soldering gun will help soften the old putty, or a small wood chisel can be used to clean it out, but take care not to damage the

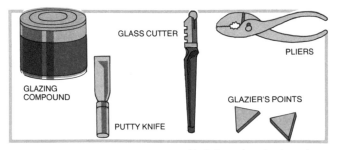

GLASS CUTTER

PLIERS

GLAZING COMPOUND

PUTTY KNIFE

GLAZIER'S POINTS

Tools to replace broken glass.

Remove old glass (above).

Remove old putty (above right).

Remove glazier's points (right).

frame. Extract the metal glazier's points with pliers.

The replacement glass should be cut 1/16 inch smaller all around than the frame opening. This is to allow for any irregularities that may exist in the frame.

Mark the glass with a sharpened crayon, then turn it over and lay it on a flat surface covered with a thickness of newspaper or an old blanket. A steel straightedge should be used to guide the cut. Any doubts about the glass cutter can be satisfied by first scoring a piece of the old glass; if the score mark shows signs of skipping, the cutting wheel is dull or chipped.

Make sure the glass is free of dust or grit before attempting the cut. The score mark should be begun just inside the edge of the glass farthest from you, then followed through with smooth, even pressure on the cutter. When the glass is scored, lay it over the straightedge and apply pressure on both sides of the score to break it cleanly. If the piece to be removed is very narrow, snap it off with the slotted head of the cutting tool.

Before the glass is installed in the frame, the groove should be painted with linseed oil in order to prevent subsequent drying out and cracking of the putty. Apply a ⅛-inch thickness of putty all around the frame. Press the glass into place, making sure it lies flat against the shoulders of the frame. Secure it with the glazier's points, pressing them in 4 to 6 inches apart on all sides.

Now roll some more putty into a "rope" about ½ inch thick. Use your fingers to press it against the wood and glass around the frame. Smooth and bevel the compound with the blade of the putty knife, making sure that you leave no breaks or separations in the seal. A coat of paint neatly finishes the job.

For metal windows the procedure varies slightly. On these the glass panes are usual-

1. Score glass.

2. Break glass along score mark.

3. If the strip is narrow, break it off with glass cutter.

4. Apply bed of glazing compound before installing the glass.

5. Press glass into frame.

6. Install glazier's points.

ly secured to the frames with small metal clips buried in the compound. These have to be removed and set aside.

Lay a bead of glazing compound into the metal frame and adjust the replacement glass so that the compound meets the glass at all sides. Install the clips, then apply the final bead of compound. If there are metal strips, screw them back in place.

7. Press in glazing compound.

8. Smooth with putty knife.

Insert new glass into storm window frame and press gasket into place.

For metal frames, install clips to hold the glass.

In numerous instances people have seriously injured themselves by walking into or putting their hands through large windows or doors. Safety and consumer agencies have been urging legislation requiring the use of less hazardous materials in such vulnerable places as sliding patio doors, storm doors, shower doors, tub enclosures, and other areas where standard glass might constitute a hazard.

Laws incorporating these recommendations have already been passed by several states. These require that "safety glazing material" be used in potentially dangerous areas such as those mentioned above.

Some of the safety materials are tempered glass, laminated glass, wire glass, and acrylic plastic.

These materials may be slightly more difficult to install than regular glass, and their cost is generally higher. By installing these materials in place of standard glass panes, however, the extra cost is offset by the sense of security in knowing one's house is safe. One thing to watch out for with the rigid plastic materials such as acrylics, though, is surface mars. Whereas their lesser hardness makes them less susceptible to breakage than glass, it also increases their chances of being nicked.

SCREEN REPAIRS

Keep your window and door screens in good condition by stacking them flat in a dry, well-ventilated area until ready for use. Wood frames should be tightened when necessary and given a fresh coat of paint from time to time to help preserve them.

A small hole in screening has a mysterious way of increasing in size if not patched as soon as it is discovered. If the hole is small enough, a drop or two of waterproof cement will do the job. The cement hardens into a film that covers the hole.

When dealing with larger tears, cut a patch of wire screen material that is wider than the hole by ½-inch. If you do not have extra screening around, patches in various sizes are available at any hardware store.

Unravel two wires at each side of the patch, then bed the end wires at a right angle on all four sides. Place the patch over the hole and thread the bent wires so that they pass evenly to the other side of the screen. They can now be bent back to fix the patch permanently and firmly.

An old or damaged wood screen frame can be renewed easily enough so that you do not have to go to the expense of purchasing a new one. When trouble occurs, it is usually at the frame joints.

A joint can be tightened by bracing the frame pieces with a ⅜-inch dowel. Drill a hole through the side member into the top or bottom piece. Coat the dowel with glue and hammer it into the hole, trimming or driving it flush, as the case may be.

A sagging screen door can be corrected with the use of a turnbuckle and cable, placed from one side of the door to the other. Fasten one end of the cable to the top side rail over the hinge; the other end should be screwed to the bottom of the other side rail. Tighten the turnbuckle until the door can swing freely.

To replace screen wire in a wood frame, you must first remove the molding. Use a paint scraper or putty knife for this job, prying gently along the length of the molding until it comes free. Remove all staples or tacks from the frame. Cut the new

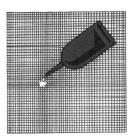

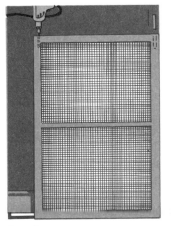

Patch a small hole
in the screen
with cement (left).

Place a patch over
the hole if it is
bigger (below left).

Fold ends under to seal
permanently (below).

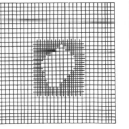

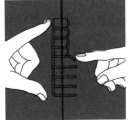

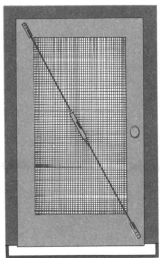

Doweling a
corner joint (above).

Repair for a sagging
screen door using a turnbuckle
and cable (right).

Home Repairs Made Easy

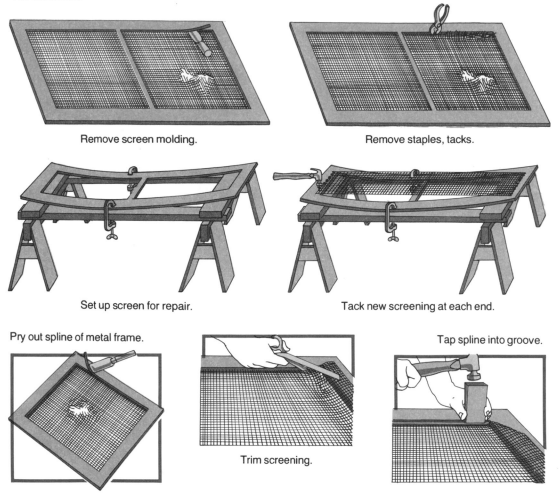

Remove screen molding.

Remove staples, tacks.

Set up screen for repair.

Tack new screening at each end.

Pry out spline of metal frame.

Trim screening.

Tap spline into groove.

screen 1 inch wider on all sides with old scissors or metal snips.

Tension must be applied to the screen when it is tacked to the frame, in order to prevent any stretching later. The best way to do this is to lay the frame across a work surface as wide as the frame (two boards across a pair of sawhorses make a good work surface). Place a board under each end of the frame, then C-clamp the sides of the frame to the work surface so that there is a slight bow formed in the middle.

Tack the new screening tautly at each end, doubling the material where you tack. Now release the C-clamps and tack the screen along the sides of the frame. Replace the molding. and trim any wire that sticks out from under it.

In metal frames, a spline holds the screening in place. This must be pried out to remove the torn screening. New screening is then laid over the framing and trimmed to size, with the corners cut at 45-degree angles. The spline is then tapped back into its groove in the frame to secure the screening.

CERAMIC WALL TILES

Ceramic tile is usually set in place with a white, waterproof tile calking used to fill the spaces around the tile. These same adhesive compounds can be used to make repairs on ceramic tile that has been cemented with portland cement, the old method of fastening.

As soon as a tile comes loose or cracks, it should be replaced. Use a chisel to cut around the damaged tile. Try not to damage the surrounding tiles. If the original fastening is cement, you will have to chisel away a part of the cement so that the replacement tile does not extend beyond the surface of the surrounding tiles.

Apply a generous bead of cement to the back of the new tile, then press it firmly into place. Wipe off all excess cement immediately. To hold the tile in place until the cement sets, support it with strips of masking tape. There should be an even space all around the tile. When the cement dries, remove the tape and fill the joints with white compound.

To cut ceramic tile to fit requires a glass cutter. Make a score along a guideline on the face of the tile, then place the tile over a nail and apply pressure on both sides to snap it clean. A file or emery cloth can be used to smooth the edge of the cut. For a curved cut, score the guideline, then make crisscross scores inside the area of the cut. Use a pliers to break out the scored section little by little.

When small, fine cracks appear in a ceramic tile the only cure is replacement. Shrinkage cracks around the wall of the tile can be filled with white plastic compound sold for that purpose. Correct such cracks as soon as they appear to prevent splash water or condensation from ruining the wall interior. Tile surfaces should never be cleaned with an abrasive agent. Warm water and a detergent are best (soap leaves a film on the tile).

1. Chisel around damaged tile.

2. Chisel cement backing.

3. Apply cement to new tile.

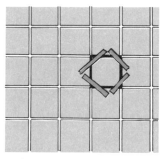

4. Support it while cement dries.

5. Fill joints with compound.

Score tile with glass cutter.

Snap over nail.

Making a curved cut.

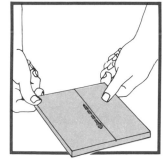

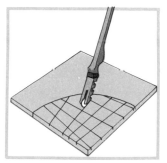

Home Repairs Made Easy

CEILING TILES

Tiles are an excellent choice for many ceiling resurfacing jobs. Acoustical tile is especially popular, easy to work with, and can do much to brighten up a ceiling. It comes in a wide variety of patterns to suit just about any decor.

Ceiling tile installation is begun at a room corner. However, since most rooms are slightly out of square or otherwise irregular, first find the center point of the ceiling by finding the midpoint on each of two opposite walls and stringing a line between these points; measure to the center of this line and describe a line at right angles to it. Measure from this center point to the walls to find the width of border tiles. In this way, if a tile must be cut to fit against the wall, it will be the same width at each side of the room, giving a balanced appearance.

If an existing ceiling is level and in sound condition, ceiling tiles can be applied right over it with adhesive. Make sure the ceiling is clean and free of grease and water-soluble paint. Dab the back of each tile with adhesive in four or five spots and place it against the ceiling in approximate position, then slide it into place, spreading the adhesive. Slight depressions in the ceiling can be compensated for by applying a thicker coating of adhesive.

Where the existing ceiling is badly cracked or peeling, and in basements, attics, and other areas where the joists or rafters are exposed, the best method of installing ceiling tiles is by stapling them to furring strips. Place the first strip against the wall, nailing it securely to each joist. The placement of the second strip depends upon the width you have determined for the border tiles. All other strips are placed on 12-inch centers (or whatever other width of tiles you may be using). Where pipes and cables are hung below the joists, a double layer of furring strips may be used to clear these obstructions. In this case, the first layer of strips may be spaced on about 24-inch centers (more or less, depending on where the obstructions fall). Pipes that are several inches below the joists should be boxed with furring strips. It is good insurance to make a sketch of your plumbing system, including the locations of valves, before enclosure so that a minimum number of tiles need be removed if you ever require access to the pipes.

The furring strips should be checked with a level and shimmed with wood wedges where necessary to provide an even, level backing for the tiles. Snap a chalk line across the furring strips as a guideline for border tiles. Measure and cut each border tile individually to assure an accurate fit. (When measuring, do not include tongues and flanges.) Cut the tiles face up with a sharp fiberboard knife. Fit the first tile in the corner, carefully aligning it with the two intersecting guidelines; staple it securely through the flanges. Install the border tiles adjacent to the corner tile, then install another border tile along each wall and begin filling in between the border tiles with full tiles, working across the ceiling. Make certain that each tile is butted tightly to and aligned properly with its neighbors before stapling. Wherever possible, light fixtures, vents, and other ceiling fittings should be positioned between furring strips so they fall in the center of a single tile, minimizing cutting and fitting. When you reach the borders on the opposite side of the room, the final tiles are face-nailed to the furring strips. A cove or crown molding at the joint between walls and ceiling conceals the nails.

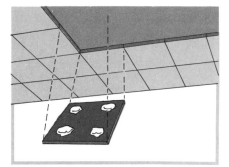

Using mastic to install ceiling tile.

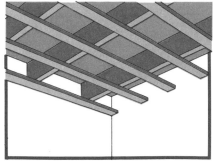

Furring for ceiling tile.

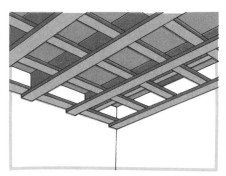

Double layer of strips to lower ceiling.

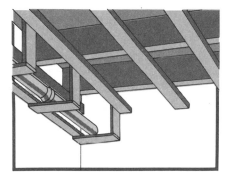

Box around obstructions.

Check furring for evenness.

Snap a chalk guideline.

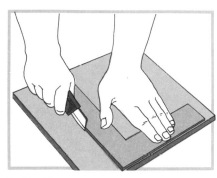

Cutting tile.

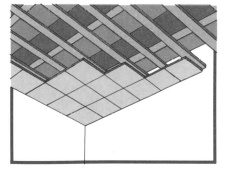

Installing tile ceiling.

Tile around ceiling fixture.

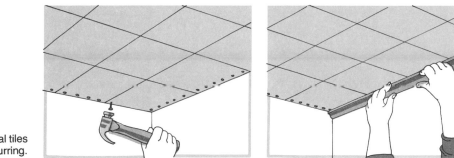

Nail final tiles to furring.

Molding to conceal nails.

Home Repairs Made Easy ● Ceiling Tiles

PLASTER REPAIRS

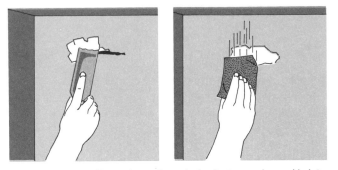

To repair small cracks in plaster, work spackle into cracks (left) and sand area smooth (right).

Plaster on ceilings and walls is generally applied over a lathing of wood, metal, or gypsumboard, the latter most common except in older homes. This lathing serves as a foundation for the plaster and is in turn fixed to the framework behind it.

Small cracks and holes in plaster can be filled with spackling compound, which is available in either dry or premixed form. First clear away all loose plaster and dust.

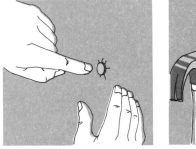

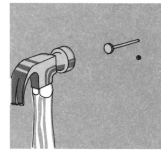

Popped nail (above left).

Drive in new nail (above right).

Drive nail below surface (left).

Work the spackle tightly into the opening with a flexible putty knife. Trim the excess flush with the wall, wiping with the knife in alternate crisscross strokes. Give the compound plenty of time to dry, then sand the area smooth, using medium sandpaper.

Gypsum wallboard is a surfacing material commonly used for both walls and ceilings. Also known as plasterboard and Sheetrock (a trade name), it is made of compressed gypsum plaster between two sheets of heavy paper or cardboard. The sheets range in sizes up to 4 by 16 feet, through 4 by 8 sheets are most favored by builders, and come in thicknesses of ⅜ and ½ inch.

Gypsum wallboard is usually nailed (or cemented and nailed) directly to the framing studs. The board is subject to dents, such as may be caused by the sharp corner of a piece of furniture. Depressions of this sort can be corrected with spackling compound or a special gypsum cement. Nail holes can be filled in this fashion also. No preparation of the surface is necessary, and the compound can be smoothed with sandpaper when it is dry.

Settling of the house's foundation or the use of green wood for backing supports can result in a vertical warping of the wallboard. When this happens, the nails that hold the panel in place may "pop" loose. This can be corrected by removing the loosened nail and driving a single nail just above or below the old nail hole, at the same time pushing the board firmly to hold it in place. Use only a screw-type nail for the fastening, and hammer it carefully so that a shallow depression is formed around the nailhead. Patch and finish the repair with spackling compound.

The joints between panels are closed with gypsum cement and a special reinforcing tape. To close a seam that has broken open, first clean out the seam with a sharp-pointed tool (a pre-pop-top beer-can opener does a good job). Pull or scrape away remnants of the old tape, then sand the seam to prepare the surface. The area you have sanded should be slightly wider than the replacement tape.

Using a broad knife with a 4-inch blade, lay the cement smoothly and evenly into the seam and around it. Before the cement has had time to dry, apply the tape over the seam, centering it and removing all wrinkles and air bubbles with the blade of the knife. Now apply more cement over the tape. Work it on smoothly, and remove all excess. After it dries, sand it smooth. To provide a smoother finish, it may be necessary to apply another coat of cement and repeat the sanding.

Since a hole in wallboard is "bottomless" because of the absence of backing, you cannot simply work patching compound into it and expect it to hold. To repair a hole, cut a piece of wire mesh a bit larger than the hole. Tie a string near the center of the mesh and work the mesh through the hole until it covers the opening from behind. Maintain a grip on the string while applying spackle to within ⅛ inch of the surface. Give the compound a chance to set, snip off the excess string, and carefully finish off the surface.

If a large section of wallboard must be replaced, you must provide backing for the new section. Use a straightedge to draw parallel lines above and below the damaged

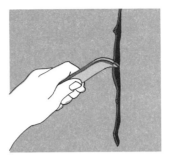

1. Clean out crack or joint. 2. Apply spackle.

3. Apply tape. 4. Apply more spackle.

5. Sand smooth after the spackle is dry.

area. With a keyhole saw, cut carefully along the lines until you encounter the studs on either side of the damage. Cut

Tie string to mesh, insert in hole (far left).

Hold string, apply spackle (center).

Snip off string, finish (left).

Home Repairs Made Easy • Plaster Repairs

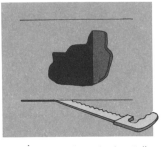

1. Cut damaged area horizontally.

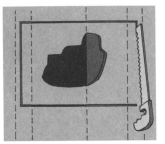

2. Cut along ends over studs.

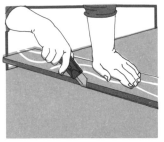

3. Score face of new board.

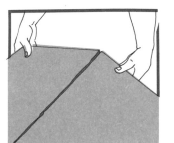

4. Snap the board.

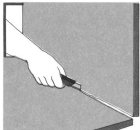

5. Score back.

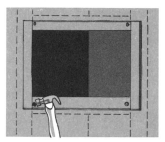

6. Provide horizontal backing.

7. Nail new section in place.

another inch of wallboard so that you are over the center line of the stud. Now cut straight down along this line on both studs. If the damaged area extends beyond the width of two studs, it is best to continue the horizontal cut to the next stud.

Measure the size of the opening and cut a new piece of board to fit. You do not have to use a saw; use a sharp knife to score the face of the board. Snap it over a straight-edge or the edge of a table, then score the rear to break it off cleanly. The new section can be nailed directly to the studs, but first you must provide horizontal backing because of the horizontal seams. Use sections of 2 x 4 or 2 x 3 lumber, sawing them to size so they can be toenailed to the studs. One support for the top and bottom of the replacement section will suffice. Nail the section into place and finish the seams as described above.

Unsightly wall surfaces can be refinished with paneling of your choice, such as wallboard, plywood, fiberboard, or hardboard, which come in various finishes and require no further covering. Or you may decide to panel a wall with wood. It all depends on the application and how much you wish to spend.

TOOLS NEEDED FOR WALL PANELING

You can probably do the whole paneling installation with tools you have on hand. It would be wise, though, to replace saws or hammers that have seen better days. Good tools last for many years and are inexpensive in the long run. Savings in wasted materials alone generally more than offset the slight additional cost of better-quality tools. Keep your cutting tools clean and sharp, and protect edges and faces when not in use. Store them carefully.

Use handsaws or time-saving power saws on paneling, whichever you prefer. If you use a handsaw, make sure it is the cross-cut type. A ripsaw will generally chip the face of the paneling. Keep the panel face up when cutting so that the saw cuts into the face on the downstroke. Start cutting carefully at the panel's edge and support the cut-off material during final saw strokes so that it doesn't break off.

For circular power saws, a combination hollow-ground blade is recommended. With a table saw, keep the paneling face up while cutting. If you use either a portable power saw or a radial arm saw, make sure the panel is face down while sawing. Whether you use a handsaw or a power saw, put masking tape along the line to be cut. This will help prevent edge splinters and chips.

You may need a compass or coping saw

Put masking tape along line to be cut.

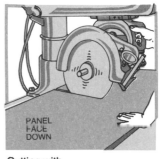
Cutting with a portable power saw.

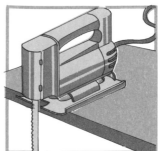
Cutting with a radial saw.

Compass saw, coping saw (top).

Saber saw.

Crosscut handsaw.

Cutting with a handsaw.
FACE OF PANEL

Cutting with a table saw.
PANEL FACE UP

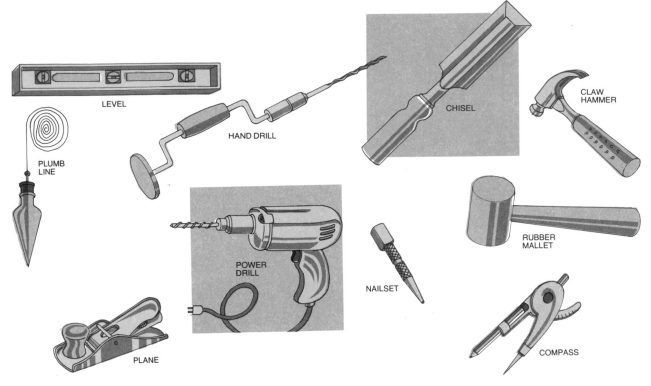

or a jigsaw (saber saw) to help you get around tricky corners and odd shapes. A level and plumb line will keep your paneling on a true line throughout the room. A drill and a chisel will be helpful for cuts within the panel's perimeter, such as one needed to accommodate a light switch. You should have a claw hammer for driving nails and a rubber mallet for pounding panels into place and setting them in adhesive. If you don't have a rubber mallet, you can make do by hitting a 2 x 4 placed over the panel-ing (protected by a rag) with a claw hammer. This will distribute the blow evenly without damaging the paneling.

If you're putting the paneling up with nails, use a nailset with 3d (1¼-inch) finishing nails. (Some types of paneling come supplied with color-head nails to match.) A plane may be needed to even off old door and window frames before paneling is installed over them. An art compass will be helpful in scribing out tricky or odd corners on the paneling (for ladders see p. 111).

TYPES OF PANELING

The do-it-yourselfer is faced with a pleasant dilemma once the walls and partitions of a home or addition have been framed and the insulation is put up, or when it is time to remodel an existing room. What type of paneling will be used? With the almost endless varieties and styles available, there is bound to be a pattern that exactly fits any designing plan.

Paneling materials are divided into three basic categories: hardboard, plywood, and hardwood-plywood. Hardboard is made from cellulose-based materials pressed under extreme pressure and then cut into planks or panels. A durable finish is added on one side. It can be purchased in thicknesses of ⅛ inch and ¼ inch.

Plastic-coated hardboard panels are a popular form of prefinished wall covering. The very strong bonded plastic finish withstands plenty of punishment and is easily maintained; a damp cloth will remove just about any dirt that hasn't been ground into the finish.

This type of paneling is available in many styles, textures, and colors. Wood finishes that simulate anything from Alpine oak to sable walnut are available. The graining and coloration of these panels make it hard to distinguish them from real wood surfaces. Most come with V grooves that divide the 4-foot-wide panels seemingly into planks of uniform or random widths. One type has slots in the V grooves so that shelves can be hung without nailing or any fuss. Matching moldings and shelving are available with this paneling.

Wood-grain paneling also comes in varying textures. Distressed wood designs like barnsiding and intricately sculptured designs like panels from the Byzantine period are included in this category.

Designer planks come in various colors

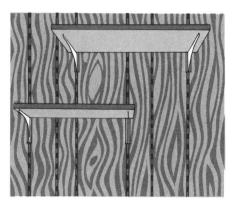

Slots in V-grooves of panels to support shelf brackets.

and patterns. Finishes range from high-gloss to satin-gloss. Some have mural or mosaic effects. The wide variety of patterns puts this type of paneling in solid competition with wallpaper.

"Masonry" paneling simulates brick-work, stone, and stucco. Some of these come in tilelike segments that the do-it-yourselfer can nail or glue to the wall. After fastening, a calking compound is put in the grooves to give a grout effect and hide nail-heads.

Suffice it to say that, whatever you can imagine in a wall finish, it has probably been done in hardboard paneling. With all the different types, installation is usually

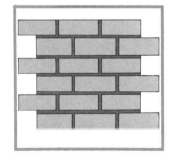

Brick-patterned hardboard paneling.

Plywood paneling.

the same (with the exception of some of the masonry patterns in which "bricks" may interlock).

Plywood paneling is made of thin layers of wood joined together with an outer veneer layer of high quality. Most of it comes prefinished. Some varieties require the installer to do the finishing, but unless you are experienced in this type of endeavor, it's better to stick with the prefinished models. The cost savings are minimal with unfinished types, and usually the factory finish will far surpass your efforts in durability and attractiveness. The panels have a more natural appearance than the hardboard wood grains, and rightly so, because they are made from actual wood.

Hardwood-plywood paneling is essentially a spin-off of the above, using specially chosen hardwood veneers. The woods range in price and quality from relatively inexpensive Philippine lauan to a very elegant (and costly) Brazilian rosewood. With the very expensive panelings, the prices are dependent on the thickness as well as the species of the wood.

There are other forms of paneling, too. Although less popular than the hardboard and plywood varieties, fiberglass paneling is attractive and versatile. It is usually textured and requires professional installation. Fire-retardant and flexible, the panels can be bent to follow the curve in a ceiling or archway. Although more expensive than most hardboard paneling, fiberglass "masonry" patterns are very realistic and offer substantial savings over actual stonework.

Solid wood paneling, somewhat the vogue in past years, has drastically declined in popularity since the advent of fine-looking, easy to handle and install, and less expensive prefinished hardboard and plywood paneling. It offers very little in the way of fire safety, compared to the newer paneling. For these reasons, solid wood paneling is not recommended for home use.

GENERAL PREPARATIONS BEFORE PANELING

Number of Panels Needed

Measure the length of all the walls, add these together, and the result will be the running length of paneling needed. In a room measuring 16 by 20 feet, the amount of paneling needed would be 72 lineal feet. If the paneling you have chosen comes in 4-foot widths, divide this dimension by 4 to find the number of panels required for the job—in this case, 18 panels.

Cutouts made for large openings (doorways, arches, windows) can often be used to panel under and over windows, for instance, or at stairways. You can estimate this use of otherwise wasted material by measuring carefully and, where possible, by planning to position a panel exactly at the edge of the opening.

As a double check, show your measurements and a sketch of your room layout to your dealer. He'll be glad to help and offer suggestions. Some types of paneling can be specially ordered in 10-foot lengths, suitable for older homes and apartments with very high ceilings. You may find, however, that the extra two feet will cost you substantially more than an additional 25 percent above the 8-foot panel's price. If this is the case, you might want to consider some other methods that will allow you to cover a 10-foot-high wall with 8-foot paneling. These methods are discussed later.

Paneling in New Construction

If you're installing paneling in new construction, the preparation required is minimal and the problems that might arise are few. There are no old moldings in the way, for one thing. You have a chance to construct closets and built-ins with proportions that are easy to panel around, for another. In paneling a new room, you're building out from relatively straight, true walls.

With new construction, the heavier

Number of Panels Needed
(Based on 8-Foot Ceiling Height)

Length of Room	Width of Room														
	6'	7'	8'	9'	10'	11'	12'	13'	14'	15'	16'	17'	18'	19'	20'
8'	7	8	8	9	9	10	10	11	11	12	12	13	13	14	14
9'	8	8	9	9	10	10	11	11	12	12	13	13	14	14	15
10'	8	9	9	10	10	11	11	12	12	13	13	14	14	15	15
11'	9	9	10	10	11	11	12	12	13	13	14	14	15	15	16
12'	9	10	10	11	11	12	12	13	13	14	14	15	15	16	16
13'	10	10	11	11	12	12	13	13	14	14	15	15	16	16	17
14'	10	11	11	12	12	13	13	14	14	15	15	16	16	17	17
15'	11	11	12	12	13	13	14	14	15	15	16	16	17	17	18
16'	11	12	12	13	13	14	14	15	15	16	16	17	17	18	18
17'	12	12	13	13	14	14	15	15	16	16	17	17	18	18	19
18'	12	13	13	14	14	15	15	16	16	17	17	18	18	19	19
19'	13	13	14	14	15	15	16	16	17	17	18	18	19	19	20
20'	13	14	14	15	15	16	16	17	17	18	18	19	19	20	20

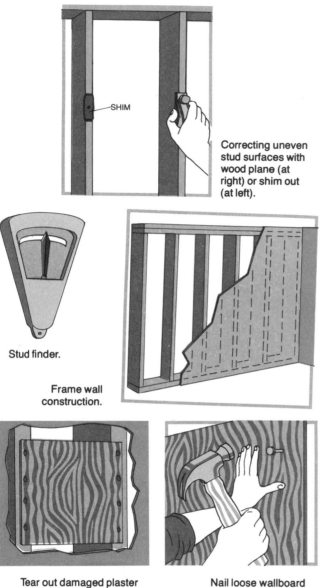

Correcting uneven stud surfaces with wood plane (at right) or shim out (at left).

SHIM

Stud finder.

Frame wall construction.

Tear out damaged plaster and build out wall.

Nail loose wallboard flat and tight.

Paneling in Existing Construction

Frame walls are normally constructed of 2 x 4 studs (verticals) and plates (horizontals) at floor and ceiling, to which the wall covering material (such as lath and plaster or gypsumboard) is fastened. Studs are set every 16 inches (center to center) and at door and window openings, where they are doubled. You must locate these studs if you are furring the wall for paneling or nailing the paneling over the existing wall. To do this, tap the wall with your fist. A hollow thump means a space between studs; a solid sound indicates a stud location. Nailheads that show in baseboards or gypsumboard also indicate stud locations. Or you can purchase a magnetic stud finder in any hardware store. The wood stud won't attract the magnetic indicator, of course, but nails driven into it to attach lath or gypsumboard will.

If the existing wall is in good shape and solidly attached, you may be able to glue the new paneling directly to it or nail through the plaster or wallboard into the studs. If there is a small area of loose plaster, you can tear out that section and build it out with furring or plywood flush with the surface of the solid part of the wall. Loose wallboard can be nailed flat and tight. Paneling will hide many minor wall defects—no need to be too fussy. Just be certain that the defect won't get worse, to spoil your paneling efforts sometime in the future.

It's best to remove moldings before you put up the paneling. Do this carefully to avoid splitting, using a chisel or carpenter's pry bar. Or you can drive the narrow-headed finish nails right through the moldings with a hammer and nailset.

If you are filling in an opening, such as where you removed a door or window, build a stud framing and fur it out or cover it with wallboard or plywood to match the vertical plane of the rest of the wall.

grades of paneling can be installed directly to smooth studs without furring. Use a wood plane to smooth imperfections, or shim out low spots if studs aren't perfectly straight. Building paper, plastic sheeting, or other vapor barrier installed against studs on outside walls will protect the paneling from moisture.

Build a simple box frame around exposed pipes or other obstructions that you don't want to relocate. Paneling will decorate almost anything. If you're planning built-ins—closets, wall shelving, cabinets—it's best to frame them out before you start to panel.

Are the Walls Even?

Paneling can readily be installed on any dry nonmasonry wall that is in good shape, but other methods are needed when a wall is uneven. Check walls carefully for flatness. An uneven wall may appear even when painted, but it will look very obviously out of kilter when paneled over. This is especially true when the paneling utilizes straight lines in its design.

An easy way to check for wall straightness is to hold a room-height length of straight 2 x 4 lumber against the wall. If the board is flush with the wall at all points, then the wall is vertically straight in that area. Repeat this process, holding the board horizontally, to check for horizontal straightness.

There are other ways of determining vertical straightness and true perpendicularity.

Remove moldings wih pry bar before putting up paneling.

Drive finishing nails through moldings.

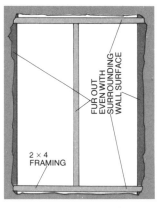

Filling in a window opening.

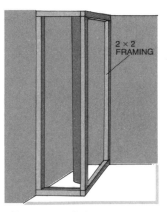

Frame around obstructions.

Check for vertical and horizontal straightness of walls.

You can use a 2-foot carpenter's level or, better yet, a 4-foot bricklayer's level. Hold the level, lengthwise up, against the wall. As with the 2 x 4 method, if the level is flush with the wall, the wall is vertically straight in that area. If the bubble is not centered in the level, however, the wall is not perfectly plumb, or perpendicular with the ground level.

A plumb line can be used for this, too. Attach the line to the ceiling with masking tape at about two inches from the wall. With a ruler, measure the distance between wall and plumb line at different points on the line. If the distances are equal, the wall is both vertically straight and plumb.

It is very rare, even in new construction, for walls to be perfectly straight and plumb. If the walls are slightly off, paneling can

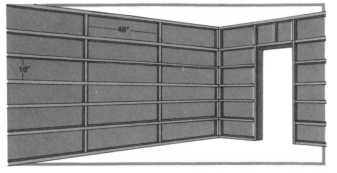

Furring strips over old wall.

usually be applied directly to them with satisfactory results. If, however, the deviations are noticeably large, compensatory measures will have to be taken before paneling is installed.

Furring

One way to combat the problem of wall deviations is with furring strips. If the paneling is thick enough not to require backing (usually ¼ inch), furring is an easy and economical solution.

Furring strips may be nailed over the old wall, directly into the studs. If the existing wall is sturdy and solid, furring strips may also be fastened with adhesive. Follow label instructions for a secure bond.

Use 1 x 2 or 1 x 3 furring strips, or cut 2-inch-wide strips from sheets of ⅝-inch sheathing plywood. Space strips every 16 inches (measure from center of one strip to center of the next). Install either horizontally or vertically, following paneling manufacturer's recommendations.

Apply additional furring at doors, windows, etc. Don't skimp—use extra furring when in doubt. Where necessary, shim out furring to establish even planes, both horizontal and vertical. Pieces of shingle are ideal for shims. On an uneven wall take special pains to provide a firm, even base for the paneling.

Backing for Paneling

When using thinner paneling, you may want to use gypsumboard as a backing (the alternative would be horizontal as well as vertical furring). In addition to its being an easily installed backing surface, it can also provide an appreciable amount of sound insulation in rooms.

Other similarly strong backings, such as plywood, particleboard, and fiberboard, could also be used for these purposes. Installation for all forms of backing is essentially the same. Gypsum wallboard, however, is the cheapest and the easiest to cut and install. Simply score both faces with a razor knife and break it off, then nail it to the studs.

Special annular-ringed nails are used for attaching gypsum wallboard. Make sure the nailheads are either flush with the board's surface or beneath it, keeping it perfectly flat so that paneling can be laid flush.

Don't forget the primary reason for using the wallboard, either. It is there to provide a perfectly flat, true surface for panel mounting. If you are nailing it over a substantial deviation in either the plaster wall or exposed studs, compensate for this.

PANEL PREPARATION AND INSTALLATION

Certain measures must be taken before you put the paneling on the wall to ensure its adjustment to the room's climate.

Have the paneling delivered a few days before it is to be used. Do not store or install it in a room or building that has been freshly plastered or where humidity is high. Be sure that the room humidity is about normal before applying the paneling.

Unpack it at least 48 hours before it is to be applied, and flat-stack it with narrow strips of wood between the sheets, or distribute it around the room so that air can reach all sides of each panel. This will permit balancing of the moisture content of the paneling with that of the air in the room.

If moisture or excessive humidity may be a problem during some seasons of the year, back-treat plywood and wood-base paneling as recommended by the manufacturer. A good practice is to brush-coat a water-repellent preservative containing 5 percent pentachlorophenol, followed 24 hours later with a coat of sealer—aluminum paint for wood; shellac, varnish, or similar material for hardboard.

If there are differences in grain and color of the paneling, distribute it along the wall and arrange the boards or sheets to get the most attractive combinations. Number the panels on the back or with a removable marking to identify the sequence for application.

Nail a temporary, level strip of wood at the bottom of the area that is to be paneled. The bottom end or edge of the paneling can be set on it, and you will be sure that the panels will be plumb.

It is generally easier to start putting up the paneling in a corner or at the end of an area. This provides a good frame of reference and means that only one side will have to be cut in order to fit into the wall's width. With some panel designs, however, such as boxes or repeating motifs, it would look better to have both ends of the wall appear symmetrical. For this reason, starting the installation in the middle would be best.

Accurate marking, measuring, sawing, and fitting are necessary for a satisfactory job. Use a compass, saber, or coping saw to cut irregular lines. A block plane, a rasp, and sandpaper are helpful for fitting and smoothing the edges. Plastic wood, colored stick putty, and other patching materials can be used to repair or fill mistakes that will not be covered by the trim.

Panels grooved to represent random-width boards generally have a groove at each 16-inch interval, which is the usual spacing for studs and furring strips. Thus, nailing can be done in the grooves to hide the nailheads. Some types of paneling have tongue-and-groove or overlapped edges, which make it possible to hide the nails in the joint.

Line up paneling for best appearance (right); nail a leveling strip at bottom (far right).

 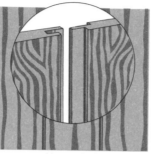

Tongue-and-groove and lapped edges make it possible to hide the nails.

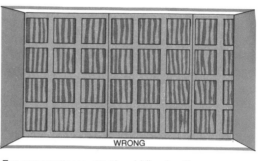

For some patterns, start in middle of wall.

Countersink nails.

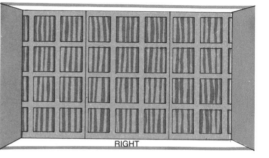

Fill holes with stick putty.

Color-coated nails that match the paneling can be used without countersinking. Otherwise, use 3d finish nails, countersink them, and fill the holes with a matching color of stick putty. The panels should be well nailed around all edges and to intermediate support studs or furring strips.

USING ADHESIVE FOR PANELING

Apply contact cement.

Press panel in place.

and push it firmly into contact with the wall covering material.

When the panel is in place, drive a few nails along the top edge, close enough to the ceiling so that the molding will cover them later.

Pull the panel away from the wall and

Apply mastic to studs.

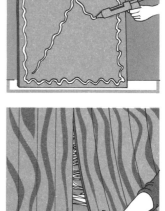

Apply mastic to back of panel.

Contact cement can be applied to both surfaces (paneling and furring strips or backing) at points of joining together. The cement can be applied with a brush or a serrated or saw-toothed spreader. The cement should dry to a nontacky condition before the panels are set in place. Position the panels accurately before joining the coated surfaces—the panels cannot be moved after the coated surfaces make contact.

Another system uses a mastic-type adhesive that is applied to the studs, furring strips, or rigid backing material. A calking gun is used to apply it to studs and furring strips. Generally, it is necessary to use a few nails at the top and bottom of each panel with the adhesive to hold the paneling snug until the adhesive dries.

If you use a mastic adhesive for paneling over a backing, run a bead with a calking gun around the edges of the panel, and then make a big "X" in the middle. Turn the panel around and stick it in place. Be sure to butt it snugly against the adjoining panel

Nail close to ceiling; molding will cover them later.

Pull away from wall and block it out with scrap wood.

Tap to make contact.

Tap at joint.

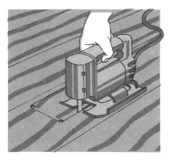

Pocket cut with
saber saw for an
electrical outlet.

block it out with a piece of scrap wood. The nails at the top will keep it from sliding out of place. When the adhesive has dried for ten minutes or so, remove the block and press the panel into place. This step is necessary for a good adhesive bond.

Using a scrap of 2 x 4 for a buffer, hammer the surface of the panel lightly to make sure the adhesive makes contact over the entire surface.

Fit all joints snugly, but not too tightly. If paneling must be forced into place, put a scrap of paneling or board over the edges and tap lightly with a hammer.

When you come to an electrical outlet, make a pocket cut in the panel with a jigsaw to expose the outlet, or drill pilot holes and make the cut with a compass saw. To locate the area to cut away, measure from the floor and front edge of the previous panel to the outlet. Transfer these measurements to the panel and make the pocket cut. To be safe and sure, measure twice, cut once. Another method is to chalk the outer edges of the electrical box, then press the panel in place against it, transferring the chalk marks to the back of the panel. The cut is then made as above.

When you have the panel attached to the wall, you can bring the outlet plug out flush with the surface of the panel by loosening the two screws that hold it in the outlet box. Replace the outlet cover with the center screw to cover the edges of the pocket cut.

As mentioned on p. 99 some paneling is available in 10-foot lengths. Because of the expense or difficulty in finding your choice of paneling in this length, you may opt for the 8-foot length, even if your walls are

Drill pilot
holes (right).

Cut with compass
saw (center).

Measuring to locate
outlet (far right).

Chalk edges of
electrical box (right).

Press paneling
against chalked
edges (center).

Bring outlet flush
with panel face (far right).

higher than 8 feet. There are a couple of tricks for horizontally butting one piece of paneling to another while still retaining a good appearance.

One involves a "shadow line." The shadow line is a stripe of black painted on the mounting surface behind the joint of the two pieces of paneling, usually at a point 8 feet below the ceiling. Then the panels are mounted about ½ to ¾ inch away from each other so that a "shadow" separates them. The shadow-line effect is especially pleasing with wood-grain paneling, less so with soft, pastel-colored paneling.

Another method of concealing a horizon-

Paint black stripe on wall and install paneling to create "shadow line."

tal joint is to place the 8-foot section of paneling on the lower portion of the wall. A shelf is then installed 8 feet up the wall along the entire width. Another piece of paneling is put above the shelf.

MOLDING AND TRIM

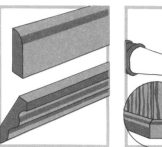

Base, ceiling moldings.

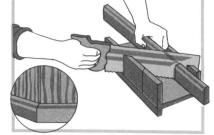

Mitering a molding.

Coping a molding.

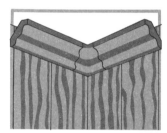

Outside corner molding (left).

Joining molding (below left).

Plastic joining molding (below).

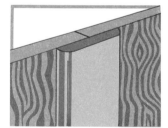

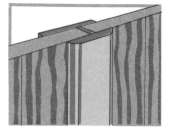

When all the panels are in place, nail molding at the ceiling line and nail on a matching baseboard molding. You can use finishing nails or nails colored to match the paneling for this job. Set colored nails flush with the surface; finishing nails should be countersunk and the holes filled with color stick putty to match the molding.

Where the moldings meet at the corners, you can either miter them (cut both at angles like a picture frame) or cope them (cut one molding to fit the curve of another). It's usually easier to miter outside corners (using a backsaw and miter box) and cope inside corners (using a coping saw).

In addition to ceiling and baseboard moldings, there are many kinds of moldings you can use to bail yourself out of tough fitting problems. Where panels meet at corners, you can use either wood or plastic moldings to make up for any slight discrepancies in fit. Outside corner moldings hide the edges of the panels and make tough wearing surfaces for the inevitable rough treatment an outside corner gets. You can butt panels together with a joining molding to hide any rough edges resulting from cutting a panel to fit a space narrower than the standard 4-foot width. With some types of plastic molding, you first put the molding on the wall with either nails or adhesive, then slide the edges of the paneling into it.

To fit paneling around windows and doorways, you should remove the trim molding and replace it to match the paneling. You can also install the paneling and nail the old molding back on. If you're really skilled, you can carefully cut the paneling to just fit up to the edge of a window or door molding, but this is a pretty tough job.

PANELING A BASEMENT

Installing paneling on a concrete or concrete-block basement wall involves a couple of extra steps, but it really is little more difficult than paneling any other room. The main difference is that you must put up furring strips (usually 1 x 2, 1 x 3, or 2 x 2 lumber) on the wall—you cannot apply the paneling directly. It is also a good idea to place insulation between the furring strips before applying the paneling, along with a vapor barrier. You may have to build a standard stud-frame wall to provide space for the insulation, depending on the type used. Your local building-supply dealer can help you with suggestions.

In many cases, especially on relatively new masonry walls, you can simply glue furring strips to the wall with special adhesive (again, consult your hardware or building-supply dealer). Glue horizontal strips along the ceiling and floor lines, then space vertical strips between them on 16-inch centers all around the room and in all corners. Check all strips with a level, and shim as necessary to plumb them.

Staple insulation between the furring strips. The store where you buy the insulation usually rents staple guns or hammers. Staple the insulation to the sides of the furrings strips to leave the faces clear for applying the paneling.

If you need additional electrical outlets around the room, have the electrician install them before you start putting up the paneling. The outlet boxes should be flush with the surface of the paneling; special shallow boxes are available for this purpose. Make pocket cuts in the panels as explained above to accommodate the outlets.

To install the paneling, apply adhesive to the furring strips, rather than to the backs of the panels. Press the panels firmly into place as previously described.

To panel around basement windows, first glue a frame of furring strips around the window recess, flush with the front edge.

Glue furring strips to masonry walls (right).

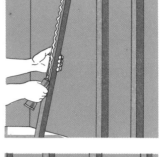

Staple insulation (below).

Shallow outlet boxes are available (below right).

Apply adhesive to furring strips (left).

Glue frame of furring strips around basement window (below left).

Apply paneling and molding (below).

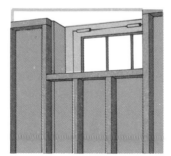

Cut the paneling to fit up to the edge of the opening. Cut pieces of paneling to line the inside of the window recess and glue them in place. Use outside corner molding to cover exposed paneling edges.

PANEL CARE AND MAINTENANCE

Fill large scratch with sticky putty.

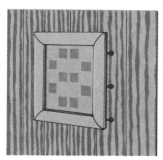

Holding picture frame away from wall with nails.

The finishes on modern plywood paneling are resistant to mars and scratches, but they do sometimes occur. They can generally be removed if they are in the finish only and have not penetrated into the wood. Use a clear wax on a damp cloth and rub the scratched area along the grain. You may have to wax the entire wall for a uniform appearance. But if the scratch goes through the finish and into the wood, a partial refinishing job will be required. Many scratches can be repaired with the use of a filler stick of the matching tone. If there is major damage, the services of a professional refinisher may be needed—or, if you were wise enough to purchase an extra panel or two when you first installed the walls, you might simply replace the damaged section.

Light has a tendency to mellow plywood wall paneling, except behind pictures, mirrors, and the like that are hung flat against the wall. This unevenness can be minimized by holding the picture or mirror out a bit—about a half inch—from the wall by means of nails placed in the backs of the frames. This allows light in behind the wall hanging so that the color tone mellows uniformly, leaving no sharp contrasts if the hanging is removed.

Low or fluctuating relative humidity can adversely affect any wood product. This is readily apparent when dry air causes a feeling of chilliness even when room temperature is 75 degrees or more. For your personal comfort as well as the health of the paneling, a humidity control system is recommended in high-humidity areas. With proper installation and care, your wall paneling will keep its good looks for years and years—a sound decorating investment.

Wiping with a damp cloth is usually all that is needed to clean prefinished paneling when it becomes dirty. On some types, an occasional application of quality liquid wax is advised—follow the directions of both paneling and wax manufacturers.

Pencil and crayon marks and other heavily soiled areas may be cleaned with a mild soap or detergent. On plywood paneling, always wipe with the grain. After soil is removed, rinse and allow to dry thoroughly. Then (unless the manufacturer advises against it) apply a clear wax to restore the desired sheen. Cleansers that contain coarse abrasives are not recommended. Cleansers or waxes that leave deposits in the pores of wood should also not be used. On textured paneling, use heavy cloth wiping rags that will not catch on the raised areas of the design.

A GOOD LADDER FOR A GOOD JOB

Of all the "tools" you need for paneling, wallpapering, and painting, perhaps none is more important than a ladder, because it involves your personal safety. Unless you limit your job to the base woodwork, or are built with the reach of a pro basketball center, you will have to get "up there," whether to do the ceiling or the upper reaches of your home's exterior. Accept no substitutes for a ladder—standing on a chair is risky business and makes the job a lot more tedious, too. The range of ladder designs, types, sizes, and materials is broad enough to fit any need.

Before you make a trip to the store to buy a ladder, think about your needs. Will the ladder be used indoors or outdoors? How high will you want to climb? Who will be using it? Where will it be stored?

If you live in an apartment, a stepladder will probably meet all your needs and will be easy to handle. Its size will depend on the highest point you want to reach, bearing in mind that you should not stand higher than the step below the ladder top. Never stand on the top of a stepladder!

If you live in a house, you may need two ladders—a stepladder for indoor work and a straight ladder or extension ladder for use outdoors. The outdoor ladder should be long enough to extend a minimum of 3 feet higher than the highest area you want to reach.

Don't let price alone guide you. Select a ladder according to your needs. And don't let the salesperson hurry you into making a quick purchase. Check the ladder for weak steps, loose rungs, or other weaknesses before you take it from the store.

Don't buy an unidentified ladder. Be sure that the name of the manufacturer or distributor is on the label. This information may be important in case of a quality problem or an accident.

Look for a seal affixed to the ladder indicating that it conforms to the standards of the American National Standards Institute (ANSI) or the Underwriters' Laboratories, Inc. (UL). The absence of a seal, however, does not necessarily imply that the ladder is of poor quality.

Wood, aluminum, magnesium, and fiberglass are the principal materials used in the construction of ladders. Each type has its advantages and disadvantages.

Wood ladders are sturdy and bend little under loads for which they are designed. They are heavier than metal ladders, and large sizes are harder to handle. When dry, wood ladders are safe to use around electrical circuits or when you are working with power tools.

If wood ladders are used indoors, or adequately protected from moisture and sunlight when used outdoors, they will last a

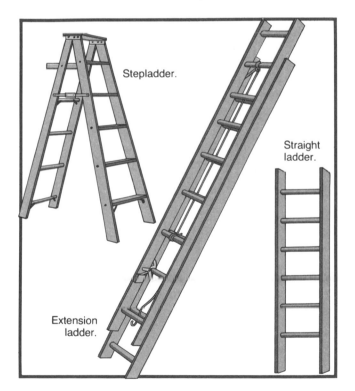

Stepladder.

Straight ladder.

Extension ladder.

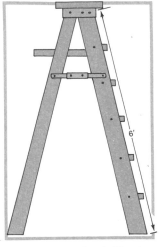

Stepladder size.

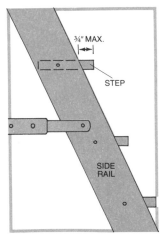

Maximum protrusion of wood steps beyond rails.

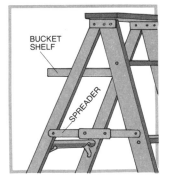

Spreader and bucket shelf.

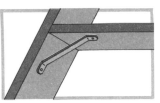

Wood stepladder metal angle brace.

Wood stepladder reinforcing rod.

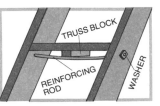

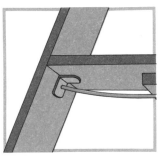

Fastening wood steps with metal angles.

Fastening wood steps in grooves.

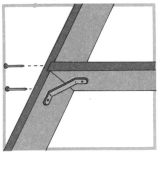

long time. Unprotected in the open, however, they may be attacked by wood-destroying insects, weakened by rot, or cracked and split by the action of sun and rain. Once weakened, wood may break easily and suddenly.

Metal ladders are generally a little more expensive than wood ladders of the same quality, but they last longer because they do not deteriorate from moisture and sunlight and are not susceptible to attack by insects. Aluminum and magnesium ladders are comparatively light, weighing only about two-thirds as much as those made of wood. The two metals weigh about the same, but magnesium ladders are somewhat more expensive. (Magnesium is actually a lighter metal than aluminum but not as strong; therefore, side rails and legs are constructed with thicker cross sections to provide comparable strength.) Magnesium corrodes (turns black) more than aluminum and has less impact resistance. Aluminum and magnesium ladders are not recommended for use around electrical circuits.

Fiberglass is the newest ladder material to appear on the market. It is used to make the side rails of high-grade metal stepladders and of straight and extension ladders. The result is a nonconductive ladder that is light, corrosion-resistant, serviceable, and practically maintenance-free. These ladders do not dry-rot or absorb moisture, and the fiberglass side rails have greater impact resistance than wood, aluminum, or magnesium. These ladders, however, are quite expensive and are used mostly by professionals.

Stepladders

A stepladder is a self-supporting portable ladder. It is nonadjustable in length, and it has flat steps and a hinged back. Size is determined by the length of the ladder measured along the front edge of the side rails.

Stepladders are useful for many indoor and outdoor jobs where the height to be reached is low and the ladder can be rested on a firm surface.

Both wood and metal stepladders are available in three categories. They are: Type I, heavy duty (250 pounds load-carrying capacity); Type II, medium duty (225 pounds); and Type III, light duty (200 pounds). These categories are accepted and widely used by the ladder industry. Look for duty rating when you purchase your new stepladder.

Steps on a wooden stepladder should be flat, parallel, and level when the ladder is open. There should not be more than 12 inches between steps, and these should be at least ¾ inch thick and at least 3½ inches deep (1 x 4 nominal size).

Each step should be braced either with metal angle braces or a metal reinforcing rod. Ends of reinforcing rods should pass through metal washers of sufficient thickness to prevent pressing into and damaging the side rails. When metal reinforcing rods are used, a wood or metal truss block should be fitted to the bottom of each step and positioned at the center between the rod and the step. The bottom step should be reinforced with metal angle braces securely attached to the step and to each side rail. Steps should not protrude more than ¾ inch beyond the front of the side rail and should have no splits, cracks, chips, knots, or other imperfections.

Steps should be fastened to the side rails with metal brackets or by grooving. At least two 6d nails (or equivalent) should be used at each end of the step, through the side rail into the step.

The metal spreader or locking device should be large and strong enough to hold the front and back sections securely in the open position. It should be resistant to rust and corrosion. The bucket shelf should be capable of holding 25 pounds and should

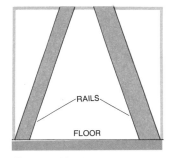

Feet should be level when ladder is open.

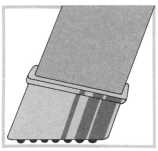

Safety shoes for wood stepladder.

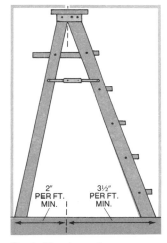

Stepladder slope when open.

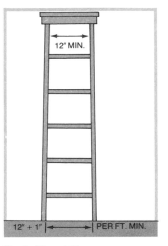

Stepladder width.

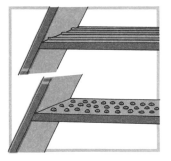

Corrugated and dimpled metal stepladder steps.

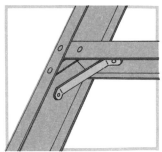

Braces on metal stepladder steps.

fold completely within the ladder. Feet should be level in open position. They can be equipped with safety shoes to prevent slippage or lateral movement.

Shoes on bottom of metal stepladder rails (top left).

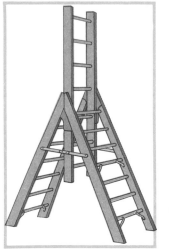

Folded bucket shelf (top right).

Extension trestle ladder.

Trestle ladder.

Platform ladder (left).

Testing stepladder stability.

The slope in the open position should be a minimum of 3½ inches per foot of length of the front section and a minimum of 2 inches per foot of length of the back section. The width between the side rails at the top step should be no less than 12 inches and should increase toward the bottom of the ladder at a minimum rate of 1 inch per foot of length.

Metal stepladder steps should be flat, parallel, and level when the ladder is open. Steps should be corrugated, have raised patterns, be dimpled, be coated with skid-resistant materials, or otherwise treated to minimize the possibility of slipping. There should be no more than 12 inches between steps, as with wood ladders.

The depth of the step or tread should be not less than 3 inches for 225- or 250-pound capacity ladders, or 2½ inches for 200-pound capacity. Steps should have no sharp edges and should not be bent or dented. The bottom step should always be reinforced with metal angle braces.

If steps have only one fastener on each side, there should be diagonal metal braces under both top and bottom steps. If steps have two fastenings on each side, the ladder should have diagonal metal braces under the bottom step.

The bucket shelf should be capable of holding 50 pounds and should fold com-

Platform ladder with guardrail.

Platform ladders used to support scaffold.

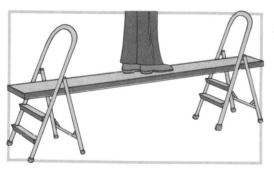

the extension trestle ladder. While these ladders are primarily for professional use, they may also come in handy for use around the home.

One type of platform ladder has a guardrail that lessens the danger of falling. It should have widely spaced legs to provide for good balance. Two of these ladders, used in tandem, provide a good, sturdy base for a scaffold.

Extension Ladders

An extension ladder consists of two or more straight sections traveling in guides or brackets arranged to permit length adjust-

Extension ladder length.

24' EXTENSION LADDER

12'

12'

3'

Overlap of extension ladder sections.

pletely within the ladder. The bottoms of the four rails should be covered for safety with insulating material, such as rubber or plastic nonslip shoes. Spreader, slope, and width specifications are the same as for wood stepladders.

Before purchasing a stepladder, test its stability by climbing to the second step from the bottom and shaking the ladder moderately back and forth while you hold onto the side rails. If the ladder feels loose, consider purchasing a heavier-duty one or one made by another manufacturer.

Stepladder Variations

There are three other types of ladders that are closely related to the stepladder: the platform ladder, the trestle ladder, and

Recommended Lengths for Different Heights of Extension Ladders	
Height You Want to Reach	**Recommended Length of Sections**
9½ feet	16 feet
13½ feet	20 feet
17½ feet	24 feet
21½ feet	28 feet
24½ feet	32 feet
29 feet	36 feet
33 feet	40 feet
36½ feet	44 feet

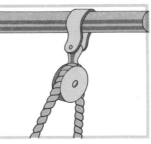

Safety boot for wood
extension ladder.

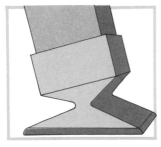

Reinforcement of bottom rung
on wood extension ladder.

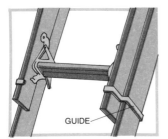

GUIDE

Side-rail slide guide.

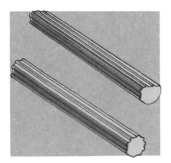

Metal ladder rungs: round,
round with flat surface.

Extension ladder pulley.

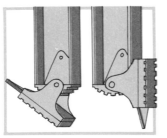

Rung lock.

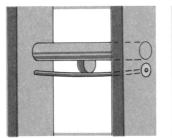

Safety shoes for metal
extension ladder.

Flat surface horizontal when
ladder is at 75° angle.

ment. Its size is designated by the sum of the length of the sections, measured along the side rails.

Each section of an opened extension ladder should overlap the adjacent section by a minimum number of feet, depending on overall length. If an extension ladder is up to 36 feet in length, the overlap should be 3 feet; if total length is between 36 and 48 feet, overlap should be 4 feet. The ladder should be equipped with positive stops to ensure that it cannot be opened too far.

To eliminate confusion in identifying the length of an extension ladder because of overlap, the Federal Trade Commission requires that the total length and working length be clearly marked. For example: "Maximum working length 17 feet; total length of sections 20 feet."

To help you choose the right size extension ladder for your needs, the table on p. 115 shows the recommended relation between working height for a ladder and total length of sections. The recommended total length of sections allows for the proper overlap plus 3 feet more than the greatest working height. The extra 3 feet is the minimum required for safe use.

Feet of wooden extension ladders may be equipped with safety boots or shoes, which are sometimes offered as an accessory. Pulleys should not be less than 1¼ inches outside diameter, and ropes not less than 5/16 inch diameter, with minimum breaking strength of 500 pounds. Rungs must be round and of hard wood, free from crossgrain, splits, cracks, chips, or knots. They should be not less than 1⅛ inches in diameter and spaced not more than 12 inches apart.

Although not required by standards of ANSI or UL, it is highly desirable that at

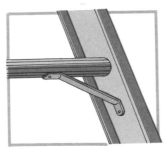

Brace for metal
bottom rung.

least the bottom rung be reinforced with a truss rod. Safety rung locks should be resistant to or protected against rust and corrosion. Locks may be of either the spring or gravity type. Side-rail slide guides should be securely attached and placed to prevent the upper section from tipping or falling out while the ladder is being raised or lowered.

Width of wooden extension ladders should be not less than 12 inches between rails of the upper section. For the lower section, width should be a minimum of 14½ inches up to and including 28-foot ladders, and 16 inches for longer ladders.

Feet of metal extension ladders should have rubber, plastic, or other slip-resistant safety treads or shoes secured to foot brackets. The brackets should pivot freely to rest squarely when the ladder is inclined for use. Rungs should be round or round with flat step surface, and with a slip-resistant tread. The flat surface should be horizontal when the ladder is placed at a 75-degree angle. The top and bottom rungs should be not more than 12 inches from the ends of the side rails to provide for extra strength and stability.

Rung braces are not required by standards of ANSI or UL, but it is highly desirable that at least the bottom rung be reinforced with a metal rung brace.

The width of metal ladders varies. The upper section should be not less than 12 inches. Bottom secions are not less than 12½ inches for ladders up to 16 feet, 14 inches for ladders up to 28 feet, and 15 inches for ladders up to 40 feet. Ropes, pulleys, and safety rung locks are the same as for wooden ladders. On most aluminum extension ladders, the side rails interlock, eliminating the need for slide guides.

Ladder Accessories

A number of useful ladder accessories can add substantially to your safety and convenience. Trays are available for at-

Safety rung lock on metal extension ladder.

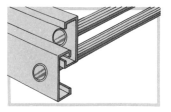
Interlocking side rails.

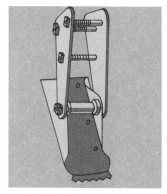
Two types of replacement safety shoes.

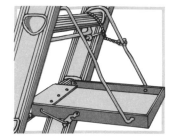
Tray for extension ladder.

Wall grips.

tachment to extension ladders to hold paint, tools, or work materials. Safety shoes should be attached to all metal ladders and to all wood ladders used in slippery or wet places. Although metal ladders are usually sold equipped with safety shoes, wear may make replacement necessary.

Safety wall-grips of rubber or plastic strips can be attached to the tops of extension ladder side rails. These strips keep the top of a ladder from slipping on the surface against which it leans.

LADDER MAINTENANCE—LADDER SAFETY— LADDER CODES

Wood ladders to be used or stored outdoors should be protected with a coat or two of clear sealer, spar varnish, shellac, or a clear wood preservative. Do not paint wood ladders since this would prevent periodic visual inspection of their condition. Linseed oil will help to rustproof metal parts such as rung locks.

Replace worn or frayed ropes on exten-

Replace worn ladder steps.

sion ladders. Check the condition of any ladder that has been dropped or has fallen before it is used again. Replace steps on wood stepladders when approximately one-fourth worn away.

Ladders should be stored where they will not be exposed to the elements. Wood ladders should be kept in a well-ventilated location, away from dampness and excessive heat. Store straight or extension ladders in flat racks or on wall brackets to prevent sag. If long ladders are stored horizontally, use three or more hangers for support.

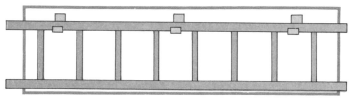

Storing ladder on wall bracket.

Wall bracket.

Inspect the ladder before each use. Oil moving parts and tighten loose fasteners. Check the rope and pulley on an extension ladder for wear and breaking strength.

Set up long straight or extension ladders by the following method to avoid muscle strain or losing control of the ladder:

• Brace the lower end of the ladder against something solid so that it cannot slide.

• Grasp the uppermost rung, using both hands, then raise the top end and walk forward under the ladder, moving your hands to grasp other rungs as you proceed.

• When the ladder is erect, move it to the desired location and then lean it forward to the top resting point.

• Place ladders at the correct angle with the wall. The base of the ladder should be one-quarter of its working length away from the wall or support. If the ladder is placed at too great an angle—that is, with the base too far out—it is subject to strain that can cause it to break or slip. On the other hand, if the base of the ladder is too close to the wall, the ladder is likely to tip backward.

• Place your ladder so that it has a firm footing. The feet of either a stepladder or an extension ladder should be level. If the ground is uneven or soft under one foot, brace the ladder. If necessary, the ladder should be lashed or held in place to prevent slippage.

• Adjust the length of an extension ladder only when your eye level is below the level of the locking device so that you can see when the lock is engaged.

When using an extension or straight ladder, be sure that it is the proper length to reach the desired height. For example, in

Brace lower end and "walk" ladder upright.

Place ladder in desired position.

Support ladder
on uneven or
unstable ground
(above and below).

Place ladder at correct angle, neither
too far away nor too close.

VERTICAL
HEIGHT

¼ VERTICAL HEIGHT

Don't go so high that you have to reach down
to rails (left) and don't overreach (right).

Home Repairs Made Easy • Ladder Maintenance—Ladder Safety—Ladder Codes

using an extension ladder to reach a roof, be sure the top of the ladder extends at least 3 feet above the roof edge. Don't climb up an extension ladder so far that you have to reach down to grasp the side rails.

Never climb higher than the step below the top of a stepladder. If you stand on the top, you can lose your balance.

Go up and down a ladder carefully, always facing the ladder. Carry your tools or other work materials in your clothing or attached to a belt. Take one step at a time.

Move the ladder to where the work can be done without reaching far to one side of the ladder. Overreaching can cause you and the ladder to fall.

Be extremely careful when using metal or wet wood ladders around electrical circuits, power tools, or appliances. Metal and wet wood conduct electricity. Always play it safe!

The stepladder and the extension ladder are the two types most commonly used around the home. Codes have been established by the American National Standards Institute to cover wood and metal stepladders and extension ladders. Any ladder you buy with an ANSI seal conforms to the code.

The code for wood ladders is a dimensional one. It covers, for example, the depth and thickness of steps. Performance tests have not been developed. The code for metal ladders is based on performance. It prescribes the methods for testing the strength of ladders, with emphasis on side rails, steps, fastening hardware, and the back legs of stepladders.

PAPERHANGING TOOLS

In order to hang wallpaper properly, you need certain tools. Some of these, like an old table or sharp razor knife, you probably already have on hand. The other items are generally inexpensive and can be purchased at your wallpaper dealer's shop. If you have a rickety old stepladder, plan on purchasing a new one (see pp. 111–120). Nothing is more annoying, or more easily preventable, than to have your wallpapering project interrupted by broken bones resulting from a fall off a broken ladder. At best you will end up on the floor wrapped like a mummy in sticky wallpaper. Avoid accidents by planning ahead.

A pasting table or other flat, hard surface at least 6 feet long is needed for cutting and pasting wallpaper. It can be rented, or you can make one by placing a sheet of ½-inch plywood on two or three sawhorses.

Two buckets, pails, or roller trays — one for paste, one for clear water — are needed. (If you're using prepasted wallpaper, just get one water tray.) A pasting brush, calcimine brush, or paint roller is necessary to apply paste if unpasted wallpaper is used.

Use a flexible metal tape ruler to measure wallpaper lengths and widths, and a trimming knife to cut wallpaper. This can be either a sharp knife or a razor blade and

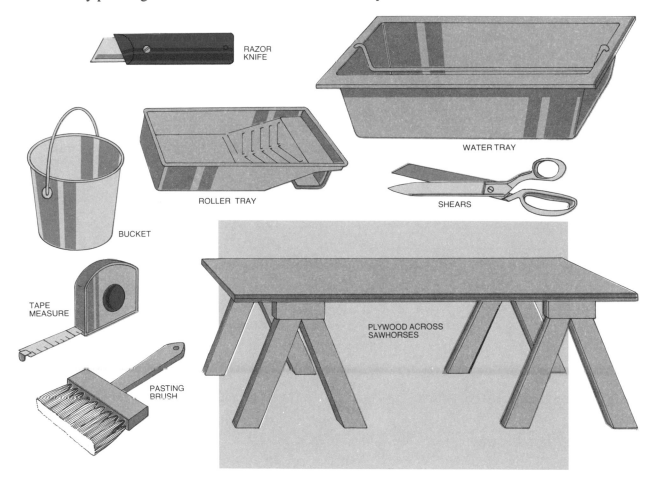

RAZOR KNIFE

WATER TRAY

ROLLER TRAY

SHEARS

BUCKET

TAPE MEASURE

PLYWOOD ACROSS SAWHORSES

PASTING BRUSH

Home Repairs Made Easy

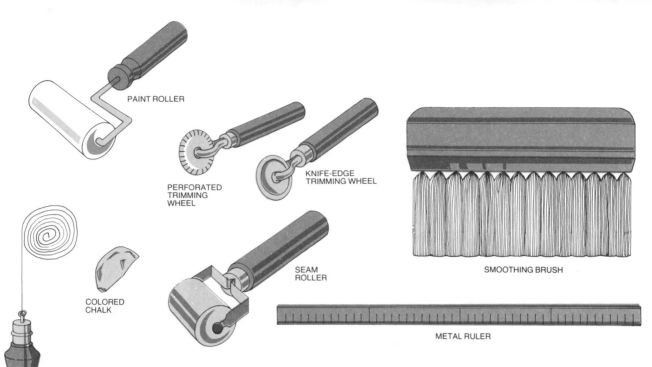

PAINT ROLLER

PERFORATED TRIMMING WHEEL

KNIFE-EDGE TRIMMING WHEEL

COLORED CHALK

SEAM ROLLER

SMOOTHING BRUSH

METAL RULER

PLUMB BOB

holder. You should also have a trimming wheel to cut paper along baseboards or trim after it is installed. Two kinds, the perforated wheel and the knife-edge wheel, are available. A straightedge is essential for cutting straight lines. A long metal ruler is best, but any long, straight object will do. A chalk line will provide a true, straight, vertical guideline. You can make one with a piece of string, some colored chalk and a plumb bob.

A smoothing brush is used to smooth wallpaper against a wall and to remove air bubbles and wrinkles. The brush should be 12 inches wide, with bristles that are firm but soft enough not to scratch the wallpaper. (On some types of wallpaper, a soft paint roller is the preferred tool for the smoothing process.)

Shears or other heavy-duty scissors can cut wet wallpaper easier than a knife can. A seam roller makes tight joints at seams and edges. Use drop cloths to protect floors and furniture not removed from the room.

WALLPAPER COLORS AND PATTERNS

The special effects that can be achieved and the seemingly endless varieties of handsome patterns reflecting just about any mood make wallpaper a valuable asset in the home or apartment owner's decorating portfolio.

The term wallpaper, it should be noted, does not apply exclusively to paper substances that are hung on a wall. It also includes vinyls, foils, grass cloth, fabrics, cork, and many other wallcovering materials available from your wallpaper dealer.

Wallpapering can be done with professional results by almost anyone willing to plan carefully and work slowly. It is not a difficult task, but it does require patience. Wallpaper can be purchased pretrimmed and prepasted so that all you have to do is soak it in water and apply it to the walls while wet. Hanging regular wallpaper, which must be trimmed and pasted, is not much harder to do.

The selection of wallpaper color and pattern is largely a matter of personal preference. Books and magazines about interior decorating are full of ideas regarding the use of wallpaper. In addition, many wallpaper dealers can give you valuable advice about how to achieve different effects— brightening a room or wall, visually lengthening a room, and coordinating carpet and furniture colors and styles.

The colors in a wallpaper vary slightly between different runs. If you have to reorder wallpaper, there is a good chance that the new order will not color-match the previous lot. Therefore, estimate your needs carefully and order enough wallpaper at one time to complete your entire job. Blank stock is an unpatterned wallpaper commonly applied to a wall to provide a smooth surface for foil wallpaper and other special applications. All other wallpaper is patterned or textured.

Some patterns—many of the vertical stripes, for example—require little or no matching. The paper can be cut almost to the exact length required. Since only an inch or two extra length for trimming is needed on each strip, there is very little waste. The same is true of randomly patterned papers such as grass cloth or burlap.

Other patterns can involve considerable waste in installation. A clue to the amount of waste can be gained from the size of the repeat. This information is provided in the wallpaper catalog from which you make your selection. For example, the catalog may state that a certain pattern is repeated every 19 inches. Assume that the distance between the baseboard and the ceiling of the room that you want to paper is 94 inches. The 19-inch pattern will go into the 94-inch wall 5 times—with 1 inch left over for trimming. This pattern would result in very little waste.

You may find that another pattern is repeated every 18 inches. For the same wall, this pattern would repeat 6 times with 14 inches left over. The 18-inch pattern results in 14 inches of trim waste required for each strip. Unless you can find a place to use these remnants (over a window or door, for example), you will have a lot of waste.

ESTIMATING WALLPAPER, TRIM, AND PASTE

WALLPAPER ESTIMATING CHART

Distance around room in feet	Single rolls for wall areas Height of ceiling			Number yards for borders	Single rolls for ceilings
	8 feet	9 feet	10 feet		
28	8	8	10	11	2
30	8	8	10	11	2
32	8	10	10	12	2
34	10	10	12	13	4
36	10	10	12	13	4
38	10	12	12	14	4
40	10	12	12	15	4
42	12	12	14	15	4
44	12	12	14	16	4
46	12	14	14	17	6
48	14	14	16	17	6
50	14	14	16	18	6
52	14	14	16	19	6
54	14	16	18	19	6
56	14	16	18	20	8
58	16	16	18	21	8
60	16	18	20	21	8
62	16	18	20	22	8
64	16	18	20	23	8
66	18	20	20	23	10
68	18	20	22	24	10
70	18	20	22	25	10
72	18	20	22	25	12
74	20	22	22	26	12
76	20	22	24	27	12
78	20	22	24	27	14
80	20	22	26	28	14
82	22	24	26	29	14
84	22	24	26	30	16
86	22	24	26	30	16
88	24	26	28	31	16
90	24	26	28	32	18

Note: Deduct one single roll for every two ordinary size doors and windows or every 30 square feet of wall opening.

Always plan on having some extra wallpaper; it may be needed for several reasons. A strip of wallpaper may be ruined in handling and need replacement. Other surfaces in a room (valances, for example) may be included in the job and require additional wallpaper. Future repairs may become necessary for which it is important to have wallpaper of the original batch. The same wallpaper, if bought later, may not exactly match the color of that on your wall.

The amount of wallpaper required to cover a surface depends not only on the size of the surface but on the wallpaper pattern as well. To make your estimate, you should know a few facts about wallpaper. It is sold in a variety of widths. Regardless of width, each single roll has 36 square feet of wallpaper (double rolls are also available). The length of each roll depends upon the width. The wider the roll, the shorter the length, and therefore fewer individual strips can be cut from the roll for hanging. When estimating the amount of wallpaper needed, count on about 30 square feet of coverage per roll, allowing 6 square feet for waste (allow for greater waste if the repeat requires it). For estimating surfaces that are interrupted by doors, windows, and fireplaces, make your estimate for the entire surface. Then reduce your estimate by 1/3 to 1/2 roll for each door, window, and fireplace, or 10 to 15 square feet each. If you estimate your needs in this way, you should have enough wallpaper to complete the job plus some left over.

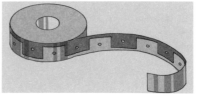

Trim.

You may prefer to have your wallpaper dealer estimate your needs. He is an expert. After you have selected a wallpaper pattern, he can tell you exactly how much you need if you give him sketches and measurements of the room.

The amount of paste needed for paper that is not prepasted depends on the number of rolls and the type of wallpaper you are using. Wheat paste can be used with most types; one pound of dry mix is generally enough to hang six to eight rolls of wallpaper. More dry mix may be needed than is recommended by the label instructions. Following label instructions sometimes results in a paste that is too thin.

Some dry-mix pastes contain mildew-resistant additives. These should always be used with coated vinyl wallpaper. The weight and type of backing on the vinyl determines the amount of adhesive needed. One gallon of vinyl adhesive is generally enough to hang two to four rolls of wallpaper. Ask your wallpaper dealer to recommend the amount and type of adhesive needed for your specific job.

Trim can be used as a decorative border, or to lessen the effects of any sudden change in patterns and colors between ceilings and walls. Trim is sold by the yard. Therefore, when measuring for trim, round off measurements to the next higher yard.

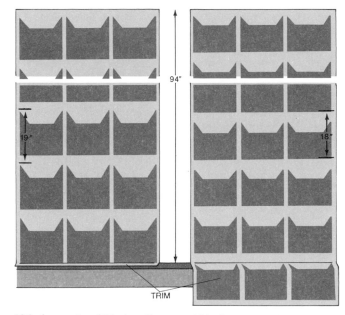

19-inch repeat on 94-inch wall.   18-inch repeat on 94-inch wall.

Papering
a valance.

SELECTION OF WALLPAPER MATERIAL

The selection of wallpaper material is partly a matter of function. Vinyl wallcoverings should certainly be used in kitchens, bathrooms, hallways, or other areas where exposure to moisture and the elements could create a problem. It is extremely durable and moisture- and grease-resistant. In an entryway, durability is not a major consideration, but dramatic appearance may be. Foils, flocks, or grass cloth can be the answer to a decorating problem here.

Vinyls

The three kinds of vinyl wallpaper commonly available are vinyl laminated to paper, vinyl laminated to cloth, and vinyl-impregnated cloth on paper backing. These vinyl wallpapers are extremely durable. They are easy to clean (scrubbable) and very resistant to damage. Most vinyl wallpapers are nonporous.

Pay close attention to labeling. Some wallpapers are vinyl-coated only. These are not particularly wear-resistant, grease-resistant, or washable.

Before hanging vinyl wallpapers, old paper on the wall should be removed. It is probably glued to the wall with wheat paste. Because vinyls are nonporous, moisture from the adhesive will be sealed in and cause the wheat paste to mildew. Also, sealed-in moisture can soak through old wallpaper and cause it to peel loose from the wall, taking along the vinyl that is pasted over it.

It is recommended that sizing be applied to surfaces before papering with vinyl. Sizing provides a good bonding surface. It also makes it easier to slide wallpaper strips into alignment for matching and making seams. The best sizing is a coat of the same vinyl adhesive you will use for applying the vinyl wallpaper. Be sure that any sizing you use is mildew-resistant.

Use mildew-resistant adhesives only. It is recommended that special vinyl adhesives be used. Paper-backed vinyl sometimes tends to curl back from the wall along edges at seams. Seams can then be difficult to finish. Use of vinyl adhesive prevents this problem.

Vinyl wallpaper stretches if pulled. If it is stretched while being applied, hairline cracks will appear at seams when the wallpaper shrinks as it dries. Be careful, therefore, to avoid stretching vinyl wallpaper. Some wallpapers find that a squeegee works better than a smoothing brush for smoothing vinyl wallpaper.

Foils

Foil wallpaper is available either with a simulated metallic finish or as aluminum laminated to paper. All foils must be handled carefully. Do not fold or wrinkle foil, because creases cannot be removed. Because of their reflective surface, foils will magnify any imperfections on the surface to which they are applied. Foils are nonporous; like vinyls, they don't "breathe."

Do not apply a cereal-based sizing to the wall; it could mildew. Sand the wall lightly with production-grade fine sandpaper to remove texture and imperfections.

It is generally recommended that the surface first be covered with blank stock. This serves two purposes: it helps smooth the surface and it absorbs moisture from the adhesive used for the foil, thus speeding the drying process. Apply blank stock with the same adhesive used for applying the foil.

Use mildew-resistant adhesives only. It is recommended that vinyl adhesives be used because the foil seals the adhesive from the air and drying is retarded. Vinyl adhesives dry relatively fast. Wheat paste could mildew and should never be used with foil.

Some foils must be hung dry. Paste is applied to the wall and the foil is positioned on the paste. Special instructions such as these would come with the wallpaper.

Grass Cloth, Hemp, Burlap, Cork

These materials are generally mounted on a paper backing. The patterns and textures are usually random and require no matching. Because of this, there is little waste. When cutting strips, you need allow only an inch or two extra length for trimming. These materials are not washable, so consider this when placing them in a much-trafficked room.

The paper backing on which these materials are mounted can be weakened from oversoaking with paste. It is recommended, therefore, that the wall first be covered with blank stock to help absorb moisture from the paste. If you decide not to use blank stock, you should apply sizing to the wall. Sizing provides a sealed surface that makes it easier to slide the wallpaper into place.

Be careful not to oversoak the backing—it can be weakened and allow the surface to separate. Rather than pasting several strips ahead, paste one strip and hang it before pasting the next strip.

These materials may be difficult to cut when wet. The job of trimming will be easier if you align the top end of the strip to the ceiling and do all the trimming at the bot-

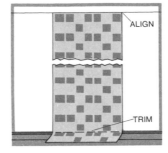
Align top end, trim only at bottom.

Align seams by pushing with the palms of your hands.

Smooth with paint roller.

Press seams with fingers.

Blot seams to remove excess paste.

Trim edges of grass cloth.

tom end of the strip. Mark it at the baseboard and cut with a scissors.

To align seams, push the wallpaper gently with the palms of your hands. Do not use a smoothing brush; the paper can be damaged by rubbing. Smooth it to the wall with a paint roller. Press seams into place with your fingers—don't use a seam roller, but firm the seams with a soft paint roller. Remove excess paste by wiping gently or blotting with a damp sponge.

In grass cloth, the color will vary slightly

between rolls and even from one part of a roll to another. It is a good idea to first cut all full-length strips and arrange them for best appearance. Then stack them in this order for pasting. The edges of grass cloth are sometimes ragged. In this case, you may wish to trim ½ inch off the edges before hanging. This will make a good, sharp edge for seams. For best results, trim the edges after the grass cloth is pasted.

Prepasted Wallpaper

Prepasted wallpaper, with water-soluble paste applied at the factory, is available in vinyl and paper materials. The wallpaper is

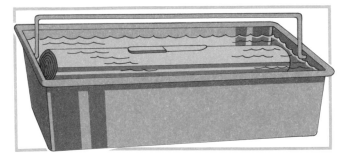

Weight paper down in water tray.

cut and soaked in water according to manufacturer's directions. Weight the paper down with a butter knife or other dull object to hold it under the water and to facilitate unrolling it. After soaking, it is ready to be hung.

No special surface preparation is required when using prepasted wallpaper — just make sure the subsurface is sound, smooth, and clean.

Flocks

Flock is made of nylon or rayon and is available on paper, vinyl, or foil wallpapers. It presents no special preparation problems. It is fairly durable but can be damaged and flattened by rubbing and pressure. Therefore, use a paint roller or squeegee (available from your wallpaper dealer) rather than a smoothing brush to smooth it on the wall. Do not use a seam roller on seams, edges, or ends. Instead, pat down edges with a damp sponge or cloth, or use a new soft paint roller.

After hanging a strip, wipe in a downward direction with a damp sponge. Then, with a clean damp sponge, fluff up all flock with upward strokes to lay all nap in the same direction. Some small fibers will come loose during this operation, but this is no cause for concern.

Wipe flock downward with damp sponge.

Wipe upward to raise nap.

GENERAL PREPARATIONS BEFORE PAPERHANGING

A few minutes spent in organizing the paperhanging area will save time, mess, and tempers. An empty room makes the best work area. However, it is seldom practical to empty the entire room. Move out what furniture you can, and move the rest away from your work area so that you have as much room as possible for the ladder and for handling strips of pasted paper. Trying to work in a cramped space is both frustrating and irritating.

Bring all tools and supplies you will need into the work area. Set up a pasting table far enough from the surfaces to be wallpapered so as not to be in the way. Cover the pasting table with clean, plain paper such as freezer paper or brown wrapping paper. Never use newsprint to cover a pasting table; the newspaper ink is likely to soil the wallpaper.

●

If old wallpaper is still in good condition, you can paper right over it. Any loose sections should be removed and the edges feathered with sandpaper. It the paper is generally loose, remove it completely with a rented steamer (following the renter's directions) or by soaking with wallpaper remover (following label directions). Where plaster is crumbling, scrape it away and patch with spackling compound, then sand smooth.

If you're papering over a low-gloss paint finish, dirt, grease, and wax must be removed. Following the label directions, mix a solution of trisodium phosphate (TSP) to wash soiled surfaces. This provides a fine receptive surface for any adhesive.

If the surface paint is a shiny, high-gloss type, wallpaper may not stick well to it. This condition can be corrected by scrubbing with a solution of TSP or by applying a commercial deglosser. Consult a paint dealer for materials and recommendations.

Remove loose sections of old paper.

Feather edges with sandpaper.

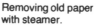

Removing old paper with steamer.

Removing old paper with chemical remover.

Apply sealer.

Apply sizing.

If the surface is not painted, it must be sealed before applying sizing. Apply an oil-base sealer to unpainted surfaces such as new wallboard, plywood, or plaster.

It is generally advised to size surfaces before papering them. Sizing further seals the surface, preventing it from absorbing water

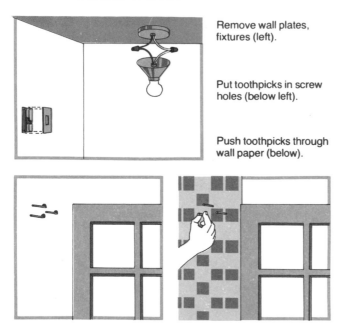

Remove wall plates, fixtures (left).

Put toothpicks in screw holes (below left).

Push toothpicks through wall paper (below).

from the wallpaper paste or glue, and thus allowing these substances to dry properly. (Vinyl adhesive should be used as sizing for nonporous wall coverings such as vinyl and foils.) Sizing also provides a roughened surface to which wallpaper paste can stick firmly.

For "breathing" wallpapers, you can use either of two sizing substances. Wallpaper paste, mixed according to manufacturer's instructions, acts as a sizing agent when applied to a surface and allowed to dry. Special wallpaper sizing is formulated specifically for this job.

Brush or roll a thin coat of sizing on the walls and allow it to dry. If the sizing turns pink in any area, it indicates a "hot spot" in the plaster; neutralize this area with a solution of zinc sulfate and water. Let dry and apply more sizing.

Take down all removable hardware that may be in your way. This includes cover plates for electrical switches and outlets and light fixtures. Since you will have to turn off the power in the room to remove the fixtures, you may find it convenient to do so only at the time you are actually papering around them.

Also remove curtain rods and brackets, drapery rods and brackets, and picture hooks. Screw holes will be difficult to find after they are covered with wallpaper. To save time and avoid having to drill new holes, place a toothpick in each hole. Remove the toothpick when papering over the hole, then push the toothpick through the paper back into the hole before going on to the next strip.

REMOVING SELVAGE

Most wallpaper today is pretrimmed. The manufacturer has mechanically cut the edges so that strips can be butted together at a seam without the need for selvage removal. (Selvage is a narrow, unprinted strip on one or both edges of a roll of wallpaper.) A few smaller companies that produce specialty wallpapers still sell their products with the selvage intact.

The removal of selvage can be a time-consuming task. You should not be dissuaded, however, from buying a roll with these margins. The time required to remove the selvage will be well worth it if the paper is appealing.

Often, selvage strips are perforated for easy removal. In this case, simply strike the selvage sharply against a hard surface while turning the roll of wallpaper. The selvage will be torn off without damaging the patterned part of the paper.

If the selvage is not perforated, it must be cut off. It can sometimes be removed by the wallpaper dealer with a special tool. If the dealer cannot do it, you must remove it yourself. It is easiest to remove the selvage before cutting the wallpaper rolls into strips. Then, when you start hanging wallpaper, this work is out of the way.

To remove selvage, unroll some wallpaper onto your table. Align a straightedge with the selvage. Using a sharp knife, cut off the selvage. Roll the trimmed paper up so the roll looks like a scroll, one side trimmed and the other untrimmed. Repeat this process on the rest of the paper until all selvage is removed. Be careful not to damage flock surfaces by rubbing or pressing hard with the straightedge.

Cut off perforated selvage and roll up trimmed paper, continuing to trim it.

PATTERN LOCATION

Before cutting the first strip, determine where the pattern should end at the ceiling. This is a matter both of pattern and personal preference. Obviously, a pattern with human figures should not end with the heads cut off or just feet showing at the ceiling.

It is also important to remember that the line formed where the wall meets the ceiling is probably uneven. On painted walls, this unevenness often goes unnoticed. However, you may choose wallpaper with a pattern that forms a strong horizontal line. If this line is located near the ceiling line, the ceiling may appear noticeably uneven and the wallpaper poorly matched.

Therefore, locate horizontal lines of a pattern as far as possible away from the ceiling line.

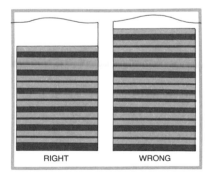

Keep horizontal lines away from ceiling to make the unevenness less visible.

Home Repairs Made Easy

HANGING WALLPAPER

Follow the manufacturer's directions carefully when mixing wallpaper paste. Stir thoroughly until the mixture is entirely free of lumps. The paste should brush on smoothly, yet be thick enough to permit sliding the paper for positioning on the wall. If the manufacturer's suggested proportions result in too thin a paste, add a small amount of the dry powder to the mix.

If all four walls are to be papered, there will almost certainly be one place where the pattern cannot be matched. You should plan to locate this mismatch in the least noticeable place in the room. The best place for the mismatch is usually the least noticeable corner. However, sometimes a door opening or built-in cupboards or bookshelves can make a break in the pattern so that a mismatch will not be noticeable.

As a general rule, you should begin papering on the wall which is most noticeable and end in the corner which is least noticeable (or at another area, as noted above). After placing the first strip of wallpaper on the wall, work from right or left to the least noticeable corner. Then work from the opposite direction to the least noticeable corner or other mismatch location.

After locating where your first strip will go, hold a partially unrolled roll of wallpaper against the wall at the ceiling joint and decide where you want the pattern to "break" at the ceiling line. Mark this point

Mark the pattern break at the ceiling line.

lightly with a pencil and place the roll on the table. Starting at your pencil mark measure off the distance from ceiling to baseboard.

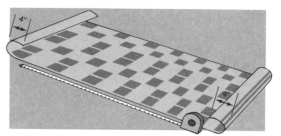
Measure and add 4 inches at top and bottom.

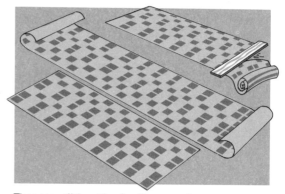
Then tear off the strip of wallpaper and tear off second strip to match first.

Add about 4 inches above your ceiling mark and another 4 inches at the base for a trim margin, then tear off the strip of wallpaper, using a yardstick or other straightedge as a guide.

Lay the roll beside the first strip, unroll, and match its pattern to the pattern on the first strip. Tear the second strip off even with the first. Place it on top of the first, pattern up. Repeat this procedure with three or four more matching strips.

Now turn the pile of strips over, pattern side down, and push it back to the end of your work table. Take the first strip off the

Apply paste to first strip.

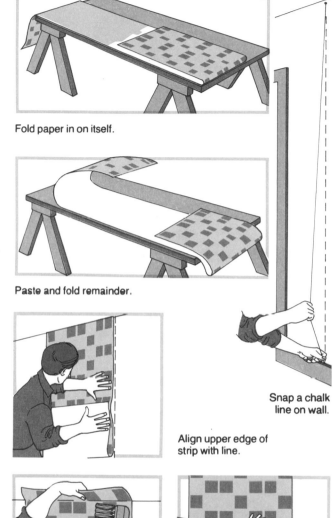

Fold paper in on itself.

Paste and fold remainder.

Align upper edge of
strip with line.

Snap a chalk
line on wall.

pile and line it up with the edge of the table nearest you. Apply paste to about two-thirds of the top of the strip.

Now fold the section in on itself—paste to paste. Align the edges of the strip carefully, but do not crease the fold. Paste and fold the remainder of the strip—again, paste to paste.

If you are using prepasted wallpaper, simply dip the strip into the water tank. Fold the strip over as described above and proceed to the next step.

The first strip must be perfectly vertical. This is important, as this strip serves as the placement reference for the entire wall. If you are starting in a corner, measure off a distance from the wall equal to one inch less than the width of the wallpaper strip. This extra inch will allow you to trim away the excess that may not be even because of the unevenness of the corner. Place a tack near the ceiling at the point you measured.

Chalk a plumb line and suspend it from the tack, allowing the weight to swing free. When it stops moving, hold the chalked line taut; pull it out at the middle and snap it against the wall.

Open the longer folded section of the pasted strip and position it at the ceiling. Align the outer edge with your chalk guideline, then give the upper area of the strip a few strokes with the smoothing brush to hold it. (For certain types of materials, as noted earlier, just press into place—do not use the smoothing brush.)

Unfold the shorter folded section and

Stroke with smoothing
brush to hold it.

Position lower end of
strip, smooth with brush.

guide it gently into place, keeping it on the chalk line. When this section is in position, brush from the center to the edges in

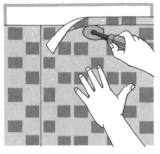
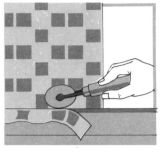

Trim at top.

Trim at bottom.

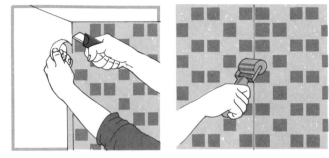

Trim at corner.

Press seams.

sweeping strokes over the entire piece. Trim at top and bottom with a razor, a sharp knife or, preferably, a wheel trimmer, then trim at the corner where necessary. Succeeding strips are hung in the same manner and in the same order in which they were cut.

After the strips have hung for 10 to 15 minutes, press the seams lightly with a seam roller. In the case of embossed or flock papers, seams are not rolled. With these wallpapers, a soft cloth pressed along the seams will serve the same end, while not crushing the flock or embossed pattern.

Remove any excess paste promptly from pattern, woodwork, etc. If the paper is a water-resistant type, wipe down the entire strip with a wet sponge. Use a clean, dry cloth on nonwashable paper.

●

Butt joints have become almost the only method used for **making seams** between strips of wallpaper. They are by far the least noticeable of joints. A butt joint is made by moving the strip being hung against the strip already in place. Firmly slide the new strip tightly against the preceding one until a tiny ridge rises at the seam. As the paste dries, the wallpaper shrinks, causing the ridge to flatten.

Hairline joints are used only for blank stock, which is applied to the wall before hanging certain types of papers. A hairline joint is made by moving the strip being hung until its edge touches the edge of the strip already hung. As the paste dries, the paper shrinks, leaving a small hairline gap between the edges. This is invisible when the wallpaper is installed.

Lap joints, once common, are rarely used for seams between strips of wallpaper. They are noticeable and unattractive on an open wall. Lap joints may be used to make seams at corners. They are also used when small pieces must be joined together, such as fitting small strips in a casement window.

Do not use overlapping joints when hanging vinyl paper. Pastes made for vinyl do not have strong adhesion for vinyl on vinyl. When hanging vinyl, use the double-cut seam method.

In this technique, a double cut is made at

Slide paper together until a ridge forms.

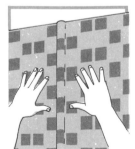

Paper shrinks to form tight joint.

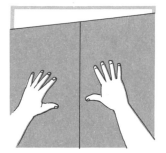

Hairline joint on blank stock.

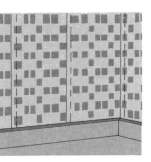

Lap joint.

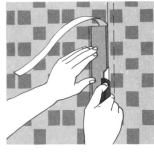

Making a double-cut seam.

seams where the wallpaper strips have been overlapped. The cutting stroke must be firm enough to cut through both layers of paper. To make the cut, place a straightedge along the center of the overlap. With one stroke of the trimming knife, cut through both layers of wallpaper. Remove the trimmed strip from the top piece of wallpaper. Carefully pull the top wallpaper from the wall until the cutaway strip of the bottom strip can be removed. Then rearrange the seam, and smooth it down.

●

Special care should be taken when **papering an outside corner.** Do not rub on the paper where it passes around the corner. The surface of the wallpaper could be damaged.

Outside corners are more noticeable than inside corners. Mismatches are far more apparent at outside corners. Because of this, seams at or near the corner should be avoided whenever possible.

To paper around an outside corner, align the corner strip with the preceding strip. Cut a slit in the 4-inch trim margins at top and bottom and wrap the strip around the corner. Trim off the excess and let set. As the paste dries, the strip will be pulled tightly against the wall.

Usually, papering inside corners results in some mismatch between strips. If the strips are carefully aligned, however, the mismatch will not be very noticeable. The

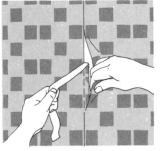

Lift top paper to remove cutaway strip below.

Smooth the seam after having it rearranged.

correct way to paper an inside corner is to cut the strip into two parts and overlap them at the corner. Never simply fold a strip and then paste it into a corner. It may pull away from the corner when it dries, becoming unsightly and subject to damage.

Measure and record the distances be-

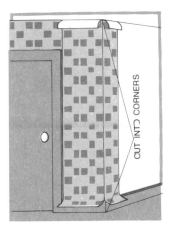

CUT INTO CORNERS

Papering an outside corner.

1. Measure distance between strip and inside corner.

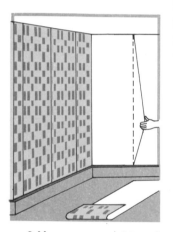

3. Measure second strip and snap chalk line

4. Hang second strip.

2. Hang first strip in corner.

You now have two strips. The strip cut to the measurement arrived at in the previous paragraph is hung first. Measure and record the second strip's width. Beginning at the corner, measure out and mark this distance onto the wall to be papered. Snap a chalk line at this point. Align the second strip with the line. Some mismatch may occur with this method, but it will not be very noticeable, especially with smaller patterns. Remember: this overlapped seam will have to be double-cut if you are working with vinyl material.

●

The procedure for **paperhanging around doors and windows** is essentially the same. The first strip to be hung around a window is aligned with the previous strip. The new strip is then pressed against the wall until it reaches the window. Don't press the top and bottom edges, however, until all cuts around the window have been made.

Using a smoothing brush (or paint roller), gently press the wallpaper into place where

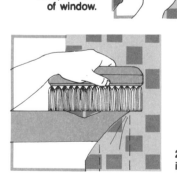

1. Cut wallpaper at top corner of window.

2. Smooth paper into joint.

tween the preceding strip and the inside corner at three different points up and down the wall. Add ½ inch to the greatest distance. Measure out the same distance on a strip of wallpaper and cut the strip to this width with a straightedge.

the wall and vertical edge of the frame meet. Cut the wallpaper at the top corner at a 45-degree angle into the outside corner of the frame. Using the smoothing brush, smooth the paper gently into place where the wall and top horizontal edge of the window frame meet. At the bottom corner, cut a 45-degree angle into the paper toward the lower outside corner of the window frame. Gently tap the wallpaper into place where the wall and bottom horizontal edge of the frame meet. Trim excess paper from around the vertical edge of the frame. Smooth the paper to the wall.

If more than one strip is required to paper around the window, repeat this procedure with the other side. The only difference between this process and papering around doors is that you needn't trim any bottom corners on door openings.

3. Cut wallpaper at bottom corner of window.

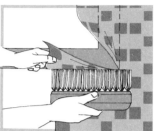

4. Press paper into place.

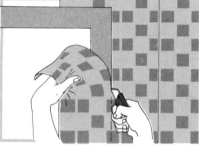

5. Trim excess paper around window.

PAINTING TOOLS

The world is full of painting experts. Because painting is a relatively easy do-it-yourself task, and because many amateurs become "professionals" merely by hanging out a shingle and advertising in the classified ad sections of the local newspaper, there is a great deal of dogmatic, if misinformed, rhetoric about proper painting methods—especially the brush vs. roller vs. spray controversy.

There are still many old-timers who disdain the roller, and as for the spray gun—well, its use should be limited by law to applying pesticides to rose bushes, and never paint to a house! For these purists, only a brush can truly communicate with a surface being coated, "working in" the paint for a properly applied finish. On the other hand, there are those who recoil in horror at the thought of picking up paint with anything other than a roller, which they regard as the greatest invention since (and an extension of) the wheel. And there are those adherents of spray painting who regard the wielders of both brush and roller as throwbacks to the age when man's use of paint was limited to decorating the walls of his cave with crude drawings of animals.

The fact is that all three methods of applying paint have distinct advantages (and disadvantages). Therefore, when it comes to selecting and using these tools, use what works best for you. There is no hard-and-fast rule to follow.

COMPARISON CHART: BRUSH vs. ROLLER vs. SPRAYER			
	Small Brush	Wide Brush	Roller	Sprayer
ADVANTAGES	Maneuverability Low price Easy to use Easy to clean	Quick application Versatile Smooth finish Can cut in around trim	Speed over large surfaces Easy to use Low price	Fast, easy to use Smoothest finish Has other uses
DISADVANTAGES	Takes more time on large jobs	Requires some experience for best results	Must cut in with brush or corner roller Difficult to clean covers	Difficult to use indoors Difficult to cut in fine line Requires some experience for good results Not worthwhile for small jobs
TYPE JOBS BEST SUITED FOR	Trim, sash Cabinetwork Radiators, blinds, etc.	Walls, exteriors, large surfaces	Large unbroken surfaces Rough surfaces (stucco, block, etc.) Floors	Large exterior surfaces "Hard to paint" surfaces (wicker, stucco, blinds)
RELATIVE COST	39¢ to $5.00	99¢ to $15.00	$1.99 to $7.50	$9.95 to $1000.00 (commercial type)

Paintbrushes

Quality is a very important factor in selecting a brush, regardless of the size or style needed for a particular project. A good brush will hold more paint and enable you to apply the paint more smoothly and with less effort.

All good brushes have bristles that are "flagged," a term denoting splits on the bristle end. The more "flags" the better, as they help retain paint. Hog bristle is naturally flagged; synthetic bristle is artificially flagged, or split.

Test for "bounce" by brushing bristles against the back of your hand. In a good brush, the bristles will feel elastic and springy. When the brush is gently pressed on any surface, the bristles will not fan out excessively.

Check the setting. Bristles should be solidly set to prevent any chance of fallout during painting. Jar the brush and fan the bristles. Any loose bristles will be apparent. The metal band holding the bristles is called a ferrule. Stainless steel and aluminum are generally used on better-grade brushes for greater resistance to corrosion.

Both the surface area and type of paint determine the size and style of brush to be used. Calcimine brushes with very long, tough, and elastic gray hog bristles are best for applying water-thinned paints to large areas. Enamel and varnish brushes, both flat and chisel-shaped, are best for applying oil-base paints and lacquers. The shape and length of the latter type help secure a smoother flow and prevent lap marks.

The following brush styles and sizes are recommended for most painting projects around the home:

• Flat wall brushes: Sizes vary from 3 to 6 inches in width with thicknesses of ¾ to 1½ inches and bristles from 2 to 7 inches long. They are best suited for painting large surfaces such as walls, ceilings, and floors.

Flagged bristles.

Wall brushes.

BAD   GOOD

Pressing the brush on a surface to test for "bounce."

Fan brush to check loose bristles.

Flat, chisel-shaped varnish brushes.

Sash, trim, artist's brushes.

• Varnish brushes: Sizes range from 1 to 3½ inches in width, with bristles from 2 to 1½ inches long. They are ideally suited for painting baseboards, window frames, narrow boards, or enameling and varnishing furniture and small panels.

• Round sash and flat trim brushes: Sizes range from 1 to 1½ inches in width. Trellises, screens, small pipes, toys, and all

Fishtailing of brush caused by not using it properly.

Standing the brush on its tip causes the edges to bend.

Cleaning brush in thinner.

Washing brush.

Storing brush in can.

Wrapping brush in paper.

Before reuse of brush, recondition it.

Priming the brush.

small areas are best painted with sash, trim, or even small artist's brushes.

In addition to these general styles, most dealers carry special brushes for bronzing, roofing, stippling, and stenciling.

A quality brush is a fine tool and should be properly used and cared for. For example, a wide brush should never be used to paint pipes and similar surfaces. This causes the brush to "fishtail." A brush should never be left standing on its bristles. The weight causes the edge to bend and curl, ruining the fine painting tips.

Always clean a brush while it is still soft after painting. Use the thinner for the product in which the brush has been used. For example, turpentine followed by naphtha or mineral spirits should be used to remove oil-base paints in which turpentine is a recommended thinning ingredient. Alcohol or lacquer thinner are used on brushes after applying shellac or alcohol-base stains. Cleaning should be followed by washing the brush in soap and water. Latex or water-base paints can be easily removed by dissolving the excess paint in water.

Once the brush is thoroughly cleaned, it should be properly stored. Drill a hole in the brush handle, insert a wire rod through the hole, then rest the rod on a paint, coffee, or shortening can taller than the length of the bristles. Bristles should not rest on the bottom of the can.

For long-term storage, make sure that the bristles are completely dry, then wrap the brush in foil or heavy paper. Hang by the handle in an out-of-the-way place.

Before reusing the brush, work it back and forth across your fingers or palm of the hand to remove dust, dirt, or loose bristling material. If the brush is to be used in shellac, water-base, or latex paint, it should be washed in soap and water and thoroughly dried before painting.

For best results prime the brush by dipping into the paint halfway to the ferrule.

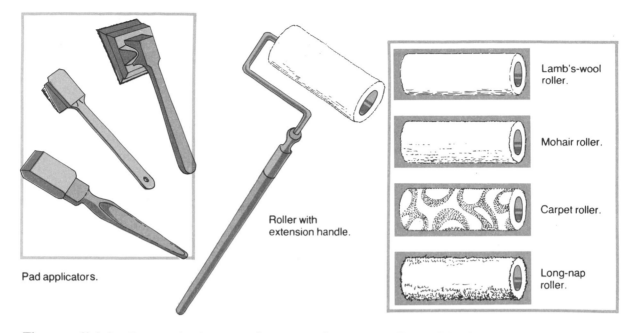

Pad applicators.

Roller with extension handle.

Lamb's-wool roller.

Mohair roller.

Carpet roller.

Long-nap roller.

Then tap lightly, five or six times, against the top edge of your paint container. The brush is now ready to use.

Pad Applicators

Relatively new are pad applicators. These are similar to brushes but generally cheaper (except for throwaway brushes). On smooth surfaces, they also apply paint much faster than brushes. Made of foamed urethane for use on both interior and exterior surfaces, some of them have replaceable pads. Others are cheap enough that it is more practical to discard them after use rather than attempt to clean them.

Paint Rollers

Painting with a roller is probably the easiest and quickest method for the average do-it-yourself decorator. It is important to use a roller that is suitable for the kind of paint to be applied. Lambs'-wool rollers, for ex-

ample, are excellent with oil-base paints, but they should not be used with enamels or water-thinned latex paints because these paints will cause the wool to mat, rendering the roller unusable.

Mohair rollers can be used with any type of interior flat paint, but they are especially recommended for applying enamel and for use when a smooth finish is desired. Rollers made from synthetic fibers can also be used with all types of flat paint, inside and out. If a stipple finish is desired, use a roller made of carpeting.

Another factor to consider is the length of the nap or pile, which can range from $\frac{1}{16}$ to $1\frac{1}{2}$ inches. A handy rule to remember is: the smoother the surface, the shorter the nap; the rougher the surface, the longer the nap. Use short-napped rollers for most walls, ceilings, woodwork, and smooth concrete. The longer naps are for masonry, brick, and other irregular surfaces.

For walls and ceilings the best size roller for the amateur is the 7- or 9-inch model. (Extension handles make it possible to paint ceilings without a ladder.) For finish-

Home Repairs Made Easy • Painting Tools

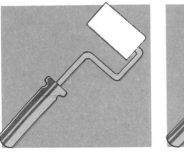

Trim roller.

Cutting-in roller.

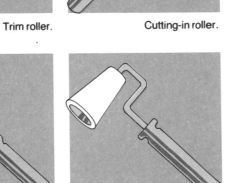

Corner roller.

Edging roller.

most vacuum cleaners; to large pressure-feed air compressors available for a low rental fee in most areas. Suction-feed spray equipment is satisfactory for most household projects. Before deciding to spray paint, however, you should consider whether the time saved will be consumed in the extra work of masking windows and other areas not to be painted.

Although practically any paint product that can be brushed or rolled on can be applied with spray equipment, spray painting is best suited for covering large wall areas, fences, or furniture items that can be painted in an open space.

The width of the spray fan should be ad-

ing woodwork, doors, and trim, the best choice is the 3-inch model. Smaller sizes are available for cutting in corners and for use on window frames and moldings. There are even V-edged rollers that coat both sides of a corner at the same time. To help you paint a wall without getting the paint on the ceiling there are special edging rollers.

Before applying paint with a roller, first cut in the edges of the wall with a brush or with an edging roller, taking care not to get paint on the ceiling or adjacent wall.

Paint Sprayers

Since the invention of the spray gun for mass-production industrial painting, it has become increasingly popular as a practical and economical means of applying paint by professional and amateur alike.

Sizes range from the small suction-feed spray-painting attachments available with

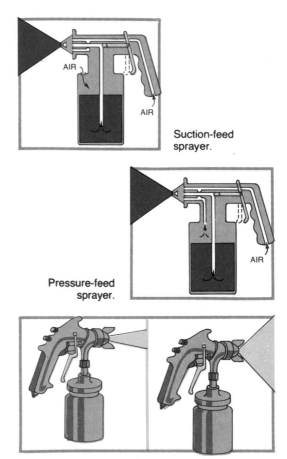

Suction-feed sprayer.

Pressure-feed sprayer.

Adjust width of fan to size of article to be coated.

justed to the size of the article being coated. A narrow fan is best for spraying small or narrow articles; a full-width fan should be used to spray walls.

Prepainting practice is important. The handyman should test the thickness of the paint, the size of the fan, and the motion of the spray gun before painting any surface. Excessive thickness can cause rippling of the wet film by the spraying air or lead to blistering later. On vertical and inclined surfaces, it can cause running or sagging.

The spray fan should be pointed perpendicularly to the surface being coated. The stroke or motion of the hand holding the spray gun should be started while the spray is pointed beyond the surface to be painted. This assures a smooth, even flow when you reach the surface itself.

Move the gun parallel to the surface, aiming beyond the edge of the surface and moving with an even stroke back and forth across the area. Corners and edges should be sprayed first.

Although a pressure-feed gun will handle heavier paint, the compressor unit poses a safety problem. Motors or gas engines of air-compressing outfits should be operated outside the spray area to avoid hazards from explosion and fire. The unit should also be placed in an area where it will receive a continuous supply of fresh, clean, dry air. Dust or vapor entering the air intake will decrease the efficiency of the unit and affect the results.

Regardless of the type of equipment used, every precaution should be taken by the spray operator. Skin should be protected. The area being sprayed should be well ventilated. A fire extinguisher should be available for use if needed, and all flammable liquids should be kept in safety cans.

Spray equipment should be thoroughly cleaned immediately after use. Simple cleaning can be done by spraying a suitable solvent through the equipment. A broom

Hold sprayer perpendicular to the surface to be coated.

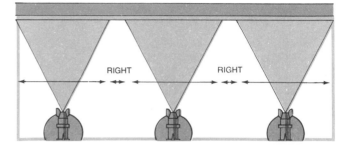

Move sprayer parallel to surface.

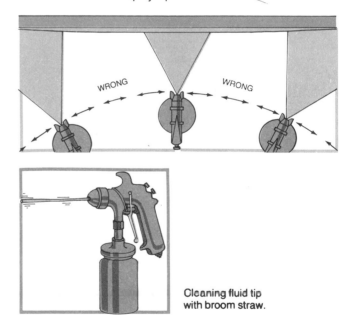

Cleaning fluid tip with broom straw.

straw can be used to unclog the fluid tip. Never use a metal wire or nail to clear air holes in the spray tip; the precision-machined openings are easily damaged.

Home Repairs Made Easy • Painting Tools

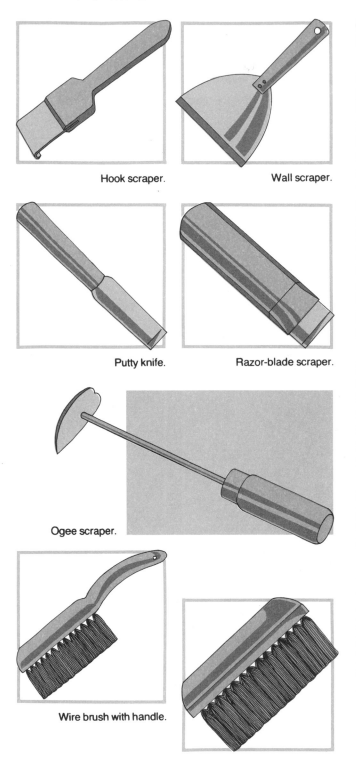

Hook scraper.

Wall scraper.

Putty knife.

Razor-blade scraper.

Ogee scraper.

Wire brush with handle.

Wire brush without handle.

Other Tools of the Painter's Trade

A variety of scrapers should be in every amateur (and professional, for that matter) painter's tool kit. Hook scrapers are good for rough exterior surfaces, and are often used with paint remover. Wall scrapers are handy for removing old paint and general scraping and cleaning. They come in various widths up to 5 inches; a 3- or 4-inch size with a stiff blade will meet most of your needs. A putty knife, similar in appearance to a narrow wall scraper, can also be used for scraping and cleaning, as well as applying and smoothing putty. An "ogee" scraper is the tool for removing old paint from crevices and recesses that can't be reached by flat scrapers. A razor-blade scraper is best for scraping paint off glass if your cutting-in is not quite perfect (and whose is?).

Wire brushes are handy for removing grime and surface dirt before applying exterior paint. Sandpaper is another important tool for smoothing surfaces. It is best used with a sanding block. When heavy sanding is required, a power belt sander may be used, followed by a finishing sander for final smoothing.

A propane torch is sometimes used to soften old paint for scraping, but this procedure entails certain obvious risks. An electric paint softener accomplishes the same end much more safely.

A calking gun is needed to seal cracks around doors, windows, corners, and other areas before exterior painting. In addition, an assortment of common tools will be helpful: hammer and nailset for driving in nails that may have come loose, a chisel for prying molding away from walls, a screwdriver for removing switch and receptacle covers, hinges, and other hardware.

(For ladders see pp. 111-120.)

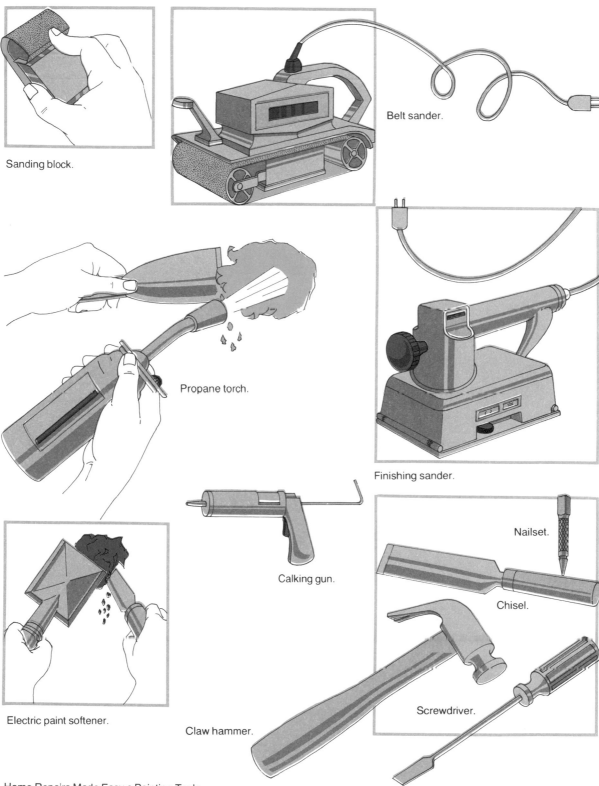

Sanding block.

Belt sander.

Propane torch.

Finishing sander.

Electric paint softener.

Calking gun.

Claw hammer.

Nailset.

Chisel.

Screwdriver.

SELECTING PAINTS FOR INTERIOR USE

Many different kinds and formulations of paints and other finishes are available for interior use, and new ones frequently appear on the market. For a specific selection consult your paint dealer. Reputable dealers keep abreast of developments in the paint industry and stock the newest formulations. The usual interior paint job consists of painting wallboard or plaster walls and ceilings, woodwork, and wood windows and doors. For these surfaces you need to choose first between solvent-thinned paint (oil-based) and water-thinned paint (commonly called latex paint, but not necessarily latex), and then between a gloss, semigloss, or flat finish. (Enamels, which are made with a varnish or resin base instead of the usual linseed-oil vehicle, are included under the oil-paint grouping.)

Oil-based paints are very durable, are highly resistant to staining and damage, can withstand frequent scrubbings, and give good one-coat coverage. Many latex paints have similar properties. The main advantages of latex paint are easier application, faster drying, and simpler tool cleanup. The brushes, rollers, and other equipment can be easily cleaned with water.

Both oil-based and latex paints are available in gloss, semigloss, and flat finishes. Glossy finishes look shiny and clean easily. Flat finishes show dirt more readily but absorb light and thus reduce glare. Semigloss finishes have properties of both glossy and flat finishes.

Because enamel is durable and easy to clean, semigloss or gloss enamel is recommended for the walls of kitchens, bathrooms, and laundry rooms. For the walls of nurseries and playrooms, either oil-based or latex semigloss enamel paint is suggested. Flat paint is generally used for the walls of living rooms and other nonwork or nonplay rooms.

Ceilings are important as light-reflecting surfaces in most rooms, and they should have dull-surfaced coatings that reflect light evenly. In bathrooms and kitchens, however, semigloss finishes are generally more desirable because of their washability. Plaster and wallboard ceilings can be coated with flat oil paints or paints of semigloss, emulsion, or rubber-base types. If the ceiling has not been previously painted, a primer should be applied before flat or semigloss paint. On acoustic tile, use flat paint, thinned in accordance with the manufacturer's recommendation. Woodwork that is new and is to be given an opaque coating requires an undercoat. For a finishing coat, you can use semigloss, enamel, or flat oil paint. Flat oil paints are easily finger-marked and are unsatisfactory for windowsills. Emulsion and rubber-base paints are also suitable for woodwork. All these coatings can be used to refinish woods that have previously been painted, varnished, or shellacked. Before refinishing, make sure that all traces of wax have been removed and that any still glossy surface has been sanded so that the new coating can adhere firmly. Where there is to be a radical change of color, more than one coat may be required. If enamel or semigloss is to be used, an enamel undercoat should be applied first. Where a transparent coating is desired so that the grain of the wood will be visible, shellac or interior varnish, followed by wax, is usually favored. Open-grain woods require a filler. Stains can be used to add color to the wood.

When an opaque finish is desired for wood paneling, use the same treatment as for woodwork. You have the choice of flat, semigloss, emulsion, or rubber-base paints. When a transparent coating is desired, a wood filler should first be applied, if it is an open-grain wood. Over this, shellac or varnish, then wax, can be used. If it seems desirable to tone the wood without concealing its grain, apply a stain after the wood is filled. Over the stain, the varnish or shellac is added, followed by wax.

In basements and recreation rooms of many homes—and in many a living room, too—there are walls of brick, stone, or cinder block. Where it is desirable to coat these masonry surfaces to obstruct the invasion of moisture or to change their appearance, there are many products to

What To Use And Where
(Interior Surfaces)

	Flat Enamel	Semigloss Enamel	Gloss Enamel	Interior Varnish	Shellac-Lacquer	Wax (Liquid or Paste)	Wax (Emulsion)	Stain	Wood Sealer	Floor Varnish	Floor Paint or Enamel	Aluminum Paint	Sealer or Undercoater	Metal Primer	Latex (Wall) Flat	Latex Gloss & Semigloss
MASONRY																
Asphalt Tile							X									
Concrete Floors						X•	X•	X		X			X			
Kitchen & Bathroom Walls		X•	X•										X			X•
Linoleum							X									
New Masonry	X•	X•											X		X	X•
Old Masonry	X	X										X	X		X	X•
Plaster Walls & Ceiling	X•	X•											X		X	X•
Vinyl & Rubber Tile Floors						X	X									
Wall Board	X•	X•											X		X	X•
METAL																
Aluminum Windows	X•	X•										X		X	X•	X•
Heating Ducts	X•	X•										X		X	X•	X•
Radiators & Heating Pipes	X•	X•										X		X	X•	X•
Steel Cabinets	X•	X•												X		X•
Steel Windows	X•	X•										X		X	X•	X•
WOOD																
Floors				X	X	X•	X•	X	X•	X•						
Paneling	X•	X•	X	X	X			X	X						X•	X•
Stair Risers	X•	X•	X	X				X	X							X•
Stair Treads			X					X	X	X	X					
Trim	X•	X•	X	X	X			X					X		X•	X•
Window Sills			X													

X• **Black dot indicates that a primer or sealer may be necessary before the finishing coat (unless surface has been previously finished).**

choose from. Both old and new masonry walls may require a sealer or undercoat if they have not been painted before. Although you can use aluminum and casein paints on old masonry surfaces, it is not advisable to use them when the construction is brand-new. These coatings can be used on both new and old masonry, regardless of its age: enamel, semigloss, flat, cement-base, emulsion, rubber-base paint.

Wood floors can be coated with a floor paint or enamel, or they can be given a transparent finish with the aid of shellac, varnish, polyurethane, or one of the various types of stains produced for the purpose. All three types of wax (emulsion, liquid, paste) are suitable.

On stair treads, floor paint or enamel can be used, as well as floor varnish, stain, or shellac. Wax is inadvisable. On stair risers, which do not have to take the same wear and tear as treads, other types of paint that are suitable for woodwork can be used.

When steel windows are to be painted, they should first be coated with one of the metal primers especially devised for the purpose. Aluminum windows usually need no primer. Both types can be coated with aluminum or rubber-base paint, enamel, semigloss, or flat paint.

Heating ducts, radiators, and heating

Light Reflectance of Various Colors

You may wish to make the most of the natural and artificial light within a room (such as a kitchen), or you may want to soften the glare that sometimes enters through large glass areas (such as a living room with southern exposure). Dark colors absorb light, whereas light colors reflect it, as indicated by this chart.

White	80%
Light ivory	71%
Apricot-beige	66%
Lemon yellow	65%
Ivory	59%
Light buff	56%
Peach	53%
Salmon	53%
Pale apple green	51%
Medium gray	43%
Light green	41%
Pale blue	41%
Deep rose	12%
Dark green	9%

pipes also require a metal primer. On them, the same types of coatings can be used that are suitable for steel windows.

Steel cabinets call for a metal primer, too. Rubber-base paint, enamel, semigloss, or flat paint can be applied over it.

HOW MUCH PAINT?

Estimating your paint needs is a matter of simple arithmetic. Finish coats of good-quality paint normally cover about 500 square feet per gallon if the surface is in reasonably good condition. Primers usually cover about 450 square feet per gallon. For specific coverage rates, refer to the label on the paint you are purchasing.

On the outside of your home, you must also consider the kind of surface to be

Surface	Square feet per gallon (approx.)	
	First Coat	Second Coat
Clapboard siding	500	550
Shingle siding	150	250
Asbestos shingles	180	400
Stucco	150	360
Cement block	180	240
Brick	200	400

painted and its condition. Some soak up paint like blotters, whereas others provide excellent bases. For example, shingles fall far below the 500-square-feet-per-gallon rule, but clapboard is more receptive to paint. The following chart shows the approximate covering ability of house paint on various surfaces.

To determine paint requirements for your home's exterior, measure the perimeter of the home. Multiply this figure by the average height from foundation to eaves, plus two feet to allow for eaves, overhangs, and the like. Do not figure in the gable ends at this point, and make no allowances for windows and doors unless they exceed 50

How to measure the exterior of a small house to determine paint needs.

1. Measure perimeter: 24′ + 40′ + 24′ + 40′ = 128′ (A)
2. Measure foundation to eave: 10′; add 2′ = 12′ (B)
3. Multiply A times B: 128′ × 12′ = 1,536 square feet
4. Measure picture window: 7′ × 10′ = 70 square feet (C)
5. Deduct 4 from 3: 1,536 sq. ft.
   − 70 sq. ft.
   1,466 sq. ft.
6. Measure roof rise = 4′ (D)
7. Measure roof run = 12′ (E)
8. Multiply D times E: 4′ × 12′ = 48′ per gable × 2 gable ends = 96 sq.ft. Add this to the square footage of the house: 1,466 + 96 = 1,562 sq.ft.
9. 1,562 sq.ft. ÷ 550 (the approximate coverage per gallon of clapboard siding for final coat) = approximately 3 gallons of paint for the house.

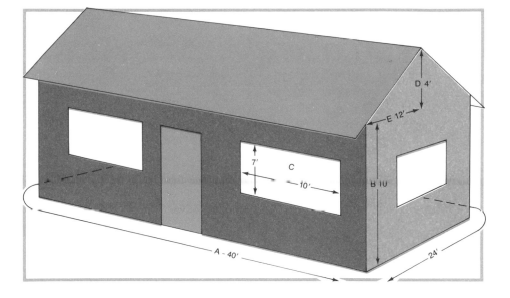

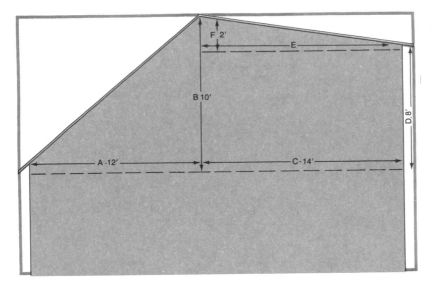

Measuring an unequal gable end of a small house to determine the paint needs:

1. Measure the roof run: 12' (A)
2. Measure the roof rise: 10' (B)
3. Multiply A times B: 10 × 12 = 120 sq.ft. As your gable is a triangle, not a rectangle, divide by 2 = 60 sq.ft.
4. As the pitch in the drawing is different on one side than on the other, measure the other side:
   Measure the run: 14' (C), multiply by the rise 8 ' (D) = 112 sq.ft.
5. Figure out the triangle above the rectangle you just measured: the run is 14' (E); the pitch is 2' (F). Multiply E by F and divide by 2: 14 × 2 = 28 ÷ 2 = 14 sq.ft.
6. Add 3, 4, 5: 60 + 112 + 14 = 186 sq.ft. for area of gable end.

square feet, as in the case of a large picture window, where you can subtract that square footage.

To figure square footage on the gable end of your house, measure the roof rise (vertical distance from eave to ridge) and the run

Total Area—Four Walls and Ceiling

In Square Feet

For Rooms with Ceilings 7 Feet 6 Inches High

	3'	4'	5'	6'	7'	8'	9'	10'	11'	12'	13'	14'	15'	16'	17'	18'	19'	20'	21'	22'
3'	99	117	135	153	171	189	207	225	243	261	279	297	315	333	351	369	387	405	423	441
4'	117	136	155	174	193	212	231	250	269	288	307	326	345	364	383	402	421	440	459	478
5'	135	155	175	195	215	235	255	275	295	315	335	355	375	395	415	435	455	475	495	515
6'	153	174	195	216	237	258	279	300	321	342	363	384	405	426	447	468	489	510	531	552
7'	171	193	215	237	259	281	303	325	347	369	391	413	435	457	479	501	523	545	567	589
8'	189	212	235	258	281	304	327	350	373	396	419	442	465	488	511	534	557	580	603	626
9'	207	231	255	279	303	327	351	375	399	423	447	471	495	519	543	567	591	615	639	663
10'	225	250	275	300	325	350	375	400	425	450	475	500	525	550	575	600	625	650	675	700
11'	243	269	295	321	347	373	399	425	451	477	503	529	555	581	607	633	659	685	711	737
12'	261	288	315	342	369	396	423	450	477	504	531	558	585	612	639	666	693	720	747	774
13'	279	307	335	363	391	419	447	475	503	531	559	587	615	643	671	699	727	755	783	811
14'	297	326	355	384	413	442	471	500	529	558	587	616	645	674	703	732	761	790	819	848
15'	315	345	375	405	435	465	495	525	555	585	615	645	675	705	735	765	795	825	855	885
16'	333	364	395	426	457	488	519	550	581	612	643	674	705	736	767	798	829	860	891	922
17'	351	383	415	447	479	511	543	575	607	639	671	703	735	767	799	831	863	895	927	959
18'	369	402	435	468	501	534	567	600	633	666	699	732	765	798	831	864	897	930	963	996
19'	387	421	455	489	523	557	591	625	659	693	727	761	795	829	863	897	931	965	999	1033
20'	405	440	475	510	545	580	615	650	685	720	755	790	825	860	895	930	965	1000	1035	1070
21'	423	459	495	531	567	603	639	675	711	747	783	819	855	891	927	963	999	1035	1071	1107
22'	441	478	515	552	589	626	663	700	737	774	811	848	885	922	959	996	1033	1070	1107	1144
23'	459	497	535	573	611	649	687	725	763	801	839	877	915	953	991	1029	1067	1105	1143	1181
24'	477	516	555	594	633	672	711	750	789	828	867	906	945	984	1023	1062	1101	1140	1179	1218

(*Note:* Deduct for doors, windows, archways, etc., over 50 square feet)

(horizontal distance covered from eave to ridge). If the roof pitch (rise divided by run) is the same on both sides (or front and back) of the house, multiply rise by run to find the square footage needed to determine paint needs for the entire gable end. If the pitch is different on one side than on the other—as in the case of a house with a full shed dormer—figure rise and run separately for each side, multiply the figures for each side, and divide by two. Other unusually shaped protrusions, such as partial shed dormers, can be figured similarly—and will put to use the knowledge you acquired in those seemingly fruitless hours you spent in high-school geometry class.

Estimating interior paint needs is done in the same way, by determining square footage of walls and ceilings, then dividing the total by the coverage shown on the paint-can label. Again, do not allow for a window or door opening unless it exceeds 50 square feet. The tables show total area for four walls and ceiling of rooms at the most common heights. If the ceiling is to be painted a different color, figure it separately and deduct the square footage from the figure given in the appropriate table.

It's always a good idea to buy an extra gallon or quart of paint to make sure that you have enough on hand when you set about doing the job—especially if you are a weekend painter. It is extremely frustrating to run out of paint with just a few more feet of wall to go; and when this happens on a Saturday evening right after the paint store has closed, the frustration is dragged out interminably. Better sufficient than sorry, and almost all paint dealers will take back unopened cans of paint.

Total Area—Four Walls and Ceiling
In Square Feet

For Rooms with Ceilings 8 Feet High

	3'	4'	5'	6'	7'	8'	9'	10'	11'	12'	13'	14'	15'	16'	17'	18'	19'	20'	21'	22'
3'	105	124	143	162	181	200	219	238	257	276	295	314	333	352	371	390	409	428	447	466
4'	124	144	164	184	204	224	244	264	284	304	324	344	364	384	404	424	444	464	484	504
5'	143	164	185	206	227	248	269	290	311	332	353	374	395	416	437	458	479	500	521	542
6'	162	184	206	228	250	272	294	316	338	360	382	404	426	448	470	492	514	536	558	580
7'	181	204	227	250	273	296	319	342	365	388	411	434	457	480	503	526	549	572	595	618
8'	200	224	248	272	296	320	344	368	392	416	440	464	488	512	536	560	584	608	632	656
9'	219	244	269	294	319	344	369	394	419	444	469	494	519	544	569	594	619	644	669	694
10'	238	264	290	316	342	368	394	420	446	472	498	524	550	576	602	628	664	680	706	732
11'	257	284	311	338	365	392	419	446	473	500	527	554	581	608	635	662	689	716	743	770
12'	276	304	332	360	388	416	444	472	500	528	556	584	612	640	668	696	724	752	780	808
13'	295	324	353	382	411	440	469	498	527	556	585	614	643	672	701	730	759	788	817	846
14'	314	344	374	404	434	464	494	524	554	584	614	644	674	704	734	764	794	824	854	884
15'	333	364	395	426	457	488	519	550	581	612	643	674	705	736	767	798	829	860	891	922
16'	352	384	416	448	480	512	544	576	608	640	672	704	736	768	800	832	864	896	928	960
17'	371	404	437	470	503	536	569	602	635	668	701	734	767	800	833	866	899	932	965	998
18'	390	424	458	492	526	560	594	628	662	696	730	764	798	832	866	900	934	968	1002	1036
19'	409	444	479	514	549	584	619	654	689	724	759	794	829	864	899	934	969	1004	1039	1074
20'	428	464	500	536	572	608	644	680	716	752	788	824	860	896	932	968	1004	1040	1076	1112
21'	447	484	521	558	595	632	669	706	743	780	817	854	891	928	965	1002	1039	1076	1113	1150
22'	466	504	542	580	618	656	694	732	770	808	846	884	922	960	998	1036	1074	1112	1150	1188
23'	485	524	563	602	641	680	719	758	797	836	875	914	953	992	1031	1070	1109	1148	1187	1226
24'	504	544	584	624	664	704	744	784	824	864	904	944	984	1024	1064	1104	1144	1184	1224	1264

(*Note:* Deduct for doors, windows, archways, etc., over 50 square feet)

Total Area Four Walls and Ceiling
In Square Feet

For Rooms with Ceilings 9 Feet High

	3'	4'	5'	6'	7'	8'	9	10'	11'	12'	13'	14'	15'	16'	17'	18'	19'	20'	21'	22'
3'	117	138	159	180	201	222	243	264	285	306	327	348	369	390	411	432	453	474	495	516
4'	138	160	182	204	226	248	270	292	314	336	358	380	402	424	446	468	490	512	534	556
5'	159	182	205	228	251	274	297	320	343	366	389	412	435	458	481	504	527	550	573	596
6'	180	204	228	252	276	300	324	348	372	396	420	444	468	492	516	540	564	588	612	636
7'	201	226	251	276	301	326	351	376	401	426	451	476	501	526	551	576	601	626	651	676
8'	222	248	274	300	326	352	378	404	430	456	482	508	534	560	586	612	638	664	690	716
9'	243	270	297	324	351	378	405	432	459	486	513	540	567	594	621	648	675	702	729	756
10'	264	292	320	348	376	404	432	460	488	516	544	572	600	628	656	684	712	740	768	796
11'	285	314	343	372	401	430	459	488	517	546	575	604	633	662	691	720	749	778	807	836
12'	306	336	366	396	426	456	486	516	546	576	606	636	666	696	726	756	786	816	846	876
13'	327	358	389	420	451	482	513	544	575	606	637	668	699	730	761	792	823	854	885	916
14'	348	380	412	444	476	508	540	572	604	636	668	700	732	764	796	828	860	892	924	956
15'	369	402	435	468	501	534	567	600	633	666	699	732	765	798	831	864	897	930	963	996
16'	390	424	458	492	526	560	594	628	662	696	730	764	798	832	866	900	934	968	1002	1036
17'	411	446	481	516	551	586	621	656	691	726	761	796	831	866	901	936	971	1006	1041	1076
18'	432	468	504	540	576	612	648	684	720	756	792	828	864	900	936	972	1008	1044	1080	1116
19'	453	490	527	564	601	638	675	712	749	786	823	860	897	934	971	1008	1045	1082	1119	1156
20'	474	512	550	588	626	664	702	740	778	816	854	892	930	968	1006	1044	1082	1120	1158	1196
21'	495	534	573	612	651	690	729	768	807	846	885	924	963	1002	1041	1080	1119	1158	1197	1236
22'	516	556	596	636	676	716	756	796	836	876	916	956	996	1036	1076	1116	1156	1196	1236	1276
23'	537	578	619	660	701	742	783	824	865	906	947	988	1029	1070	1111	1152	1193	1234	1275	1316
24'	558	600	612	684	726	768	810	852	894	936	978	1020	1062	1104	1146	1188	1230	1272	1314	1356

(Note: Deduct for doors, windows, archways, etc., over 50 square feet)

Total Area — Four Walls and Ceiling
In Square Feet

For Rooms with Ceilings 10 Feet High

	3'	4'	5'	6'	7'	8'	9'	10'	11'	12'	13'	14'	15'	16'	17'	18'	19'	20'	21'	22'
3'	129	152	175	198	221	244	267	290	313	336	359	382	405	428	451	474	497	520	543	566
4'	152	176	200	224	248	272	296	320	344	368	392	416	440	464	488	512	536	560	584	608
5'	175	200	225	250	275	300	325	350	375	400	425	450	475	500	525	550	575	600	625	650
6'	198	224	250	276	302	328	354	380	406	432	458	484	510	536	562	588	614	640	666	692
7'	221	248	275	302	329	356	383	410	437	464	491	518	545	572	599	626	653	680	707	734
8'	244	272	300	328	356	384	412	440	468	496	524	552	580	608	636	664	692	720	748	776
9'	267	296	325	354	383	412	441	479	499	528	557	586	615	644	673	702	731	760	789	818
10'	290	320	350	380	410	440	470	500	530	560	590	620	650	680	710	740	770	800	830	860
11'	313	344	375	406	437	468	499	530	561	592	623	654	685	716	747	778	809	840	871	902
12'	336	368	400	432	464	496	528	560	592	624	656	688	720	752	784	816	848	880	912	944
13'	359	392	425	458	491	524	557	590	623	656	689	722	755	788	821	854	887	920	953	986
14'	382	416	450	484	518	552	586	620	654	688	722	756	790	824	858	892	926	960	994	1028
15'	405	440	475	510	545	580	615	650	685	720	755	790	825	860	895	930	965	1000	1035	1070
16'	428	464	500	536	572	608	644	680	716	752	788	824	860	896	932	968	1004	1040	1076	1112
17'	451	488	525	562	599	636	673	710	747	784	821	858	895	932	969	1006	1043	1080	1117	1154
18'	474	512	550	588	626	664	702	740	778	816	854	892	930	968	1006	1044	1082	1120	1158	1196
19'	497	536	575	614	653	692	731	770	809	848	887	926	965	1004	1043	1082	1121	1160	1199	1238
20'	520	560	600	640	680	720	760	800	840	880	920	960	1000	1040	1080	1120	1160	1200	1240	1280
21'	543	584	625	666	707	748	789	830	871	912	953	994	1035	1076	1117	1158	1199	1240	1281	1322
22'	566	608	650	692	734	776	818	860	902	944	986	1028	1070	1112	1154	1196	1238	1280	1322	1364
23'	589	632	675	718	761	804	847	890	933	976	1019	1062	1105	1148	1191	1234	1277	1320	1363	1406
24'	612	656	700	744	788	832	876	920	964	1008	1052	1096	1140	1184	1228	1272	1316	1360	1404	1448

(Note: Deduct for doors, windows, archways, etc., over 50 square feet)

SURFACE PREPARATION FOR INTERIOR PAINTING

In general, walls, ceilings, woodwork, and other surfaces to be painted should be clean, dry, and smooth. But read the label on the paint can before you start painting; it may contain additional or special instructions for preparing the surface.

New **plaster walls** should not be painted with oil-base paint until they have been thoroughly cured—usually after about two months. Then a primer coat should be applied first.

If necessary to paint uncured plaster, apply only one coat of a latex paint or primer. Latex, or water-base, paint is not affected by the alkali in new plaster and allows water to escape while the plaster dries. Subsequent coats of paint—either oil-base or latex—can be added when the plaster is thoroughly cured.

Unpainted plaster readily picks up and absorbs dirt and is difficult to clean. The one coat of latex paint or primer will protect plaster walls.

On new wallboard or drywall, a latex primer or paint is recommended for the first coat. Solvent-thinned paints tend to cause a rough surface. After the first coat of latex paint, subsequent coats can be of either type. Clean or dust new surfaces before you apply the first coat of primer or paint.

Most homes built in the past 25 to 30 years have walls and ceilings covered with wallboard, also known as **gypsumboard**, drywall, or plasterboard. Before painting, make minor or major repairs as necessary. Look in particular for cracks around windows and door frames, nails that have raised the surface, and just plain holes. Wood in heated homes contracts in the winter and expands in the summer, and this can cause nail "popping."

Drive popped nails back below the surface of the wallboard. Reinforce weak areas by driving a ringed drywall nail into the panel below or above a popped nail about an inch or two away. Drive the nail until it dimples the surface and no more; use a nailset to avoid banging up the wallboard and causing major damage.

Use spackle to patch the dimples and even the surface. Spackle comes in powdered or ready-mixed form. Apply it with a broad knife or putty knife, filling the area, scraping off the excess, and sanding to an even surface when dry.

Cracks can be sealed with fiberglass tape or with perforated drywall tape and joint cement. Sand the area of the crack 4 inches or so to each side when using perforated tape, then apply joint cement over the crack. Center the strip of perforated tape over the crack, pressing it flat with a broad knife. Remove excess cement, feathering the edges so they're smooth. Allow to dry, then apply another coat of joint cement a couple of inches beyond the first coat. Feather the edges and let dry overnight. You can then sand and paint. Fiberglass tape is somewhat similar in application— just follow the directions on the package you buy (see also p. 92).

A hole in wallboard can be repaired by plugging it with a wad of newspaper and then using spackle to fill in until you have a flat surface that can be sanded even. It may

Cracks around door frames.

Stuff newspaper
into hole (above).

Fill with spackle (at right).

Apply final coat of spackle
to surface (below).

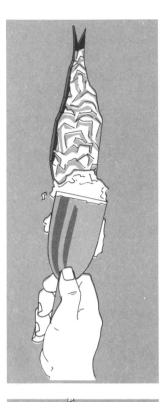

Chip away loose plaster.

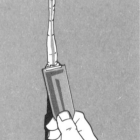

Fill part way to surface.

Apply plaster up to
wall surface.

"Cut" surface with steel wool
to give new paint firm hold.

take a couple of coats of spackle to do the job properly.

Plaster is repaired in much the same manner as wallboard. With cracks more than ¼-inch wide, chip away the loose plaster and wet down the area. Fill it half way to the surface with plaster and let it dry. Then wet it again and apply another coat to the surface of the wall. When it is dry, spackle where needed and sand.

After repairs are completed, clean the surface of dirt and grease. A dry rag or mop will remove dust and some dirt. You may have to wash the surface with a household cleanser to remove stubborn dirt or grease.

Kitchen walls and ceilings usually become covered with a film of grease (which may extend to the walls and ceilings just outside the entrances to the kitchen), and bathroom walls and ceilings may have steamed-on dirt. The grease or dirt must be removed—new paint will not adhere to it. To remove grease or dirt, wash the surface with a strong household cleanser, turpentine, or mineral spirits.

The finish on kitchen and bathroom walls and ceilings is usually a gloss or semigloss. This finish must be "cut" so that the new paint can get a firm hold. Washing with a household cleanser or turpentine will dull the gloss, but for best results, rub the surface with fine sandpaper or steel wool. After using sandpaper or steel wool, wipe the surface to remove dust.

Woodwork (windows, doors, and baseboards) usually has a glossy finish. First wash the surface to remove dirt and grease, and then sand it lightly to "cut" the finish. After sanding, wipe the surface to remove the dust.

You can buy liquid preparations that will soften hard, glossy finishes to provide good adhesion for new paint.

If there are any bare spots in the wood, touch them up with an undercoat or with pigmented shellac before you paint.

PAINT APPLICATION AND CLEANUP

Lap paint over previous
strip of paint.

Cut in ceiling-wall joints
before you paint the walls.

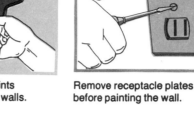

Remove receptacle plates
before painting the wall.

Use drop cloths or plastic sheeting to protect floors and furniture. Paint the ceiling first. Don't try to paint too wide a strip at a time. The next strip should be started and lapped into the previous one before the previous one dries.

If you are putting two coats on the ceiling, apply the second coat, and "cut in" at the junction with the walls, before you paint the walls.

Remove all electric switch and receptacle plates from the walls to avoid smearing. Use a cardboard or metal shield to avoid smearing the trim if the trim is to be another color. Or you can use masking tape if you prefer. Wipe spills up immediately.

Start painting a wall at the upper left-hand corner and work down toward the floor (left-handed persons may find it more convenient to start at the upper right-hand corner).

When using a roller, paint over a section of wall about 3 feet wide in a "W" pattern. Fill in the W with horizontal strokes of the roller. Then smooth out with vertical strokes in one direction.

Paint the woodwork last—preferably after the walls are dry.

Flush doors can be painted with a roller. On paneled doors, some parts can be painted with a roller, but other sections require a brush. (You may prefer your doors and other trim in natural color. See p. 157.)

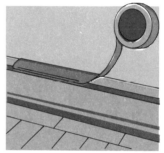

Use a shield to protect trim
(above).

Masking tape to protect trim
(above right).

Paint a "W" pattern
(right).

Fill in the "W", then smooth out with vertical strokes.

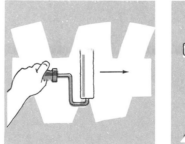

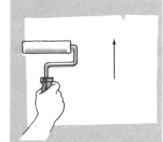

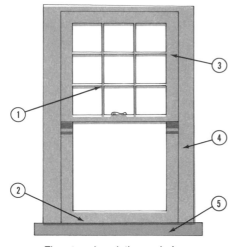

Five steps in painting a window.

Paint the parts of a window in this order: mullions, horizontals of sash, verticals of sash, verticals of frame, horizontal frame, and sill. Windows are easier to paint and to clean afterward if the glass is masked. Both masking tape and liquid masking are available at hardware and paint stores.

A simple way to protect the glass is to cover it with a piece of wet newspaper. The moisture will paste the newspaper to the glass and also prevent paint from soaking into the absorbent paper. When you strip the paper from the glass after painting, the paint will come with it.

●

Brushes, rollers, and other equipment should be cleaned as soon as possible after being used.

Equipment used to apply latex paint can be cleaned easily with soap and water. Rinse thoroughly.

Equipment used to apply oil-base paint may be a little harder to clean. Soak brushes in turpentine or thinner long enough to loosen the paint. Then work the bristles against the side and bottom of the container to release the paint. To release the paint in the center of the brush, squeeze or work the bristles between the thumb and forefinger. Rinse the brush in the turpentine or thinner again, and, if necessary, wash it in mild soap suds. Rinse in clear water.

Protecting a window with masking tape.

Protecting glass with newspaper.

Soak brushes in thinner. Work bristles against side of can. Squeeze brush between fingers.

NATURAL FINISHES FOR TRIM AND UNUSUAL EFFECTS

Some doors, particularly flush doors, are attractive in their natural finish. However, they will become discolored and soiled easily unless protected. Your paint dealer can offer suggestions on how to finish and protect your doors. Many kinds of products are now on the market, and new ones are constantly appearing.

The first step in finishing doors is to obtain the proper color tone. This is usually acquired by staining. Sometimes, however, no staining is required—the preservative finish is enough to bring out the desired color tone. With new doors, you can experiment on the trimmings or shavings to help you make a decision.

The next step is sealing. One coat of shellac is usually adequate. When the shellac is dry, the surface should be sanded smooth, wiped free of dust, and varnished. Rubbing the surface with linseed oil, as is done in furniture finishing, provides a nice soft finish but requires more work. Also, surfaces so finished collect dust more readily.

For a natural finish of other interior trim, you need to specify the desired kind and grade of wood at the time of construction. This can add substantially to the construction costs. If you already have handsome naturally finished woodwork in your home, consider yourself fortunate. And make sure you think twice, then twice more, before painting over it.

●

The beauty of paint lies in its adaptability to your decorating whims. How about textured paint to give your room a new personality? This treatment adds depth to the walls, and its rough finish blends beautifully with various decors. In addition, the heavy consistency of textured paint fills small holes and cracks, making it the perfect camouflage for old, scarred walls that would normally require replastering.

Draw design on textured paint.

Fill impressions with deeper color.

While the paint is still wet, create a random pattern by going over the surface with a special roller, a whisk broom, a comb, or other object that will make a design. Decorators often give a textured finish an individual touch by drawing stylized birds, plants, and other figures and designs. You, too, can do it. Simply draw freehand an outline of whatever you choose, using an unsharpened pencil or similar object. If you wish to make the impressions more outstanding, fill them in with a slightly deeper color when dry.

Striping is another fashionable wall treatment. Paint the walls in the chosen background color and let them dry. Then, using masking tape (which must be securely fas-

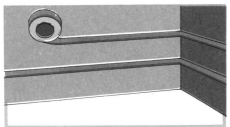

Masking walls for striping.

Stippling a wall.

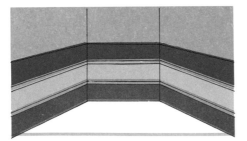

Stripe effect.

tened to the surface), mark off the areas to be striped in the desired widths. Paint these designated areas in a contrasting color. Let

dry thoroughly, then remove the strips of masking tape. The walls are no longer a backdrop; they are one of the most exciting features in the room. Striped walls do wonders to increase the visual size of a small room.

Stippling the walls produces a very decorative effect and gives them dimension. Paint the walls the background color and let dry completely. Then, using a stippling roller (available in a wide assortment of design-producing sleeves), go over the dry walls in a contrasting color of your choice.

COLOR CAMOUFLAGE

The right paint can have a magic effect in emphasizing the good points and hiding the defects of a home. Light colors reflect and tend to create a cheerful atmosphere—they are effective in making small rooms seem larger. Dark colors absorb light and, when used extensively on large surfaces, tend to be depressing. They can be used to make a large, well-lighted room seem smaller and more intimate. If a ceiling is too high, painting it a dark color may give a better sense of proportion to the room. Bright colors attract the eye and may be employed to distract attention from an unattractive feature—they may also, if improperly used, become irritating. Warm colors—reds, oranges, yellows—convey a cozy feeling and are stimulating, whereas the cool colors—blues, greens, violets—are relaxing and cooling.

Red is stimulating. It makes a room look smaller and dominates in large doses, but it may provide just the excitement you are looking for. Green has the opposite effect; it is smooth and tranquil. Yellow is cheerful, blue is soothing, purple is subduing and somewhat regal. White, gray, brown, and beige are neutral colors that make fine backgrounds but can be dull when used as the principal decorating schemes. These neutral colors have found a certain popularity among modern designers, however.

Decide which features of the room you feel should be accented, which you wish to minimize. A fireplace or some other feature of interest might be made the focal point of the decorating scheme; accent it by painting the surrounding wall a contrasting color. A long, narrow room may take on seemingly improved proportions if one of the end walls is painted a darker hue than the other walls, visually drawing it closer to the center of the room. Painting the walls and woodwork the same color gives a sense of spaciousness and trimness—painting the woodwork in an accenting color can complement the walls and point up some special characteristic.

A room should also be considered in terms of its function as well as its relation to neighboring rooms. An entryway, for example, should be painted in friendly, inviting tones, and in tones that will blend naturally with those of the living areas into which it leads the visitor. If you entertain formally, or enjoy dining by candlelight, dining-room colors should help to enhance the moods that are sought. And, of course, the colors on a room's walls must harmonize with the furniture and accessories of that room. If you proudly display bright modern paintings on your walls, determine what wall colors will best show off the pictures without distracting attention from them.

Often, a favorite drapery material or a cherished couch or other piece of furniture is the key to the decorating scheme for a given room—and, ultimately, the color scheme for the entire home.

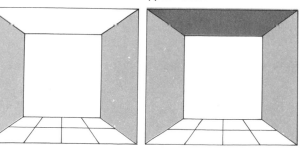

Painting a too-high ceiling in a darker color makes room appear lower.

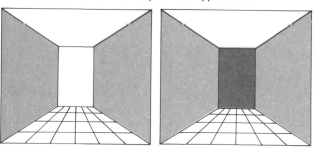

Painting one of the end walls of a long, narrow room in a darker color improves its appearance.

Painting Tips

- Do the painting when the room temperature is comfortable for work—between 60 and 70 degrees F. Provide good cross-ventilation both to shorten the drying time and to remove fumes and odors.
- Check the label on the paint can for any special application and drying instructions.
- Preferably, remove all furnishings from the room. Otherwise, cover the furniture, fixtures, and floor with drop cloths or newspapers. No matter how careful you may be, you will spill, drip, or splatter some paint.
- Remove all light switch and wall plug plates. If you wish, paint the plates before you replace them after painting the room.
- Dip your brush into the paint no more than one-third the length of the bristles. This will minimize splattering and dripping.
- When using latex paint, wash your brush or roller occasionally with water. A buildup of the quick-drying paint in the nap of the roller or at the base of the bristles of the brush can cause excessive dripping.
- Wipe up spilled, splattered, or dripped paint as you go along. Paint is easier to clean up when it is wet.
- Do not let the paint dry out in the can or in brushes or rollers between jobs or during long interruptions in a job. After each job, replace the can lid securely, and clean brushes or rollers. During long interruptions in a job, also replace the can lid, and either clean brushes or rollers or suspend them in water.

Safety Tips

- Never paint in a completely closed room, and use caution when painting in a room where there is an open flame or fire. Some paints give off fumes that are flammable or dangerous to breathe or both.
- Avoid prolonged exposure to paint fumes for a day or two after painting. Such fumes can also be harmful to canaries or other pet birds.
- Use a sturdy stepladder or other support when painting high places. Be sure that the ladder is positioned firmly, with the legs fully opened and locked in position
- Face the ladder when climbing up or down it, holding on with at least one hand. Lean toward the ladder when painting.
- Do not overreach when painting. Move the ladder frequently rather than risk a fall. And, to avoid spilling the paint, take the few seconds required to remove the paint can from the ladder before you move it.
- When you finish painting, dispose of used rags by putting them in a covered metal can. If left lying around, the oily rags could catch fire by spontaneous combustion.
- Store paint in a safe, but well-ventilated, place where children and pets cannot get to it. A locked cabinet is ideal if well ventilated. Unless needed for retouching, small quantities of paint may not be worth saving.

Color Do's and Don'ts

DO

• Remember that large areas of color emphasize the color. Choose a lighter shade for such areas.

• Use light colors in a small room to increase apparent size.

• Emphasize reds and yellows in windowless rooms.

• Make use of horizontal and vertical lines for giving visual balance to rooms with high or low ceilings.

• Aim for a continuing colorflow through your home—from room to room—using harmonious colors in adjoining areas.

• Paint the ceiling of a room in a deeper color than the walls if you want it to appear lower; paint it in a lighter shade for the opposite effect.

• Study color swatches in both daylight and nightlight. Colors often change under artificial lighting.

DON'T

• Use too large a pattern, or too much pattern in an area.

• Use equal proportions of colors; always use more of one color than another.

• Choose neutral or negative colors simply because they are safe and "mix well."

• Paint woodwork and trim of a small room in a color different from the background color, or the room will appear small and cluttered.

• Paint radiators, pipes, or similar projections in a color that contrasts with walls, or they will be emphasized.

• Use glossy paints on walls or ceilings of living areas, since the shiny surface creates undesirable glare.

If You Have the Painting Done

You may prefer to have all or part of your painting done by a professional painter. When you hire a contractor, it is a good idea to get a signed agreement specifying:

• The specific price for the job.

• Exactly what areas or surfaces are to be painted.

• The types, brands, and quality of paints to be used and the number of coats, including primer coats, to be applied.

• The measures to be taken to protect floors, furnishings, and other parts of the house.

• A complete cleanup guarantee.

• A completion date (allowing for possible delays—because of bad weather, for example).

Check the contractor's work with friends or neighbors who may have hired him in the past. Be sure that he is fully insured (Workmen's Compensation and Employer's Liability Insurance, Public Liability, and Property Damage Insurance). Otherwise, you could be held liable for accidents that occurred on your property.

SELECTING PAINTS FOR EXTERIOR USE

Several types of paint for house exteriors are available. Ideally, a white house paint should have a clean, highly reflective whiteness. It should remain clean and white at all times during the life of the coating.

The ideal paint should not be affected by moisture. It should be resistant to staining by rust and other residues of metal corrosion. It should also resist mildew and should not be discolored by industrial gases. The paint should wear away at an even rate, leaving a smooth adherent film, suitable for repainting after a reasonable number of years.

Although no house paint on the market has all of these desirable characteristics, many modern paints of high quality can be depended upon to provide excellent performance under most of these conditions. You should be aware of the climatic and atmospheric conditions to which house paints are subjected in your area. Through your paint dealer, you should determine the types of house paint that perform best under local conditions and the performance characteristics that are most important to your paint job.

No one type of house paint is "better" than another in every respect. Within each type, almost any quality of paint may be made, depending upon the grades of ingredients used, their relative proportions, and the care used in compounding the product. Regardless of type of paint selected, there will be greater assurance of satisfactory service if the particular paint was produced by a reputable manufacturer and sold through a reputable dealer. No type of paint formulation will guarantee a high-quality product; this can be insured only by the integrity of the maker.

Paints used on house siding are mostly based on linseed oil—that is, they have linseed oil "vehicles" to carry the pigment. These paints have a long history of satisfactory service. Many improvements have been made by modifying the linseed oils and by changing the pigmentation. Further, since no one paint can satisfy all requirements under different conditions, paints have been specialized to produce the best result for various use requirements.

For example, white paints may be self-cleaning—free-chalking—for use where siding covers the lower portion of a house; or they may be chalk-resistant for use where chalk rundown will mar brick or stone below the siding. This should be kept in mind when buying white house paint, since chalk rundown on masonry is unsightly. Another type of white paint is fume-resistant. It is used where industrial or other fumes may be present and could stain the paint. For warm, humid conditions in most latitudes, mildew-resistant paints are used to discourage mildew discoloration.

If the old paint is sound but dirty, a one-coat paint will give a gleaming new surface. Chalk-resistant, pastel-colored paints can be made from white one-coat paints. All pastel tints must be made with chalk-resistant or tint-based paints to avoid early fading. Dark-colored paints cannot be made from white paint; they are colored during manufacture. There are shingle and shake paints and clear finishes for houses sided with shingles or shakes. The choice depends on whether or not the grain pattern of the wood is to remain visible. Clear finishes need refinishing more frequently than opaque paints, but they reveal the beauty of the wood.

All the paints mentioned above, except clear finishes, require a primer when new wood is painted. For repainting, the primer is necessary only if the old paint is in bad condition. The primer should be the one recommended for the topcoat selected.

What To Use And Where
(Exterior Surfaces)

	House Paint (Oil or Oil-Alkyd)	Cement Powder Paint	Exterior Clear Finish	Aluminum Paint	Wood Stain	Roof Coating	Trim Paint	Porch and Deck Paint	Primer or Undercoater	Metal Primer	House Paint (Latex)	Water Repellent Preservative
MASONRY												
Asbestos Cement	X•								X		X	
Brick	X•	X		X					X		X	X
Cement & Cinder Block	X•	X		X					X		X	
Concrete/Masonry Porches And Floors								X			X	
Coal Tar Felt Roof						X						
Stucco	X•	X		X					X		X	
METAL												
Aluminum Windows	X•			X			X•			X	X•	
Steel Windows	X•			X•			X•			X	X•	
Metal Roof	X•									X	X•	
Metal Siding	X•			X•			X•			X	X•	
Copper Surfaces			X									
Galvanized Surfaces	X•			X•			X•			X	X•	
Iron Surfaces	X•			X•			X•			X	X•	
WOOD												
Clapboard	X•			X					X		X•	
Natural Wood Siding & Trim			X		X							
Shutters & Other Trim	X•						X•		X		X•	
Wood Frame Windows	X•			X			X•		X		X•	
Wood Porch Floor								X				
Wood Shingle Roof					X							X

X• Black dot indicates that a primer, sealer, or fill coat may be necessary before the finishing coat (unless surface has been previously finished).

Over the past decade or so, exterior paints have been developed in which the solvent for the vehicle is water, instead of turpentine or mineral spirits—the solvents used for linseed oil. The first of these water-thinned products were the so-called latex paints, which are emulsions of the vehicle in water. After the paint is applied, the emulsion coalesces, permitting the water to evaporate, leaving the vehicle and pigment. More recent are paints in which the linseed oil vehicle is in true water solution. The oil

Self-cleaning paint may stain brick or other surfaces below it.

had to be altered to accomplish this, but such paints have the properties of both water and oil paints. The advantages of both the emulsion and the linseed-oil solution include ease of application, cleanup with water, good tint retention, and easy cleaning. Emulsion paints dry faster than do the solution paints. As repaints, emulsion paints may not adhere well to chalky surfaces. The procedure recommended by the manufacturer must be followed. It will likely call for a primer for emulsion types to insure adhesion to chalky surfaces.

Moisture is the cause of much unsatisfactory paint service. Under certain conditions, the effects of moisture can be controlled best by using special blister-resistant paints. They may be oil- or water-base paints, and must be used as directed to obtain their maximum efficiency.

Exterior trim paints are used principally on wood trim, screen frames, shutters, and other small areas of the home. Dark, medium, and light greens are among the most popular colors. Good leveling or freedom from brush marks, rapid drying, high gloss, good color- and gloss-retention, one-coat hiding, and good durability are important properties of exterior trim paints. They are usually solvent-thinned.

Some paint manufacturers market special undercoats in a gray or other neutral color as a primer for the trim and dark-colored house paints. The regular primer for white and light-tinted house paints is also satisfactory as a primer for the dark-colored paints. This primer, generally white, may be tinted to a neutral gray or any other color with pastels in oil when used under dark-colored paints.

Exterior latex masonry paint is a standard paint for masonry. Cement-base paint may be used on nonglazed brick, stucco, cement, and cinder block. Rubber-base paint and aluminum paint with the proper vehicle may also be used.

Ordinary house or trim paints may be used for the finish coats on gutters, downspouts, and hardware or grilles. A specially recommended primer must be used on copper or galvanized steel. Use house paint, aluminum paint, or exterior enamel on steel or aluminum windows. Paint window screens with a special screen enamel.

Porch-and-deck paint may be used on both concrete and wood porches and steps. On wood, a primer coat is applied first. On concrete, an alkali-resistant primer is recommended. Rubber-base paints are excellent for use on concrete floors. Hard and glossy concrete surfaces must be etched or roughened first. (For quantity of paint see p. 149.)

SURFACE PREPARATION FOR EXTERIOR PAINTING

In general, a surface that is to be painted should be firm, smooth, and clean. With oil-base paint, it must also be dry. Latex or water-base paint can be applied to a damp surface (but not to a wet one). The paint-can label may contain additional or special instructions for preparing the surface.

Apply calking compound around windows and doors and wherever dissimilar materials abut (wood–masonry, wood–metal, wood siding–trim, etc.). Tightly calked joints helped to weatherproof your house and prevent moisture seepage with its subsequent damage to paint film.

Wood siding preferably should not contain knots or sappy streaks. But if new siding does, clean the knots and streaks with turpentine and seal with a good knot sealer. The knot sealer will seal in oily extractives and prevent staining and cracking of the paint.

Smooth any rough spots in the wood with sandpaper or other abrasive. Dust the surface just before you paint it.

Old surfaces in good condition—just slightly faded, dirty, or chalky—may need only dusting before being repainted. Very dirty surfaces should be washed with a mild detergent and rinsed thoroughly with water. Grease or other oily matter may be removed with mineral spirits.

Remove all nail rust marks. Set nailheads below the surface, prime them, and putty the holes. Fasten loose siding with galvanized or other nonrusting nails. Fill all

1. Seal knots so they won't show through paint.

2. Set nailheads below surface.

3. Fill holes with putty.

4. Fill cracks in siding.

5. Spot-rime before painting.

6. Feather edges of sound paint.

cracks; compounds for that purpose are available from paint and hardware stores. Sand smooth after the compound dries.

Remove all rough, loose, flaking, and blistering paint. Spot-prime the bare spots before repainting. If the cracking or blistering of the old paint extends over a large

Calk joints tightly.

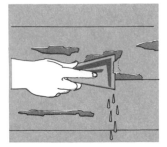

Scraping old paint from rough surfaces (above).

Sanding smooth surfaces (above right).

Using an electric paint softener (right).

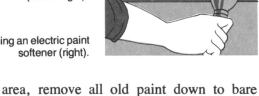

area, remove all old paint down to bare wood. Prime and repaint the old surface as you would a new wood surface. Sand or "feather" the edges of the sound paint before you repaint.

Before you repaint, be sure to correct the

Patch masonry cracks (left).

Replace crumbling mortar (below).

Wire-brushing masonry surface (below right).

condition that caused the blistering, cracking, or peeling of the old paint. Otherwise, you may run into the same trouble again. It may be a moisture problem. See pp. 174-177 for causes and cures.

Old paint may be removed by sanding, scraping, or burning, or with chemical paint remover. Scraping is the simplest but hardest method. Sanding is most effective on smooth surfaces. Chemical paint remover can be expensive for large areas. Only experienced persons should attempt burning. An electric paint softener is much safer.

●

New galvanized **steel surfaces** (such as gutters and leaders) should weather for about 6 months before being painted. If earlier painting is necessary, first wash the surface with a vinegar solution and rinse it thoroughly. This will remove any manufacturing residue and stain inhibitors. Apply a special primer before painting.

Rust and loose paint can usually be removed from old surfaces with sandpaper or with a stiff wire brush. Chipping may be necessary in severe cases. Chemical rust removers are available.

Oil and grease may be removed with a solvent such as mineral spirits. Rinse the surface thoroughly.

●

New concrete should weather for several months before being painted. If earlier painting is necessary, first wash the surface with a solvent such as mineral spirits to remove oil or grease. Fresh concrete may contain considerable moisture and alkali, so it is best to paint with latex paints.

Patch any cracks or other defects in masonry surfaces. Pay particular attention to mortar joints. Mortar and concrete patching compounds are available at hardware stores. Follow label directions for use.

Clean both new and old surfaces thoroughly before painting. Remove dirt, loose particles, and efflorescence with a wire brush. Oil and grease may be removed by washing the surface with a commercial cleanser or with a detergent and water. Loose, peeling, or heavily chalked paint may be removed by sandblasting. This is normally a professional operation.

If the old paint is just moderately chalked but is otherwise "tight" and nonflaking, coat it with a recommended sealer or conditioner before you repaint with a water-base paint. Some latex paints are modified to allow painting over slightly chalked surfaces. Follow the manufacturer's directions for use.

After cleaning the surface, wash or hose it—unless efflorescence was present.

VARIOUS WAYS TO APPLY EXTERIOR PAINT

Exterior paint may be applied by brush, roller, or spray. You can paint faster with a roller than with a brush; however, a brush may give better penetration on wood surfaces. With a roller, you still need a brush for "cutting in." This means extra tools to clean after the job is finished.

Rollers work well on masonry and metal surfaces. Proper depth of the pile on the roller cover is important and varies from one surface to another. Follow the manufacturer's recommendations.

Spraying is the fastest method. But you may not get proper penetration on wood surfaces. On masonry surfaces, voids that

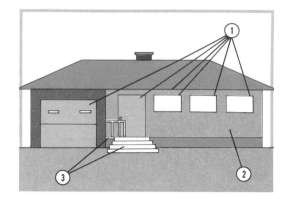

House painting sequence:
1-Windows, trim, doors;
2-Body of house;
3-Porches, steps.

Spray-painting masonry is the fastest method.

are difficult to fill with a brush or roller can be coated adequately by spraying. Surrounding surfaces must be well protected when spray-painting.

Paint the windows, trim, and doors before you paint the body of the house. Paint wood porches and steps last.

Read the paint-can label carefully before you start to paint. It will contain specific directions for application.

Home Repairs Made Easy

HOW MANY COATS AND WHEN TO PAINT?

For the original paint job on new wood surfaces, three coats are recommended. A three-coat system will perform better and last much longer than a two-coat job. However, most original paint jobs are two-coat applications. If you plan to limit yours to two coats, be certain to apply both generously, toward the lower spreading rate of the range specified by the manufacturer on the label of the container. Again, manufacturer's instructions for use of primer and topcoat should be followed. On factory-primed sidings, the factory primer will take the place of one of the required coats.

Repaint work is best limited to a single coat of topcoat paint of a similar color. If you plan a color change, two coats of topcoat paint may be required. If bare wood is exposed, areas should be spot-primed before the topcoat paint is applied.

Use a good-quality oil-base exterior primer with solvent-thinned paint. Most manufacturers recommend use of a solvent-thinned primer with latex or water-base paint. A solvent-thinned primer may be applied to a dry surface only. Prime after you clean and repair the surface, but before you putty cracks or other defects.

Allow the primer coat to dry according to the manufacturer's label instructions. Allow longer drying time in humid weather. Apply the finish coats as soon as the primer has dried sufficiently. Allow about 48 hours' drying time between oil-base finish coats. Two coats of latex paint may be applied in one day.

On metal surfaces, prime both new metal and old metal from which the paint has been removed. Good primers usually contain zinc dust, red lead, zinc yellow, blue lead, iron oxide, or some rust-inhibiting pigment as one of the ingredients. After the primer has dried sufficiently, apply one or two finish coats of paint.

New wood should be painted promptly (within two weeks) after its installation. If you find that this cannot be done, it is advantageous to protect the bare wood as soon as possible against the entrance of rain and heavy dew and mildew by brushing a paintable water-repellent preservative solution on the siding, trim, and into all joints. Wood so treated should be allowed to dry for a few days prior to painting or staining.

The best time to paint is during clear, dry weather. Temperatures must be above 50 degrees F. Latex paints may be applied even though the surface to be painted is damp from condensation or rain. Solvent-thinned paints should be applied only to a dry surface.

If the outside temperature is high (70 degrees F. or higher), it is best to paint those surfaces already reached by shade. This is known as "following the sun around the house." To avoid the wrinkling and flatting of solvent-thinned paints, and water marks on latex paints, do not paint late in the day in the early spring or late fall when heavy dew is common.

Do not paint in windy or dusty weather or when insects may get caught in the paint. Insects are usually the biggest problem during fall evenings. Don't try to remove insects from wet paint, as this would damage your new paint job; brush them off after the paint dries.

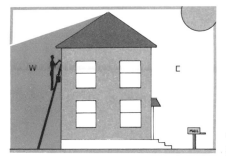

"Following the sun around the house."

A COAT OF PAINT CAN ALTER
THE PHYSICAL APPEARANCE OF YOUR HOUSE

Exterior sleight of hand can easily be accomplished by a coat of paint. A fresh, crisp appearance can give a formerly drab and tired-looking home a new lease on life—and a definite psychological lift to its inhabitants. But it can do even more than that—it can alter the entire physical appearance of the house.

Often, the roof color sets the tone for the rest of the house. If it is a neutral hue, the home can be brightened up by the use of a bolder, warm color such as red. Low homes can be made to look higher by emphasizing vertical lines with trim paint.

Top-heavy, boxy structures benefit from color-accenting of horizontal lines such as fasciae and windowsills. Painting the upper story a darker color than the lower achieves the same effect. Split levels look better when they are not too "split." The different levels should usually be the same color. Large homes, particularly if they are well landscaped, lend themselves better to the cooler hues of the spectrum. Many vintage homes suffer from the visual weight of a profusion of gables and other projections. These should be camouflaged by painting them to match their surroundings, so that there is at least a suggestion of harmony and continuity in the home's lines.

Color is highly personal. Certain rules and color schemes can be suggested, but don't be afraid to use your own good taste and initiative. It's your house and your money. If it turns out to be a visual atrocity, you can always repaint. But chances are good that, with a little forethought and the careful selection of colors, a fresh coat of paint, both indoors and out, will do your home proud.

Painting a low house by emphasizing
the vertical lines makes it appear higher.

A high, boxy house
benefits by emphasizing
the horizontal lines
(right).

The same effect can be
achieved by painting
a high, boxy house
in two colors (far right).

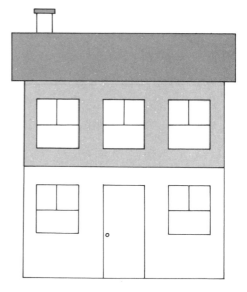

Home Repairs Made Easy

PUTTING ON THE PAINT

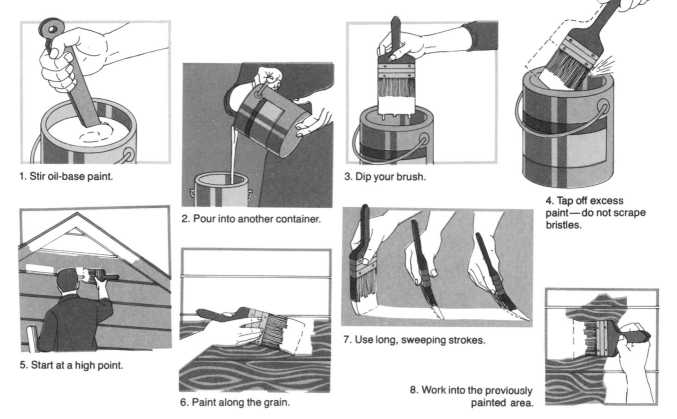

1. Stir oil-base paint.

2. Pour into another container.

3. Dip your brush.

4. Tap off excess paint—do not scrape bristles.

5. Start at a high point.

6. Paint along the grain.

7. Use long, sweeping strokes.

8. Work into the previously painted area.

Stir or shake oil-base paint thoroughly before you start to paint. Stir it frequently while painting. Latex or water-base paint should not be shaken—it foams.

If you are using a gallon of paint, transfer it to a larger container or pour about half into another container. It will be easier to handle, and there will be room to dip the brush.

Dip your brush about one-third the length of the bristles. Tap off excess paint on the inside of the can; do not scrape the brush across the rim.

On windows, paint the wood dividing the glass first. Then paint the frame, trim, sill, and apron in that order. Shutters and storm sash are easier to paint if removed from the house and laid flat on supports. Wipe off dust and dirt before painting them.

On siding, start painting at a high point of the house—at a corner or under the eave. Paint from top to bottom. Complete one sidewall before starting another.

Paint along the grain of the wood. If you are painting with a brush, use long sweeping arm strokes, keeping an even pressure on the brush. Apply both sides of each brushful. End each stroke with a light lifting motion.

Apply paint to an unpainted area and work into the wet edge of the previously painted portion. When you finish an area, go over it with light, quick strokes to smooth brush marks and to recoat any thin spots.

Clean your brushes immediately after painting. The how-to differs for the various types of paint and is described on p. 156.

NATURAL FINISHES AND SOLID-COLOR STAINS

Natural finishes help to retain or enhance the natural color and grain of wood. Such finishes are most extensively used on the more attractive siding woods such as redwood, western red cedar, and Philippine mahogany but are not limited to use on these species. They are relatively easy to apply and economical to maintain. The natural-finish family includes water-repellent preservatives, bleaches, and penetrating or semitransparent stains. All are either unpigmented (clear) or pigmented very slightly, hence the term "natural finishes."

Paintable water-repellent preservatives (WRP) repel liquids such as rainwater and dew and thereby reduce the swelling and shrinking of wood. They also protect wood against mildew and decay.

The WRPs are easy to apply by brush or roller, or by dipping the wood before installation. They penetrate wood, leaving its appearance relatively unchanged except for an initial slight darkening reaction. Treatment with WRP slows the weathering process and protects against water staining as well as mildew.

Where paintable water-repellent preservative is the sole treatment to be applied to exterior wood surfaces, two coats are recommended. The best results are obtained when the first coat is applied to the back, face, edges, and ends of the wood before it is nailed into place. After installation, the second coat should be brushed over all exposed wood surfaces. As weathering progresses, the color of WRP-treated wood may lighten.

The frequency with which the water-repellent preservative needs to be renewed is dependent upon climatic conditions. In relatively dry areas, the treatment retains its effectiveness longer than in areas subject to extensive rainfall, and it may not need to be renewed for three to five years. Where the treated wood is subject to frequent wetting, renewal may be required after 12 to 18 months. Successive retreatment may be extended to two years or more. Darkening of the wood or the appearance of blotchy discoloration are indications that the treatment has lost its effectiveness. This may be verified by splashing half a cup of water against the treated wood surface. If the water balls up and runs off, the treatment is still effective. If the water soaks quickly into the wood, it is time to refinish. A single recoat should suffice.

Some homeowners want their houses to have a weathered appearance sooner than natural weathering provides. This can be

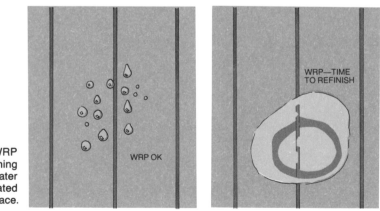

Checking to see if WRP is still effective by splashing half a cup of water against the treated wood surface.

WRP OK

WRP—TIME TO REFINISH

achieved by applying a bleach or bleaching oil. Bleaching oils are available in many paint stores. In addition to a bleaching chemical, the better bleaching oils contain pigments to impart a grayed appearance to wood and an agent to protect the finish against mildew.

By means of chemical reaction with the wood, bleaches hasten the natural color changes brought on by weathering and eliminate the darkening that often occurs when wood weathers naturally. On new wood, two coats of bleach are recommended. The original application is often the last. Reapplication of bleach is required only if the wood begins to darken or if the bleaching becomes uneven.

Since the bleaching action is aided by moisture, together with sunlight, it is helpful to spray bleached surfaces periodically with water from the garden hose.

Semitransparent stains, sometimes called penetrating stains, contain a small amount of pigment that allows them to alter the natural color of wood but only partially obscure the grain or texture. They are generally offered in natural wood-tone colors and are available in either solvent-thinned or water-thinned types.

Two coats of penetrating stain are generally recommended on new wood, and application is best done by brush or flat applicator. Roller or spray application, followed by brushing, may be used on smooth wood and textured surfaces. Care should be taken on windy, dry days to avoid lap marks due to fast absorption.

Penetrating stains leave a flat or dull finish. They are a "breathing" type of finish, since they do not form a continuous film or coating on the surface of the wood. A penetrating stain finish is gradually worn away by the weather. When the erosion progresses to the point that portions of the wood show through, it is time to refinish. A single refinish coat is generally adequate.

●

The increasing use of textured wood sidings, an ideal surface for stains, has added to the popularity of **solid-color stains.** Also called heavy-bodied stains, they are made with a much higher concentration of pigment than penetrating stains. As a result, solid-color stains have higher hiding power, sufficiently high to obscure the natural color and grain of wood. They are more like paint than stain.

As a rule, only a single coat of solid-color stain is applied, but two coats provide better and longer service. Any of the conventional methods of application may be used to apply the stain to smooth wood surfaces, but brush application is best.

PAINT FAILURES—CAUSES AND CURES

The interior paint, preparation, and application have all been the best. Why do the ceilings peel, the walls blister? It will probably pay to have a plumber check for leakage somewhere in the water supply or sewage systems. Just a tiny leak can have a devastating effect upon the surrounding walls. Moisture in the plaster causes blistering, peeling, and eventual ruination of the entire wall. If you suspect a leak behind the wall, no matter how slight, by all means have it corrected.

Ceilings, of course, can be ruined in the same manner, but many times the affected area is confined to that part of the ceiling which is underneath a toilet, tub, or washbasin. Frequent spillage of water from these sources seeps into the plaster or wallboard and causes moisture difficulties that are difficult to eradicate. Sometimes a more moisture-resistant floor overhead (ceramic tile, for example) will help, though this solution may require extensive and expensive structural modifications.

Blistering, peeling wall (at left).

Scrape away all damaged paint (below left).

Install a hood and fan above range (below).

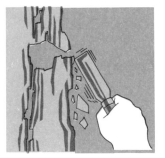

Even after you have sealed off the moisture source, the trouble may persist, because the dampness stays in the plaster or wallboard for a long time after the original soaking. This can usually be overcome by using an aluminum paint under a primer. If care is taken to scrape all affected paint from the surface, and the directions on the label of the aluminum paint are carefully followed, the problem should be solved.

Often paint cracks and peels above a kitchen range. The cure is a range hood with a fan to draw off the hot, moist vapors.

●

More serious problems occur in exterior paint. There are many types of failure and as many causes.

Blistering occurs when moisture trapped in siding is drawn from the wood by exposure to the sun and pushes paint from the surface. First you must find and eliminate sources of moisture. Is there seepage or leakage from eaves, roofs, or plumbing? Is the area near a bathroom or kitchen? Consider installing moisture-escape devices such as louvers, exhaust fans, or vents.

Scrape off old paint around the blistered area. Sand the surface to bare wood and spot-prime with an undercoat. Seal all seams, holes, and cracks against moisture with calking compound. Apply a topcoat of quality house paint according to the directions on the label.

Chalking is normal, and even desirable, since it keeps paint clean. But when paint chalks excessively, it will not last long. The cure: be more generous with paint. Don't spread it too thin. Use two coats. Use chalk-retardant paints above masonry.

Flaking or chalking paint on masonrysurfaces is caused by inadequate surface preparation. The paint flakes off in "scales" or powders and chalks off. The solution is first to remove flaking and chalking paint by wire-brushing. Seal all surface cracks against moisture with concrete patch. Apply a masonry conditioner according to the manufacturer's directions, then apply two topcoats of latex house paint or exterior masonry paint.

Cracking and alligatoring usually indicate that paint was applied in several heavy coats without sufficient drying time between coats, or that the undercoat used was not compatible with the finish coat. Sand the cracked or alligatored surface smooth. Then apply one coat of undercoat and one topcoat of recommended quality house paint according to label directions.

Checking is most commonly found on plywood veneer and is caused by expansion and contraction as it weathers and ages. To correct the problem, sand the surface smooth. If the cracked area is not extensive, spot-prime the exposed bare wood with an exterior undercoat. Fill primed cracks with calking compound. Apply a topcoat of recommended quality paint.

Should the problem be extensive, the best procedure is to replace the plywood. To prevent the problem on new plywood, sand the surface smooth, then apply one coat of latex wood primer and two coats of quality latex house paint according to label directions.

Peeling, like blistering, is caused when moisture trapped in siding is drawn from the wood by the sun's heat and pushes paint from the surface. The solution is to find and eliminate sources of moisture, following the same procedures as for blistering. Then scrape and repaint.

Flaking occurs when siding alternately swells and shrinks as moisture from behind it is absorbed and then dries out. The brittle paint film cracks under the strain and pulls away from the wood. Corrective measures are the same as for blistering.

Topcoat peeling is usually found on over-

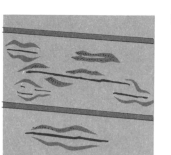
Blistered siding.

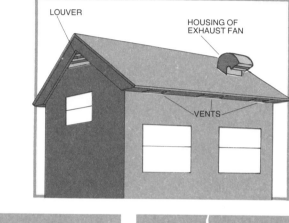
Install louvers, vents, exhaust fans.

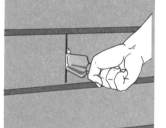
Seal seams, cracks.

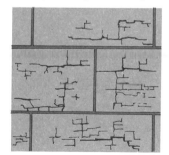
Flaking, chalking on masonry.

Excessive chalking.

Cracking and alligatoring.

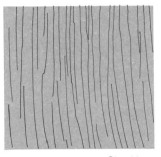

Checking.

Fill primed cracks.

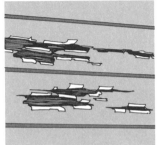

Peeling.

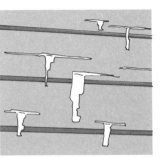

Flaking.

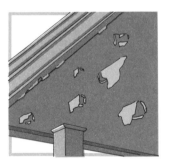

Topcoat peeling on overhanging horizontal surfaces.

Peeling, cracking on metal surfaces.

hanging horizontal surfaces and other areas protected from the weather. It is caused by poor adhesion to the previous coat of paint because built-up salt deposits have not been washed away by rain. Sand the surface thoroughly to remove all peeling paint. Wash the sanded surface with a solution of three heaping tablespoons of trisodium phosphate to one gallon of water. Rinse well and allow to dry. Apply one coat of undercoat and one topcoat of quality house paint according to label directions.

Peeling or cracking of paint on galvanized metal gutters and downspouts indicates the use of improper metal primer or no primer at all. The paint film has little or no adhesion. Strip off all loose paint by scraper, wire brush, or power wire-brushing. It is very important that all loose paint be removed, or succeeding coats of paint will subsequently peel away too. When finishing with oil-base topcoat, prime bare spots with a metal primer. When finishing with latex topcoat, apply latex paint directly to bare galvanized areas after cleaning with a solvent and allowing the solvent to evaporate.

Fading is normal, but if it is excessive, salt air from the seashore is very often the cause. Sometimes heavy pounding of wind-driven rain or snow, followed by bright sunlight, will cause one side of the house to fade more quickly than the others. Not much can be done about it, but be sure to

Bleeding.

Mildew.

Staining.

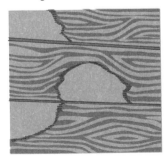

buy the best brand of paint, since it will invariably contain more and better pigment than cheaper types and thus hold out a bit longer.

Bleeding sometimes occurs on redwood and cedar siding and shingles. Sap runs or bleeds through paint and stains the surface. It is caused by inadequate sealing at the first paint application. If shake/shingle paints don't do the trick, the cure may be drastic. Stained areas may have to be scraped to raw wood and coated with knot sealer. If the staining material is creosote from an earlier application, the stain is blotchy rather than runny. Scraping down to bare wood is then the only cure. It's a tough one, but it can be done.

Mildew thrives on high humidity and high temperature, which stimulate fungus growth on paint film. If left on the surface and painted over, it will grow through the new coat of paint. The cure is to scrub the entire surface with a solution of one-third cup of trisodium phosphate and eight tablespoons of household bleach in four quarts of warm water. Then apply a wood undercoat. Mildew-resistant additive may be added to the undercoat if mildew conditions are severe and an oil-base topcoat is used. The additive in a finish coat should be avoided. The topcoat should be a quality mildew-resistant house paint.

Staining occurs when moisture in the siding dissolves coloring matter in the wood.

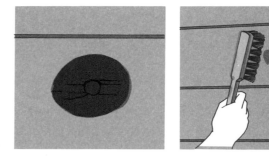

Rusting nails. Wire-brush stained area.

Colored water escapes onto the surface through breaks in the paint film and drips from underneath overlapping boards. Stain is deposited as the water dries. The solution is first to find and eliminate sources of moisture. Then wash the stained surface with a mixture of 50 percent denatured alcohol and 50 percent clean water. Allow the surface to dry for 48 hours. Then apply two coats of quality house paint.

Excessive moisture may cause rusting of uncoated steel nails used in construction. After finding and eliminating sources of moisture, sand or wire-brush the stained paint and remove rust down to the bright metal of the nailhead. Countersink the nailhead ⅛ inch below the surface of the siding. Immediately spot-prime the nailhead with undercoat. Fill the countersunk hole with calking compound or putty (see p. 165). Apply two coats of quality house paint according to label directions.

CONDENSATION

Condensation is the change in moisture from a vapor to a liquid. In homes not properly protected, condensation caused by high humidity often results in excessive maintenance costs. Water vapor within the house, when unrestricted, can move through the wall or ceiling during the heating season to some cold surface where it condenses, collecting generally in the form of ice or frost. During warm periods the frost melts. When conditions are severe, the water from melting ice in unvented attics may drip to the ceiling below and cause damage to the interior finish. Moisture can also soak into the roof sheathing or rafters and set up conditions that could lead to decay. In walls, water from melting frost may run out between the siding laps and cause staining, or it may soak into the siding and cause paint blistering and peeling.

Wood and wood-base materials used for sheathing and panel siding may swell from this added moisture and result in bowing, cupping, or buckling. Thermal insulation also becomes wet and provides less resistance to heat loss.

The cost of heat loss, painting and redecorating, and excessive maintenance and repair caused by cold-weather condensation can easily be reduced or eliminated by proper construction details.

Estimates have been made that a typical family of four converts 3 gallons of water into water vapor per day. Unless excess water vapor is properly removed in some way (ventilation usually), it will either increase the humidity or condense on cold surfaces such as window glass. More serious, however, it can move in or through the construction, often condensing within the wall, roof, or floor cavities. Heating systems equipped with winter air-conditioning systems also increase the humidity.

Most new houses have from 2 to 3½ inches of insulation in the walls and 6 or more inches in the ceilings. Unfortunately, the more efficient the insulation is in retarding heat transfer, the colder the outer surfaces become and, unless moisture is restricted from entering the wall or ceiling, the greater the potential for moisture condensation. Mositure migrates toward cold surfaces and condenses or forms as frost or ice on these surfaces.

Inexpensive methods of preventing condensation problems are available. They mainly involve the proper use of vapor barriers and good ventilating practices. Naturally it is simpler, less expensive, and more effective to employ these during the construction of a house than to add them to existing homes.

Condensation takes place any time the temperature drops below the dew point (100 percent saturation of the air with water vapor at a given temperature). Commonly, under such conditions some surface accessible to the moisture in the air is cooler than the dew point, and the moisture condenses on that surface.

During cold weather, visible condensation is usually first noticed on window glass, but it may also be discovered on cold surfaces of closet and unheated bedroom walls and ceilings. Condensation may also be visible in attic spaces on rafters or roof boards near the cold cornice area, or it might form as frost. Such condensation or melting frost can result in excessive maintenance costs, such as the need for refinishing of window sash and trim, or even decay. Water from melting frost in the attic can also damage ceilings below.

Another area in which visible condensation can occur is in crawl spaces under occupied rooms. This area usually differs from those in the interior of the house and in the attic because the source of the moisture is usually from the soil or from warm

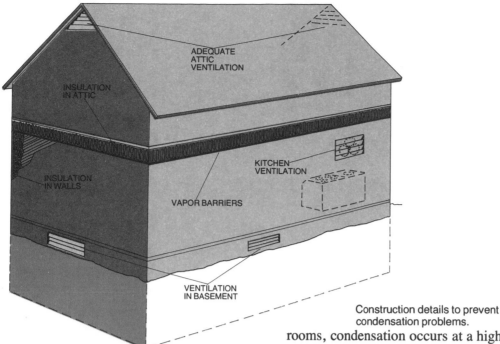

Construction details to prevent condensation problems.

moisture-laden air that enters through foundation ventilators. Moisture vapor then condenses on the cooler surfaces in the crawl space. Such conditions often occur during warm periods in late spring.

An increase in the relative humidity of the inside atmosphere increases the potential for condensation on inside surfaces. For example, when the inside temperature is 70 degrees F, surface condensation will occur on a single-thickness glass window when the outside temperature falls to -10 degrees F and the inside relative humidity is 10 percent. When the inside relative humidity is 20 percent, condensation can occur on the single glass when the outside temperature falls only to about +7 degrees F. When a storm window is added or insulated glass is used, surface condensation does not occur until the relative humidity has reached 38 percent when the outdoor temperature is -10 degrees F. These conditions apply only if storm windows are tight and there is good circulation of air on the inside surface of the window. If draperies or shades restrict circulation of air, storm windows are not tight, or lower temperatures are maintained in such areas as bed-

rooms, condensation occurs at a higher outside temperature.

Condensation in concealed areas, such as wall cavities, often is first revealed by stains on the siding or by paint peeling. Water vapor moving through permeable walls and ceilings is normally responsible for such damage. Water vapor also escapes from houses by constant outleakage through cracks and crevices, around doors and windows, and by ventilation, but this moisture-vapor loss is usually insufficient to eliminate condensation problems.

Moisture that is produced in or enters a home changes the relative humidity of the interior atmosphere. Ordinary household functions that generate a good share of the total amount of water vapor include dishwashing, cooking, bathing, and laundry work; add to this human respiration and evaporation from plants. Houses may also be equipped with central winter air conditioners or room humidifiers. Still another source of moisture may be from unvented or poorly vented clothes dryers.

Condensation problems can best be eliminated by specifying proper construction details during planning of the house. Correct placement of vapor barriers, adequate insulation, the use of attic ventilation, and

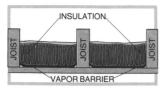

Vapor barrier between
attic joists.

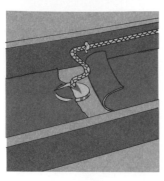

Make sure the vapor
barrier fits tightly around
ceiling fixtures.

other good practices can be incorporated at this time. When these details have not been included in an existing house and condensation problems occur, they are often more difficult to solve. Nevertheless, there are methods to minimize such problems after the house has been built.

●

Visible condensation on the interior glass surfaces of windows can be minimized by the use of storm windows or by replacing single-thickness glass with insulated glass. When this does not prevent condensation, however, the relative humidity in the room must be reduced. Draperies or curtains across the windows hinder rather than help. Not only do they increase surface condensation by keeping the glass surfaces colder, but they also prevent the air movement that would warm the glass surface and aid in dispersing some of the moisture.

Condensation or frost on protruding nails, on the surfaces of roof boards, or other structural members in attic areas normally indicates the escape of excessive amounts of water vapor from the heated rooms below. If a vapor barrier is not already present, place one between joists under the insulation. Make sure the vapor barrier fits tightly around ceiling lights and exhaust fans, calking if necessary. In addition, increase both inlet and outlet ventilators. Decreasing the amount of water vapor produced in the living areas is also helpful.

Surface condensation in unheated crawl spaces is usually caused by excessive moisture from the soil or from warm, humid air entering from outside the house. To eliminate this problem, place a vapor barrier over the soil; if necessary, increase the amount of ventilation.

Concrete slabs without radiant heat are sometimes subjected to surface condensation in late spring when warm humid air enters the house. Because the temperature of some areas of the concrete slab or its covering is below the dew point, surface condensation can occur. Keeping the windows closed during the day, using a dehumidifier, and raising the inside temperature aid in minimizing this problem. When the concrete slab reaches normal room temperature, this inconvenience is eliminated.

●

Reducing high relative humidities within the house to permissible levels is often necessary to minimize condensation problems. It is helpful to discontinue the use of room-sized humidifiers or reduce the output of automatic humidifiers until conditions are improved. The use of exhaust fans and dehumidifiers can also be of value in eliminating high relative humidities within the house. When possible, decreasing the activities that produce excessive moisture, as discussed previously, is sometimes helpful.

●

Concealed condensation is essentially a surface or similar condensation that takes place within a component such as a wall cavity when a condensing surface is below the dew point. In cold weather, condensation often forms as frost. Such conditions can cause staining of siding and peeling of the paint and possibly decay in severe and sustained conditions. These problems are usually not detected until spring, after the heating season has ended. The remedies should be taken care of before repainting or re-siding is attempted. Several methods may be used to correct these problems: reduce or control the relative humidity within the house; add a vapor-resistant paint coating such as aluminum paint to the interior of walls and ceilings; improve the vapor resistance of the ceiling joists; and improve attic ventilation.

DAMPNESS IN BASEMENTS

Almost all basement dampness problems can be traced to one of three causes: leakage, seepage, or condensation.

Leakage is usually obvious, occurring during a heavy rainfall or when snow is melting. An excessive amount of water builds up in the soil around the foundation walls, forcing its way through cracks or other defects in poured concrete walls (such as small holes around form wires), or through poor mortar joints in a concrete-block wall. If the area around the foundation has been improperly backfilled or graded, the situation is aggravated. In very wet periods, considerable flooding may result.

Seepage is evidenced by large areas of dampness on the foundation walls, rather than by water leaking through a particular spot. Usually, it will be greatest along the lower parts of the wall. Like leakage, it is caused by excessive water pressure on the outside of the basement walls. It may also be due to capillary action, which draws water from the moist soil through porous sections of the masonry.

Condensation looks very much like seepage, but here the moisture comes from air inside the basement, not from water outside (although seepage from outside may be a factor in creating the conditions for condensation). Condensation usually occurs during warm, humid weather, when the cool masonry walls seem to "sweat." It can also happen during colder months when warm air is discharged by a clothes dryer or similar appliance; moisture from this air collects on the cooler walls in the form of droplets, which may be mistaken for seepage from outside.

There is a simple test to determine whether a damp wall is the result of seepage or condensation. Tape a small mirror or a piece of sheet metal to the wall (or use a waterproof mastic if it is too wet for tape to

stick). Leave it there overnight and inspect it the next day. If the surface of the mirror is fogged or the sheet metal damp, the moisture came from inside the basement, indicating that condensation is to blame. If the surface of the patch is dry and clear while the surrounding wall is damp, seepage is the problem.

Test indicating condensation.

Test indicating seepage.

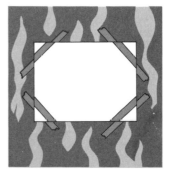

Leakage in poured concrete (above) and concrete block walls (above right).

Seapage or condensation (right).

Home Repairs Made Easy

1. Cut hole for vent of clothes dryer.

2. Insert hooded fitting through the hole.

3. Attach flexible pipe to the fitting of dryer's exhaust port.

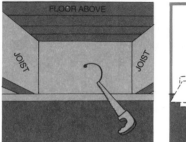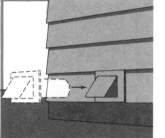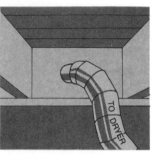

CURES FOR CONDENSATION IN BASEMENTS

If condensation is the cause of your moisture miseries, the remedy is to dry out the air in the basement as much as possible.

Adequate ventilation is essential for a dry basement. In cool, dry weather, keep the basement windows open whenever possible. On hot, humid days, keep them closed; warm, moist air may even cause mildew to form on the cooler masonry walls. If your basement has too few windows to provide needed ventilation, a small exhaust fan installed in a window or ducted to the outside will help.

Pipes that tend to sweat in hot weather should be wrapped with insulation. This is especially important if finishing off the basement ceiling is part of your plans. Otherwise, moisture dripping from the pipes will ruin your ceiling tile or panels.

Clothes dryers should always be vented to the outside. This is a relatively easy do-it-yourself job. The vent pipe is normally run through a hole in the header joist or stringer joist (these are the joists that rest on the sills, which in turn are bolted to the top of the foundation walls). The hole can be cut either from inside the basement or, with careful measurements, from outside. Its diameter will depend on the size of the exhaust port on your dryer. Use a saber saw or keyhole saw to cut the hole, after first drilling a ½-inch or larger pilot hole. Insert a hooded fitting through the hole from the outside, then connect the dryer's exhaust port to this fitting with flexible pipe, which can be bought at most hardware stores.

If you do not have a clothes dryer, try to avoid hanging clothes to dry in the basement. The moisture from the wet clothes will enter the air and show up as condensation on the walls.

When basement condensation persists, an electric dehumidifier or chemical drying agents may be needed to remove moisture from the air and keep the basement dry.

●

If you are one of the fortunate few who have been able to move into brand-new houses in this time of skyrocketing costs and astronomical-interest mortgages, chances are that your condensation problems are greater than most. Condensation is at its maximum in new houses. During construction, literally tons of water are used—in concrete, mortar, plaster, wallpaper paste, tile work, and even many types of paint. This water gradually evaporates, giving a higher moisture content than normal to the air throughout the house and ending up as condensation on basement walls and windows in every room.

All the steps described above (especially providing adequate ventilation) should be employed to assist this normal drying-out process. In addition, be patient. Do not try to accelerate the process by turning up the furnace to extremely high temperatures. This will only cause uneven drying, exaggerating the effects of normal materials shrinkage and almost surely resulting in greater patch-and-repair problems later on.

HOW TO CURE SEEPAGE AND STOP LEAKS IN BASEMENTS

If seepage is the cause of your basement dampness, a simple coat of paint may be the solution. Not just any paint, of course, but one that is resistant to water, alkali, and mildew and has good adhesion to concrete. This will provide a watertight coating that is durable and decorative.

Most such paints can be applied to both damp and uncured concrete as well as to previously painted surfaces. As with any paint job, the key to success is careful preparation.

Unpainted concrete, new or old, must be clean before application of paint. Grease, oil, and dirt should be removed with a strong cleansing agent such as trisodium phosphate. After scrubbing with a stiff-bristled brush, rinse the surface thoroughly with water to remove all residue. Allow to dry for 24 hours.

On a previously painted wall, all paint that is flaking, blistering, cracking, or chalking must be removed. This is done by scraping and brushing with a wire brush. Chemical removers can also be used. As with new concrete, the surface should then be scrubbed clean, rinsed, and allowed to dry thoroughly.

If the walls are whitewashed, scrub them with a dilute mixture of muriatic acid (10 parts water to 1 part acid). Wear rubber gloves and protective glasses or goggles for this job, and be careful not to splash any of the mixture on your skin or in your eyes. If you do, wash it off immediately with plenty of water. Again, rinse the surface thoroughly after scrubbing, and allow it to dry.

Before painting, patch large cracks and holes in the concrete, following the directions given below for plugging leaks. Hairline cracks and pores or pinholes need not be filled; the full-bodied paint will cover them.

Apply the paint with a brush or roller, covering the surface evenly and thoroughly. Normally, a single coat does the job, but if the concrete or concrete block is very porous a second coat may be required.

A more serious seepage problem suggests a structural fault that will probably have to be corrected from outside the wall. You may prefer to leave this project to the professionals, since it involves excavating a trench wide enough to allow working space and deep enough to reach the problem area. The masonry surface must then be scrubbed clean before a coating of cement plaster is troweled on. This is followed by a second coating and, finally, a coating of asphalt cement or plastic sealer.

Where subsoil moisture is present in excessive amounts, causing the seepage problem, drain tile should be laid around the foundation footings to carry water away from the house—another digging project. Tiles should be pitched downward ¼ inch per foot toward the drainage point. Joints between tiles should be covered with strips of tar paper to keep out dirt, and the tiles should both rest on and be covered by a layer of gravel or crushed stone.

●

When water is trickling through the basement wall, your first step is to plug the leak. This is best done with a quick-setting hydraulic cement that can be applied even when a crack is under pressure—that is, when water is pouring through it. Apply the cement with a trowel or wide-blade putty knife, holding it in place until the flow of water is stopped.

Such patches are usually only temporary and should be replaced when the crack is dry. For a normal dry repair, first chisel out the crack to form an inverted V-groove, about ½ inch at the surface and wider beneath so that the patching material will be locked in place. Use a cold chisel and a 1-pound ball peen or mash hammer for this job (your claw hammer should be reserved for carpentry and woodworking projects). Clean away all loose rubble and dust, and wire-brush clean. Flush with water to remove all dust particles.

Mix together 1 part cement to 2½ parts of clean sand. Add enough water to make a stiff mixture, making sure to wet all parts of the sand-cement. Dampen the area to be patched, then force the mixture into the crack with a trowel, filling it completely. Keep the patched area slightly damp for a few days to allow the cement to cure thoroughly. If that doesn't solve your leakage problem, you will probably have to attack it from outside, as described for seepage.

In a concrete-block foundation wall, water may leak through a defective mortar joint between blocks. To repair this, first scrape away all loose and crumbling mortar, using a cold chisel or an old screwdriver. Clean out the joint with a wire brush and rinse with water to remove all dust parti-

cles. Make a mortar mix of 1 part masonry cement to 3 parts clean, dry sand. Add enough water to make a workable but fairly stiff mixture. Force the mortar into the joint with a trowel, striking it off flush with the surface of the block. Allow the mortar to dry thoroughly.

Leaks at the wall-floor joint can similarly be corrected with cement. Even more effective is a two-part epoxy resin compound that forms a durable seal against hydrostatic pressure at this point. Once again, the area should be thoroughly cleaned before making the repair. The material is mixed immediately before use and brushed or troweled into place. Two coats are usually recommended.

Leaks in concrete floors are repaired in the same way as wall leaks: undercutting, cleaning, and patching with a sand-cement mixture. However, floor leaks may be indicative of more serious problems. Your home may be in a very low, wet location or be built over a marshy area or an underground stream. In that case, a drainage tile system may have to be installed as described above for major seepage problems.

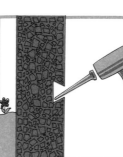

Plugging the leak with cement.

Chiseling crack.

Fill crack with patching cement.

Scrape defective mortar joint.

Force mortar into joint.

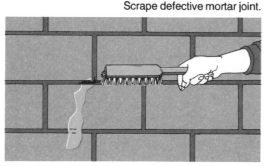
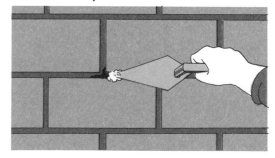

DAMPNESS IN CRAWL SPACES

Crawl spaces present some special problems because cold and dampness commonly invade these areas. Occasionally, unpleasant odors result. These conditions make living on the floor above somewhat less than ideal. The conditions are usually curable.

Again, adequate ventilation is essential. There should be vents or louvers on at least two opposite sides of the crawl space to provide cross-ventilation. If necessary, you can install vents by cutting holes through the header joists similar to installing a dryer vent, described on p. 182. If the foundation is of concrete block, you can simply knock out a block to emplace a vent. Louvered vents, which can be closed off in damp or cold weather, are best. Most of them are also screened to keep out rodents and other small animals.

Cold floors in rooms over crawl spaces present another problem. The best solution is to install 4-inch insulation batts between the floor joists. Staple the batts to the bottoms of the joists, forming air space between the subfloor and the insulation. (Don't block vents with the insulation.) Below the insulation, staple a vapor barrier of heavy felt paper. This will seal out any moisture. Make sure that the entire area beneath the floor is covered.

If dampness persists, cover the ground in the crawl space with tar paper. Overlap the joints 3 to 4 inches, and seal the tar paper to the foundation walls with asphalt

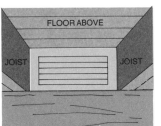

Install vent in leader joist.

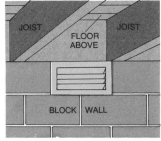

Install vent in block wall.

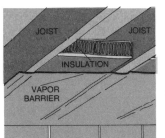

Insulation to prevent cold floors over crawl spaces.

compound. Then spread a 2-inch layer of dry sand over the tar paper. This should insure that the area above the crawl space will be cozy and dry the year round.

PREVENTING DAMPNESS PROBLEMS

Patching holes and cracks and waterproofing basement walls solve the immediate problems of leakage and seepage, but since the ultimate cause is excess water accumulation in the ground around the foundation walls, this situation should also be corrected. This is done by making provision to divert surface water before it can come into contact with the foundation.

Check gutters and downspouts for leaks or improper pitching that may cause water to collect along the foundation wall. Gutters that are clogged with leaves and other debris may also divert water onto the ground beside the house and, eventually, into the basement. Downspouts should be connected to a storm sewer or to an underground dry well located at least 10 feet away from the foundation. Downspouts not so connected should empty onto concrete splash blocks that carry the water runoff away from the house walls.

To carry away rainwater as quickly as possible, the ground surface should slope away sharply at foundation walls, then more gradually to at least 10 feet from the walls. If such is not the case, fill in with new soil, taking special care in areas where puddles form during rainy weather. Tamp the soil firmly and sow it with good grass seed or sod rolled down evenly and firmly. If the new grading extends above basement windows, protect each one with a curved metal shell or concrete wall. Gravel in the bottoms of these protected areas will facilitate drainage. Hinged plastic covers may be provided to admit light but keep out rain and snow.

Where concrete walks or driveways are adjacent to the foundation wall, they should also slope away gradually. The walk-wall joint should be concave or sharply angled to keep out water. If the joints are not so protected, or if they are broken or otherwise damaged, they should be fixed.

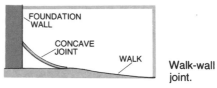

Walk-wall joint.

Chip away loose or damaged concrete. Scrub clean both the wall and the walk, and roughen both surfaces with a cold chisel and peening hammer. You can then apply an epoxy resin compound to the joint, as described above for basement wall-floor joints. Or you can use a mixture of 1 part cement to 2½ parts sand. Moisten the concrete surfaces, then trowel the cement-sand mixture into the joint, sloping it sharply away from the foundation wall for a minimum of 2 inches.

If all else fails and you must call in a professional to try to solve your basement dampness problem, exercise a degree of caution and beware of "miracle cures." There are many highly reputable firms in the basement waterproofing business, but there are also some of lesser repute. Follow the usual practice of checking with the local Better Business Bureau, consumer protection groups, and other homeowners who have dealt with the firm before you sign any contract. As ever, let the buyer beware.

Downspouts should carry water away from foundation.

INSULATION

Homeowners around the country are faced with a serious problem—conserving energy and money without sacrificing on comfort in the home. Although the problem is serious, the solutions are fairly simple. There are several energy-saving steps the average do-it-yourselfer can take without having a garage full of tools or laying out big bucks.

We all know that heating and cooling the home is taking a bigger and bigger bite out of the personal budget each year, and it probably won't get better. A few energy conservation steps can ease those monthly bills as well as add resale value to the home. With the dwindling natural resources of our country, the nation as a whole will also benefit.

It's an interesting fact that most homes, built in the days when energy was plentiful and cheap, don't have enough insulation, and some don't have any at all. The expression "better late than never" surely applies here.

No matter where you live, insulation is a hidden but most important part of your house. During the heating season, insulation keeps warmth indoors where it belongs, and your family is comfortable and snug. Insulation is equally important in hot weather, since it helps keep the extreme heat of the sun from penetrating. And, in air-conditioned homes, insulation eases the task of the cooling system.

A properly insulated house costs far less to heat and cool than its noninsulated twin. Less fuel is burned, and at the same time a higher level of comfort is experienced. By the same token, air conditioners that work less use less electricity. It can truthfully be said that insulation pays for itself over and over again.

An insulated home is also a far more pleasant place in which to live. Indoor temperatures can be kept more constant. Inside surfaces of walls, floors, and ceilings, insulated from outdoor extremes, are closer to room air temperature and therefore conducive to comfort and well-being. Annoying drafts are minimized or eliminated, and the whole living area stays comfortable in the coldest, or hottest, weather.

In the heating season alone, adequate insulation in the attic floor generally saves up to 30 percent on fuel bills and can save up to 50 percent. In an air-conditioned home, summer savings are comparable.

The most common kinds of insulation for

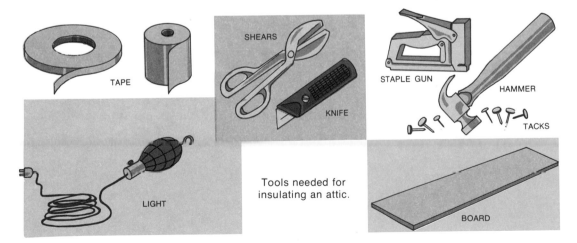

TAPE

SHEARS

KNIFE

STAPLE GUN

HAMMER

TACKS

LIGHT

Tools needed for insulating an attic.

BOARD

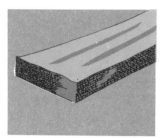

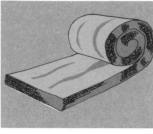

Blanket.

Batt.

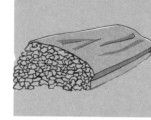

Loose fill
insulation.

the home are mineral fiber, cellulose fiber, plastic foam, and aluminum foil sheets. These types can be divided into categories according to how they are installed.

Mineral fiber insulation is purchased in batts or blankets and is the most widely used type. Mineral fiber, whether fiberglass or rock wool, is used to insulate unfinished attic floors, attic rafters, and the underside of floors. Batts come precut in widths of either 15 or 23 inches and in lengths of 4 or 8 feet. Blankets are purchased in the same widths and are cut to the desired length. All mineral fiber insulation can be bought with or without a vapor barrier backing and is fire- and moisture-resistant. Installation of this type is very easy.

Loose fill insulation comes in glass fiber, rock wool, cellulose fiber, vermiculite, and perlite. Basically, this type is used only for unfinished attic floors and is best suited for areas that are irregular or have many obstructions. If a vapor barrier is needed, it must be bought and installed separately with this type. Cellulose fiber is chemically treated to be fire- and moisture-resistant but has not yet been proven to be heat-re-

sistant. This means that the insulation could break down in a hot attic. Check to be sure that bags indicate that the material meets federal specifications. Because this type of insulation is simply poured into place, installation is no problem.

Glass fiber, rock wool, and cellulose fiber can also be blown into place. Generally used for attic floors and finished frame walls, this type has the same physical properties as poured-in loose fill. Because it consists of smaller tufts, cellulose fiber gets into small nooks and corners more consistently than rock wool or glass fiber when blown into closed spaces such as walls or joist spaces. Professional installation is required with this insulation.

Ureaformaldehyde can also be used for unfinished attic floors or finished frame walls. Foamed in place, it may have higher insulating value than blown-in materials, but it is more expensive. The quality of application to date has been very inconsistent, so choose a qualified contractor who will guarantee his work.

Regardless of the type of material from which insulation is manufactured or the physical form in which it is applied to the house, the principle remains the same. Between the fibers are tiny air spaces. There are untold numbers of these in each piece of insulation, and each one is a tiny insulator in its own right. The cumulative effect is what does the job. By creating an extremely effective barrier to the passage of heat, the insulation isolates the house from exterior weather influences.

Your money's worth in insulation is measured in R-Value. R-Value is a number that tells how much resistance the insulation presents to heat flowing through it. The higher the R-Value, the better the insulation. One brand of insulation might be slightly thicker or thinner than another, but if they're marked with the same R-Value they'll resist heat flow equally well. If you have a choice of insulating materials, simply price the same R-Value for both and get the better buy. Pay more only for more R-Value. The R-Value is marked on the outside of the package.

Insulating the attic floor, where savings generally will be greatest, usually can be done by the homeowner himself. The amount of insulation needed depends entirely upon how much insulation, if any, is already there. To find out, go up into the attic and measure the depth with a tape measure or yardstick.

If there is 6 inches or more, no additional insulation is needed. Insulation with an R-Value of R-11 should be used in attics with between 2 and 6 inches of insulation already in place. If there is no insulation at all present, new insulation should have an R-Value of R-22. If you can't get into your attic or don't want to do the work yourself, call a reputable contractor and get an estimate for the needed R-Value. These amounts will make certain that your home meets current Federal Housing Administration standards for new houses.

Amounts greater than these may be necessary if your climate is substantially colder or warmer than average or a high amount of attic insulation will have to partially compensate for poorly insulated walls.

A minimum of tools and experience are needed to insulate an attic properly. Besides the insulation, the materials needed are: tape (2 inches wide), staple gun or hammer and tacks, heavy-duty shears or

Use board to form walkway on joists.

Watch out for nails!

What the well-dressed insulator will wear: gloves, breathing mask, long-sleeved clothing.

knife to cut insulation, and temporary lighting and flooring.

Some simple safety steps should be taken when working in the attic with insulation of any type. Provide good lighting (it's dark up there!). Lay boards or plywood sheets down over the tops of the joists or trusses to form a walkway. Be careful of roofing nails protruding through the roof sheathing. If you use glass fiber or mineral wool, wear gloves, a breathing mask, and long-sleeved clothing. Because most insulation comes wrapped in a compressed state, it should be kept wrapped until ready for use.

A vapor barrier is usually necessary

Measure present insulation in floor.

Polyethylene sheet as vapor barrier.

Lay batts or blankets in place.

Pour in loose fill insulation.

Level loose fill insulation.

Do not cover
fixtures.

Do not
cover vents.

Noncombustible
material should
be used for
insulation around
chimneys.

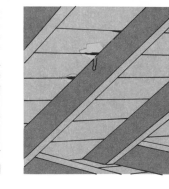

Check for
roof leaks.

when insulation is installed. This is a material that will block moisture and not absorb it. If warm, moist air from inside the house is allowed to pass through the wall covering and meet the cool dry air from outside, the resulting water vapor can wet the insulation, robbing it of its insulating qualities. Excessive moisture can also cause rotting in the wood used to build the house. Added ventilation will remove water vapor before it gets a chance to condense and will also increase summer comfort by cooling your attic.

If you are installing batt or blanket insulation, buy the type with the vapor barrier attached (unless you are adding more insulation on top of existing insulation, in which case no vapor barrier should be used). Install it with the vapor barrier side toward the living space.

For loose fill insulation, lay down polyethylene sheets between the joists before pouring in, or blowing in, the insulation.

The actual job of insulating an attic is quite simple. If batts or blankets with vapor barrier attached are used, merely lay the insulation between joists or trusses. Loose fill insulation is poured between the joists up to the top of the joists. Use a rake or board to level it. Fill all the nooks and crannies, but don't cover recessed light fixtures or exhaust fans. The National Electrical Code requires that insulation be kept at least 3 inches away from light fixtures.

Extra precautions must be taken not to cover any vents that would block the flow of air into the attic. The space between the chimney and the wood framing should be filled with noncombustible material, preferably unfaced batts or blankets.

While insulating the attic, it's a good idea to check for roof leaks by looking for water stains or marks. If you find leakage, make repairs before you insulate. Wet insulation is ineffective and can damage the structure of the home.

Insulating a finished or partially finished attic is a little harder because some parts are inaccessible. A contractor can do a complete job, and in some cases this is the best course. If you can get into the unfinished parts of the attic to do the work, you can do the job yourself.

Insulating an attic that is unfinished but has a floor is usually a job for a contractor. Assuming there is less than 4 inches of insulation under the floor, insulation can be blown under the floor boards. If there is more than 4 inches, the job is not economical.

The do-it-yourselfer can insulate the rafters, end walls, and collar beams of an unfinished, floored attic. This is the best way if you are planning to finish the attic. Batts or blankets are installed between the rafters and collar beams, and between the studs on the end walls. At ceiling height, 2×4 beams must be installed between each roof rafter, if the attic doesn't already have them. This gives a ventilation space above the insulation and forms the roof of the attic. Between the collar beams, add insulation with an R-Value of at least R-22. Rafters and end walls require insulation thick enough to fill up the rafter and stud space. Insulation for the rafters should be R-19,

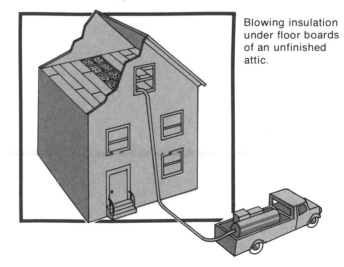

Blowing insulation under floor boards of an unfinished attic.

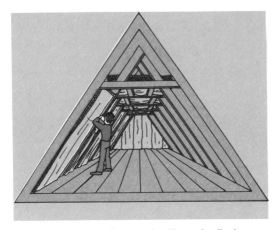

Insulating rafters, end walls, and collar beams.

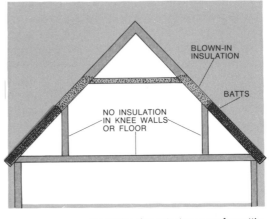

Insulating the outer spaces of an attic.

and the end walls should have at least R-11 insulation.

The homeowner with a completely finished attic is more limited as to what he can do himself. Insulating an attic without tearing down the finished walls is almost always a job for a competent contractor. A contractor will blow insulation into the open joist spaces above the attic ceiling, between the rafters, and into the floor of the outer attic space, then install batts in the knee walls. If you want the outer attic spaces heated for storage or any other purpose, have the contractor install batts between the outer attic rafters instead of insulating the outer floors and knee walls. Insulating

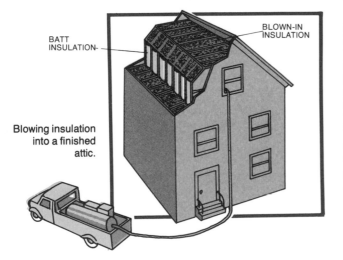

Blowing insulation into a finished attic.

this type of attic is not worth considering unless there is less than 4 inches of insulation already installed.

You can insulate wherever you can get into unfinished spaces. Installing insulation in the attic ceiling is the same as installing it in an unfinished, floored attic. If you want to insulate the outer attic spaces, install batts between the rafters and the studs in the small triangular end walls. If there is no existing insulation, use R-22 for the ceiling and R-11 for the end walls.

The next step toward easing your energy bills and adding to the comfort of your home is to insulate the walls. This depends on what type of walls you have and how much, if any, insulation is already there.

To find out what's inside the wall, turn off the principal electric switch or a circuit breaker or fuse for a convenient outlet or switch box on an outside wall. Remove the cover plate and the electrical box (usually nailed to a framing member) to get a look inside the wall cavity. You'll be able to see or feel any insulation that's in the wall stud cavity space. If you are in doubt as to the amount of insulation, or whether it will be adequate, your best bet is to call an insulation contractor.

Most frame houses have a wood struc-

Installing insulation in the attic ceiling.

ture—usually 2 × 4s—even though they may have brick or stone on the outside. If you have this type of walls, you should consider insulating them if they are not already insulated. A contractor can fill them with insulation and cut energy waste by about two-thirds. This job is not for the do-it-yourselfer.

The contractor will measure the area you want insulated to determine how much material he will need and to estimate the cost. To install the insulation, the contractor must be able to get at all the spaces in the wall. For each space, he must drill a hole, usually in the outside wall, after removing the the finish layer (usually clapboard or shingle). This amounts to a lot of holes, but once the job is complete, a good contractor will leave no traces behind.

If you have brick veneer on the outside, the procedure is much the same, except that it may be cheaper to do the job from the inside.

Once the holes have been made in the walls, the contractor will blow the insulation material under air pressure through a big flexible hose into the area to be filled. If the contractor uses foam-type insulation, he'll pump the foam into the wall spaces with a flexible hose and an applicator. With either method, each space will be completely filled, and the siding replaced.

Before you sign an agreement with the contractor, define what you're buying and make sure it's spelled out in the contract. Insulation material properly installed will add an R-Value of 8 for rock wool, 10 for cellulose fiber, or 11.5 for ureaformaldehyde in a standard wood-frame wall. You should agree with the contractor on what the R-Value is before the job begins. Next, check a bag of the type of insulation he intends to use (there will only be bags of mineral fiber or cellulose fiber—there's no good way to check quantity with foam). On it will be a table indicating how many square feet of wall space that bag is meant to fill while giving your house the desired R-Value. The information may be in dif-

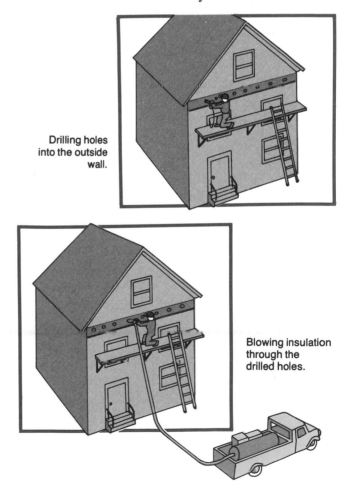

Drilling holes into the outside wall.

Blowing insulation through the drilled holes.

ferent forms (number of square feet per bag or number of bags per 1,000 square feet), so you may have to do some simple arithmetic to interpret the number correctly. Knowing this and the area of the walls to be insulated, you should be able to figure out about how many bags should be installed to give you the desired R-Value.

This number should be agreed on between you and the contractor before the job is begun. While the job is in progress be sure the correct amount is being used. There's nothing wrong with having the contractor save the empty bags so you can count them. Four or five bags more or less than the amount you agreed on is an acceptable difference from the estimate.

Some houses have structural brick or masonry walls without a wooden frame behind. Insulating this type of wall is more complicated than frame walls but may be worthwhile if there is no insulation already there. Call a contractor to get an estimate and find out what's involved.

If you are adding a room or have unfinished walls, the job of insulating them is relatively simple. If stud spacing is standard (16 inches, center to center), push blankets or batts into the space between the studs until they touch the sheathing or siding. Be sure to place them so that the vapor barrier faces inward. Fit flanges tightly against the sides of the studs and begin sta-

pling at the top with a heavy-duty stapler. Space staples about 6 to 12 inches apart. To fill a stud space that is less than standard, cut the insulation lengthwise about an inch wider than the space and then staple normally.

To help prevent condensation in insulated walls, seal any openings that could afford a path to moisture, especially around the window and door frames. Painting the interior walls with a low-permeability paint, such as high-gloss enamel, will also help in this respect. Discuss this matter with a paint dealer before purchasing paint.

If you live in a climate where your heating bills are big enough to be a major hassle, it's a good idea to insulate the underside of your house. It won't save much on air conditioning, but it certainly will save on heating expenses.

If your house (or part of it) sits on top of a crawl space that can be tightly sealed off from the outside air in the winter, the cheapest and best place to insulate is around the outside walls and on the ground inside the space. This should be considered only if there is no existing insulation and if the crawl space is big enough to allow plenty of room to do the work.

First cover the earth inside the crawl space with a layer of 6-mil polyethylene plastic, sealing it to the walls and at seams with 2-inch-wide duct tape or masking tape.

Insulating a new wall.

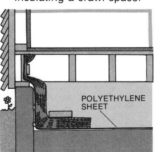

Insulating a crawl space.

POLYETHYLENE SHEET

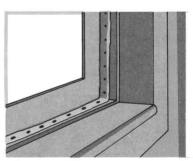

Seal all openings around windows and door frames.

Install batt or blanket insulation (R-11) around the walls of the crawl space, fastening it to the sills by nailing through ¼ × 1½-inch strips of lattice. Cut the insulation long enough to allow it to overlap the floor by 2 feet. When all the insulation is in place, secure it by laying 2×4s along the wall-floor bend. Force insulation against the header joists and the end joists to insure a good weather seal.

Even with a plastic vapor barrier on the floor, the air in the crawl space will be too damp if fresh air doesn't get in. This will mean that the new insulation will be wet and won't keep the house as warm. It will also mean that wooden framing members will be wet, and they'll rot. Proper ventilation will prevent both of these problems.

If the crawl space is part of the forced-air heating system, seal it as tightly as possible—the air moving through it from the furnace is enough ventilation in winter. If the crawl space has vents, keep them shut in winter, open in summer. If there are no vents, run the blower on the furnace three or four times during the summer to keep the air in the crawl space from getting too damp, preventing wetting the insulation.

All other crawl spaces should have vents that can be opened in summer to clear out the damp air and closed very tightly in winter to make the most of your new insulation. A word of caution: Your furnace may get its combustion air from the crawl space. If so, some of the vents should be left open year-round. Check with your fuel oil dealer or gas utility if you are not sure.

Insulating crawl spaces should not be done if you live in Alaska, Minnesota, or northern Maine. The extreme frost penetration in these areas can cause heaving of the foundation if the insulation method described here is used. Residents of these areas should contact local building code officials or government agencies for advice.

Insulating the floor of your house is a

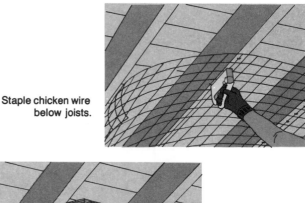

Staple chicken wire below joists.

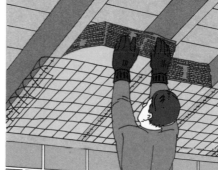

Slide batts or blankets on top of the wire.

good idea if you have a crawl space that you can't seal off in winter, or if you have a garage, porch, or other cold unheated space with heated rooms above it. Install batts or blankets, preferably with foil facing, of R-11 rating between the floor joists. Staple wire mesh or chicken wire to the bottom of the joists, and slide the batts or blankets in on top of the wire, leaving an air space between the vapor barrier and the floor.

Check your floor joist spacing—this method will work best with standard 16- or 24-inch joist spacing. If you have irregular spacing there will be more cutting and fitting and some waste of material.

If you have a basement that you use as a living or work space and that has air outlets, radiators, or baseboard units to heat it, you may find that it will pay to add a layer of insulation to the inside of the wall. You only need to insulate the parts of the walls that are above the ground down to about 2 feet below ground level.

Check walls for dampness
from the ground outside.

Seal cracks with epoxy
patching compound.

Before insulating, check to see whether moisture is coming through the walls from the ground outside. If it is and your walls are damp, eliminate the cause of dampness to prevent the insulation you're about to install from becoming wet and ineffective.

If the dampness is caused by water seeping through cracks in the foundation walls, seal these cracks with an epoxy patching compound, available at most hardware stores. Follow manufacturer's directions for application. If seepage covers a large area, it may indicate a more serious problem of excessive water pressure against the outside of the foundation. The solution here may involve digging down outside the foundation and applying bituminous coatings to the outside of the walls, and laying drain tiles to carry ground water to a drywell or other location away from the house. It's hard labor that you will probably want to leave to an experienced contractor.

Install a framework of 2×3 studs along the walls to be insulated. The bottom plate of the frame should be nailed to the floor with concrete nails, and the top plate nailed to the joists above. Studs should be placed 16 or 24 inches apart between the top and bottom plates.

Batt or blanket insulation rated R-7 should be cut into sections long enough to extend from the top plate to about 2 feet below the ground line. Staple the sections

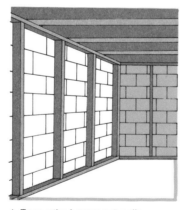

1. Frame the basement walls.

2. Staple insulation to studs.

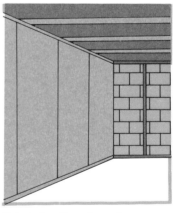

3. Install wallboard over framing.

into place between the studs, with the vapor barrier toward the living space. Only in very cold northern climates will there be added benefits by installing the insulation the full height of the wall.

To finish the basement, install wallboard or paneling over the new insulation and furring. Add molding at the top plate and baseboard at the bottom for a basement that's fit for a king—a comfortable king at that!

As in insulating a crawl space, residents of Alaska, Minnesota, and northern Maine should check local practices before insulating basement walls.

In recent years the family of insulation products has grown to include merchandise for such specialized requirements as sound control, window sealing, and insulating suspended ceilings. Insulation can now be purchased for any purpose, leaving the homeowner no excuse for not wrapping his home with a warm blanket of insulation and saving on fuel bills at the same time.

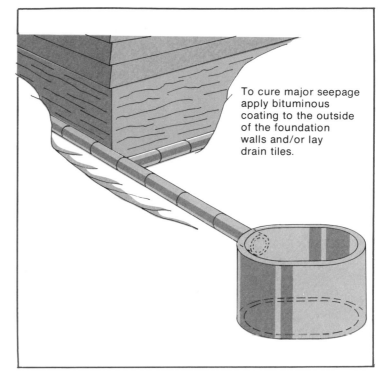

To cure major seepage apply bituminous coating to the outside of the foundation walls and/or lay drain tiles.

WEATHERSTRIPPING AND CALKING

Calk around windows.

Calk around faucets.

Calk around chimney.

Calk between house and porch.

In a well-insulated house the largest source of heat loss is air leaks, especially around windows and doors. Weatherstripping and calking of window and door frames not only reduces the heat loss in winter and heat gain in summer, but reduces uncomfortable drafts as well.

Weatherstripping and calking a home are generally worthwhile and economical projects in all climates. The average homeowner can seal his home against the elements for a minimal cost and almost without working up a sweat. Materials are available at most hardware stores.

Calking should be applied wherever two different materials or parts of the house meet. The best way to approach this job is to load up the calking gun and make a thorough examination of the outside of the house, looking for any areas where outside air could leak in.

Common problem areas are around windows and doors, where water faucets, pipes, or wires penetrate the outside house surface, around the chimney, and between the main body of the house and porches.

Calking compound is available in a variety of types and prices to fit anyone's budget. Decide on the type best suited for your needs and the easiest to work with.

Oil- or resin-base calk is readily available and will bond to most surfaces, including wood, masonry, and metal. This type is not the most durable, but it costs the least.

Latex, butyl, or polyvinyl-based calk is also readily available and will bond to most surfaces. It is more durable but more expensive than oil- or resin-based calk.

Elastomeric calks are the most durable and also the most expensive. These include silicones, polysulfides, and polyurethanes. The instructions provided on the labels should be followed.

To fill extra-wide cracks or as a backup for elastomeric calks, use oakum, calking cotton, sponge rubber, or glass fiber.

Lead-based calk is not recommended, because it is toxic. Many states prohibit its use.

Calking a house usually requires the use of a ladder to do the job right. Be sure you use it safely. Carry the calking gun in a sling

Carry calking gun in a sling when climbing (left) and don't overreach (right).

so that you can use both hands climbing the ladder, and don't try to reach for that extra little bit—get down and move the ladder.

Estimating the number of cartridges of calking compound required is difficult, since the number will vary greatly with the size of the cracks to be filled. If possible, it's best to start with a half dozen cartridges and then purchase more as the job continues and you need more.

Before applying calking compound, clean the area to be sealed of paint build-up, dirt, or deteriorated calk, using solvent and a putty knife or other scraping tool.

Drawing a good bead of calk with the gun will take a little practice. First attempts may be a bit messy, but don't get discouraged. Make sure the bead overlaps both sides for a tight seal. Sometimes a wide bead is necessary to do the job right.

Fill extra-wide cracks like those at the sills (where the house meets the foundation) with oakum, glass fiber insulation strips, or similar material, then finish the job with calk.

Calking compound also comes in rope form. This type is forced into cracks with the fingers and is especially good for extra long cracks.

Weatherstripping is another project the homeowner can do to keep the winter chill from entering his domain and to ease high energy costs. A minimum of tools, skills, and cash is required to properly seal doors and windows in a home.

Three types of weatherstripping are commonly used to seal windows. All are readily available at hardware stores or building supply outlets.

Thin spring metal is installed in the channel of a window so that it is virtually invisible when installed. Although somewhat difficult to install, it is very durable.

Rolled vinyl weatherstripping is available with or without a metal backing. It is visible when installed. This type is durable and easy to install.

Foam rubber with adhesive backing is the easiest of all to install, but it breaks down and wears rather quickly. It is not as effective a sealer as metal strips or rolled vinyl and should never be used where friction occurs.

Weatherstripping is purchased either by the running foot or in kit form for each window. In either case, measurements of all windows must be taken to find the total length of weatherstripping needed for the

Various kinds of weatherstripping.

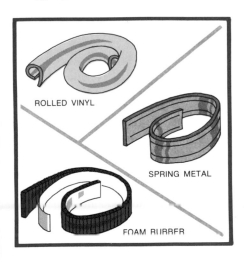

ROLLED VINYL

SPRING METAL

FOAM RUBBER

Clean area before calking.

Fill wide cracks before calking.

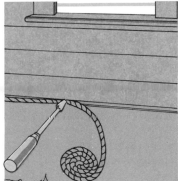

Home Repairs Made Easy • Weatherstripping and Calking

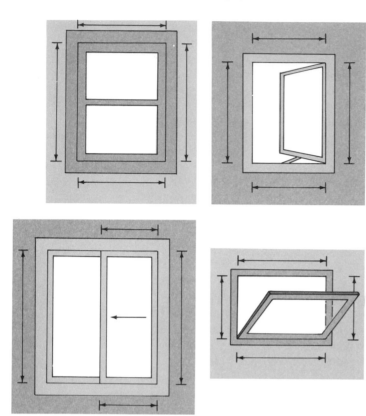

Measuring windows for weatherstripping: double-hung window (top left), casement window (top right), hopper- or awning window (above right), sliding window (above left).

Then attach a strip the full width of the window to the upper sash bottom rail. Countersink the nails slightly so they won't catch on the lower sash top rail.

Nail vinyl strips on double-hung windows so that when the window closes the vinyl will seal any possible air leaks. A sliding window is much the same and can be treated as a double-hung window turned on its side. Casement and tilting windows should be weatherstripped with the vinyl nailed to the window casing so that, as the window shuts, it compresses the roll.

Install adhesive-backed foam, on all types of windows, only where there is no friction. On double-hung windows, this is

1. Installing spring metal in side channels.

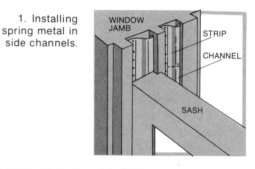

2. Installing spring metal on top and bottom of sash.

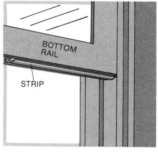

3. Installing spring metal between sash.

job. Measure the total distance around the edges of the moving parts of each window to be sealed. Be sure to allow for waste. If a window kit is purchased, be sure the kit is intended for the correct type and size of the window.

Thin spring metal is installed by moving the sash to the open position and sliding a strip in between the sash and the channel. It is then tacked in place into the window casing. Do not cover the pulleys in the upper channel.

Strips should also be installed the full width of the sash on the bottom of the lower sash bottom rail and the top of the upper sash top rail.

only on the bottom and top rails. Other types of windows can use foam strips in other places.

You can weatherstrip your doors even if you're not an experienced handyman. There are several types of weatherstripping for doors, each with its own level of effectiveness. Select the type best suited for your needs.

Foam rubber with either an adhesive or a wood backing can be purchased for the sides and top of a door. Both types are installed on the door jamb to prevent air leaks when the door is closed. They are easy to install, but not very durable.

Rolled vinyl with an aluminum backing is installed much the same as foam to reduce drafts. It is also very easy to install and is much more durable than foam.

The third type of weatherstripping designed for use on the sides and top of a door is spring metal. This is the best type for do-it-yourselfers to use when sealing doors. It is easy to install and extremely durable. After installation in the door jamb, a screwdriver should be used to lift the outer edge for a positive seal.

Accomplished handymen and carpenters can install fitted interlocking channels, the best weather seal available for doors. This technique for sealing doors uses two metal channels, called J-Strips, that interlock when the door is closed, all but eliminating air leaks around the door.

Door sweeps that fit either on the outside or inside of the door are easy to install and are useful for flat thresholds. A drawback is that the sweep will drag on the carpet or rug when the door is opened or closed. Check the supplied instructions for installation.

If you feel courageous enough to remove the door, door shoes can be installed. These are useful for wooden thresholds that are not worn, and they are very durable. Remove the door by knocking out the hinge pins with a hammer and screwdriver. If the

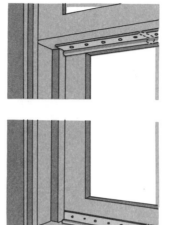

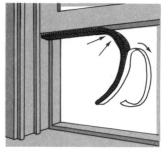

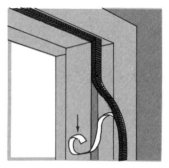

Installing adhesive-backed foam rubber.

Installing vinyl strips on double-hung window.

Installing foam rubber weatherstripping on door jamb (right)

Installing rolled vinyl weatherstripping on door (below).

Installing interlocking channels on a door (below right).

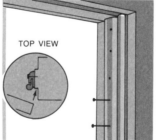

TOP VIEW

TOP VIEW

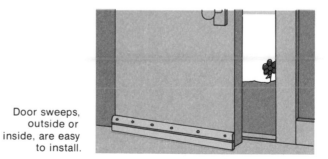

Door sweeps, outside or inside, are easy to install.

1. Knock out hinge pins.

2. Unscrew hinges.

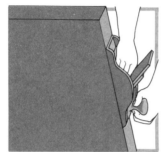

3. Plane bottom of door.

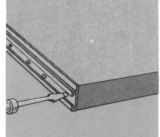

4. Screw on door shoe.

pins are jammed and can't be removed, unscrew the hinges from the door jamb to take off the door. The shoe is installed by removing a small amount of wood from the bottom of the door with a plane, then screwing the shoe into place.

A vinyl bulb threshold to seal the bottom of the door also requires the removal of the door. If there is no threshold, or the wooden one is worn, this is the best kind to use. A vinyl bulb, similar to the door shoe, is installed on the threshold, and the bottom of the door is beveled with a plane to seal against the vinyl with the door shut. The vinyl will eventually wear out but can be replaced.

An interlocking threshold much like the metal channels for the sides and top of a door can be purchased. Although this type is an exceptionally good weather seal, it is very difficult to install, and the job should be done only by a skilled carpenter.

Installing a vinyl threshold after having removed door (right).

An interlocking threshold is a very good weather seal (far right).

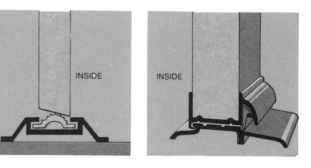

INSTALLING STORM SASH

Windows and doors can be big energy wasters. This is because doors and windows that open have cracks all around them allowing air to pass through the joints and around window and door frames if they are not tightly sealed. Another reason is that glass itself is a highly heat-conductive material.

Storm windows and doors cut heat loss (or heat gain) at these points about in half. Insulating glass (two panes of glass sealed together at the edges) has approximately the same effect. Triple glazing (insulating glass plus a storm window) is even more effective and often is used in extremely cold climates.

According to the National Bureau of Standards, an investment in storm windows will pay for itself in a decade, including interest costs at 6 percent, and thereafter return an annual dividend of 13 percent. This is based on a climate where winter temperatures are similar to those of Washington, D.C. In regions of the country where snow lies on the ground all winter, payback will occur in less than 7 years, the NBS says. And with fuel costs rising rapidly, this time period will shrink considerably.

There are basically three kinds of storm windows, each providing about the same effectiveness. The more expensive ones are more attractive and convenient, but not more effective.

Plastic sheeting, available in hardware stores, makes effective storm sash. At a cost of only about 50 cents per window, no home located in a cold region should go without at least this type of storm sash. Because of the low price, this type is also ideal for people who rent homes.

Measure the width of your larger windows to determine the width of the plastic rolls to buy. Measure the length of your windows to see how many linear feet and therefore how many rolls or the kit size you need to buy.

Attach to the inside or outside of the frame so that the plastic will block airflow that leaks around the movable parts of the window. If you attach the plastic to the outside, use ¼ × 1¼-inch wood slats and tacks around the edges. If you decide to

Single-pane storm windows built to your specification.

Triple-track combination storm window for double-hung windows.

Insulating glass prevents heat loss or gain (right).

Plastic sheeting attached to the outside of the window (center).

Plastic sheeting attached to the inside of the window (far right).

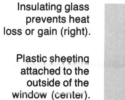

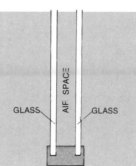

GLASS   AIR SPACE   GLASS

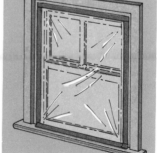

Drill drainage holes, if your units don't have them already.

attach it to the inside, masking tape will work.

Inside installation is easier and provides greater protection to the plastic. Outside installation is more difficult, especially on a two-story house, and the plastic is more likely to be damaged by the elements.

Be sure to install tightly and securely, and remove all excess. Besides looking better, a clean installation will make the plastic less susceptible to deterioration during the course of the winter.

Storm window suppliers will build single-pane aluminum storm windows to your measurements that you can install yourself. Cost is about $10 to $20 per window. This type of storm sash is taken down at the end of winter.

Corner joints should be strong and airtight.

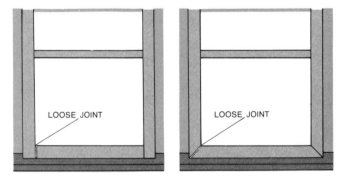

LOOSE JOINT   LOOSE JOINT

Determine how you want the windows to fit in the frame. Your measurements will be the outside measurements of the storm window. Be as accurate as possible, then allow ⅛ inch along each edge for clearance. You'll be responsible for any errors in measurement, so do a good job.

When the windows are delivered, check the actual size against your order. A poor window fit will mean possible air leakage.

Install the windows and fix in place with movable clips so that you can take them down easily. The side of the aluminum frame that touches the window frame should have a permanently installed weatherstrip or gasket to seal the crack between the window and the single-pane storm window frames.

Single-pane storm windows aren't as expensive as the double-track or triple-track combination windows. The disadvantage of the single-pane windows is that they can't be opened easily once they are installed.

A mill finish (plain aluminum) will oxidize quickly and degrade appearance. Windows with an anodized or baked enamel finish look better.

Triple-track combination (windows and screen) storm windows are designed for installation over double-hung windows only. They cost about $30 to $45 per window. They are permanently installed and can be opened any time with a screen slid into place for ventilation.

Double-track combination units are also available at a lower cost. Both kinds are sold almost everywhere, and can be bought with or without the cost of installation.

You can save a few dollars (10 to 15 percent) by installing the windows yourself, but in most cases it is better to have the supplier install the windows for you, even though it costs a bit more.

When the windows are installed, make sure that both the window sashes and screen sash move smoothly and seal tightly when closed. Poor installation can cause misalignment.

Be sure there is a tightly calked seal around the edge of the storm window. Leaks can hurt the performance of storm windows considerably.

Most combination units come with two or three small holes (or other types of vents) drilled through the frame where it meets the window sill. This is to keep winter condensation from collecting on the sill and causing rot. Keep these holes clear, or drill them yourself if your units don't already have them.

The quality of construction affects the strength and performance of storm windows. Corners are a good place to check construction. They should be strong and airtight. Normally, overlapped corner joints are better than mitered. If you can see through the joints, they will leak air.

Storm windows are supposed to reduce air leakage around windows. The depth of the metal grooves (sash tracks) at the sides of the window and the weatherstripping quality make a big difference in how well storm windows can do this. Compare several types before deciding.

Combination (windows and screen) storm doors are designed for installation over exterior doors. They are sold just about everywhere, with or without the cost of installation. In most cases, it is easier to have the supplier install the doors.

Before the installer leaves, be sure the doors operate smoothly and close tightly. Check for cracks around the jamb, and make sure the seal is as airtight as possible. Also, remove and replace the exchangeable panels (window and screen) to make sure they fit properly and with a weathertight seal.

The same rules apply to judging the quality of storm doors as apply to storm windows. Corner joints, weatherstripping, and hardware quality should be checked.

Storm doors of wood or steel can also be purchased within the same price range as the aluminum variety. They have the same quality differences and should be similarly evaluated. The choice between doors of similar quality but different materials is primarily up to your own taste.

MAKING ROOF REPAIRS

When a leak develops, it is important that repairs be made without unnecessary delay. If repairs are neglected over a long period, interior plaster may crack, loosen, and eventually fall. Drywall becomes soggy and crumbly, and the whole roof structure below the shingling may rot. Even small leaks often cause discoloration of wall coverings and stains on finished floors. Although it may not be possible to apply a new roof or to do extensive repair work, the do-it-yourselfer may be able to patch leaky spots until permanent repairs can be made or the old roof can be replaced.

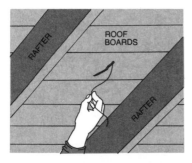

1. Locate hole from beneath and mark with wire.

2. Coat leak with asphalt.

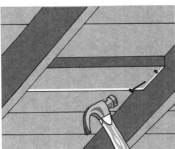

3. Nail board beneath leak.

It is often difficult to locate the point of leakage from a wet spot on the ceiling, especially if the underside of the roof is not easily accessible, because water may flow along the roof boards or rafters before dripping down. It is equally difficult to locate a hole from the top of the roof. If the attic has no ceiling, however, most holes may be found readily from the inside of the attic on a bright day. Even small holes will be plainly visible, and their location can be marked by pushing wires through to the surface.

You can make a temporary repair from underneath to hold until you can do the job properly from above. Coat the leaking area with asphalt roofing cement. Cut a 1 x 6 or similar board to fit between the rafters, and toenail it in place beneath the asphalt patch.

When making repairs on the roof, wear sneakers or rubber-soled work shoes. Avoid unnecessary walking on the roof, as this can damage the surface.

Make sure your ladder is sound before using it. Place the ladder flat on the ground and walk along the rungs from one end to the other to make sure they are all solid. Check the hooks on an extension ladder to make sure they engage fully (see p. 118).

To raise a long ladder, set its foot against a wall. Starting at the opposite end, lift it over your head and walk it, rung by rung, until it is upright. Then move the foot away from the wall one-quarter of the height the ladder is to reach. Make sure that the ladder rests on a firm footing. If necessary, place it on a secure board or boards to make the footing level (see p. 119).

Don't attempt to work on a steep roof without some additional support. One way to provide this is with a second ladder (not the one you use to get up to the roof). Nail or screw a piece of 2 x 4 to each leg of the ladder, following the angle of the roof. Nail or screw braces of 1-inch lumber or ¾-inch

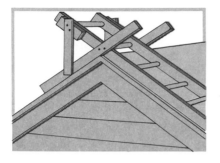 

Nail braces to end of ladder and hook over roof ridge (far left).

Ladder held by rope (left).

plywood across the joint (you will have to back these up with blocks of 2 x 4 affixed firmly to the ladder legs). Then "hook" the braced end of the ladder over the peak of the roof.

Another means of support is a strong rope tied to a ladder. Of course it must be firmly anchored or it will be worse than worthless. Tie one end to the top of a flat ladder laid across the roof and secure the other end to a stout tree or other support.

●

In North America, where the weather ranges from tropical to arctic, many types of roofing are used. Most of the United States and Canada, however, lie in the temperate zone, and roofs are very similar in all but the extreme hot and cold zones of these countries. In practical terms, this means that most roofs are of peaked wood trusses, or rafters, covered by either plywood or wood sheathing and finished with a layer of mineral-surfaced asphalt shingles. There are other types, of course, wood shingles, slate, tile, and asbestos-cement being fairly common. Other materials such as metal, metal-bound gypsum, reinforced concrete, or concrete planks are sometimes used mostly on flat roofs.

Roofings of various types may be and frequently are applied over old roofs, but it is usually advisable to remove the old roofing before applying an entirely new roof—particularly if one roof has already been

applied over the original. The homeowner then has the opportunity to have defective or rotted sheathing replaced, thus providing a smoother roof deck with opportunity for better nailing.

Sometimes the do-it-yourselfer prefers to leave roofing repairs to the professional. Unless the roof is low or flat, there is certainly some danger in climbing around on it. Even so, it pays to know something about roofing—if only to keep an eye on the roofer and his bill.

Built-up roofing is used when the roof is flat or has a very low pitch. It consists of several layers of bituminous-impregnated felt, lapped and cemented together with a bitumen that is usually heated. Fine gravel or slag is then spread over the top layer to provide a weathering surface. If properly applied, built-up roofings should not require major repairs for a long time.

The application of built-up roofing is a specialized operation that requires particular experience and special equipment. It is therefore advisable to employ an experienced roofing concern to lay or repair this type of roofing.

Slate is a rigid roof material that gives good service and long life with very little need for repair. Though originally more costly, it is usually worth the extra expense. Slate is dense, nonporous rock used on roofs to produce a good-looking, highly durable covering. Only responsible and experienced slate roofers should be engaged to lay such a roof.

ASPHALT ROOFINGS

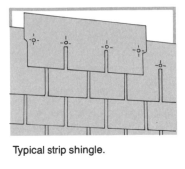

Typical strip shingle.

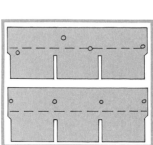

Improper shingle nailing.

Asphalt-prepared roofings are manufactured in three forms: mineral-surfaced shingles, mineral-surfaced roll roofing, and smooth-surfaced roll roofing. Mineral-surfaced asphalt shingles and roll roofing are composed of roofing felt, made of organic fibers saturated and coated on both sides with asphalt, then surfaced with mineral granules on the side exposed to the weather. The other side may be dusted with mica or talc. Smooth-faced roll roofing is dusted on both sides with fine mineral matter such as mica, talc, or fine sand and is usually lighter in weight than mineral-surfaced roll roofing. Mineral-surfaced asphalt shingles and roll roofing are usually available in a variety of colors; smooth-surfaced roll roofing is usually black or gray.

Mineral-surfaced asphalt shingles are made in strips of two to four (usually three) units or tabs joined together, as well as in the form of individual shingles. When laid, strip shingles furnish virtually the same pattern as individual shingles, and they have become the standard method of application today. Most shingles come in varying sizes and patterns.

The principal cause of damage to asphalt shingle roofs is the action of strong winds on shingles that have been nailed too close to the upper edges. Most shingles today are impregnated on the edges with a material that softens in the sun and seals the edges to the shingles below.

The shingles most likely to be affected by winds are those in the four to five courses near the ridge or in the area extending about 5 feet from the sloping area at the edge or rake of the roof. To fasten loose shingles correctly, use a putty knife or trowel to place a small quantity of asphalt cement under the center of each tab about

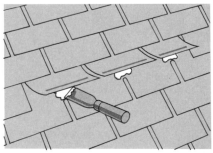

Force cement under shingle tabs.

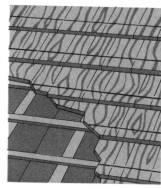

Mark wood shingles for nailing surfaces.

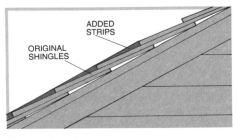

Nail beveled strips for uniform surface at the base of the old shingle.

Home Repairs Made Easy

one inch from the lower edge. Press the shingle down firmly after application. Too much cement will prevent the tab from lying flat. Also, be careful not to seal the lower edge completely.

Asphalt shingles are frequently applied over old wood shingles or other roofing, provided that the surface of the old covering is in reasonably good condition. If not, the old covering should be removed. A wood shingle roof is laid over intermittent wood strips, so be sure to mark the location of the strips to make sure that the new nails will strike a solid surface below. All defective or missing shingles should be replaced, and beveled strips ⅜ inch x 4 inches (the same thickness as the old wood shingles) should be nailed at the base of the old shingles to assure a uniform surface.

If the old covering is completely removed, the roof deck should be made smooth and solid, and all loose material should be swept off. Any defects in the sheathing or plywood should be corrected, and, if the old material is in very bad shape, the entire surface should be recovered with exterior plywood to form a solid new underlayment.

Mineral-surfaced roll roofings are made in various colors, both solid and blended. The mineral granules on the surface protect the asphalt coatings from the weather and increase the fire-resistant qualities of the roofing. The manufacturer's directions should be followed with respect to storing, handling, and temperatures at which roll roofing should be laid.

Minor damage to mineral-surfaced roll roofing such as nail holes or small breaks may be repaired by applying asphalt cement. To repair large breaks, the horizontal seam below the break should be opened and a strip of roofing of the type originally used slipped in under the break, allowing the strip to extend at least 6 inches beyond the break on either side. The lower edge

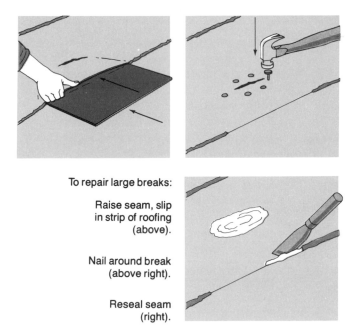

To repair large breaks:

Raise seam, slip in strip of roofing (above).

Nail around break (above right).

Reseal seam (right).

should be flush with the horizontal exposed edge. Asphalt cement should be applied liberally on the upper surface of the repair strip before inserting it. After the strip has been inserted, press the edges of the roofing down firmly and nail securely with rustproof nails. Space the nails 2 inches apart about ¾ inch from the edge of the break. Apply asphalt cement to the horizontal seam and renail; cement over nails.

Leaks at the seams of roll roofing are caused principally by inadequate nailing and cementing of the roofing, by loose

Cut buckled areas of roll roofing.

Pull loose nail, fill hole before recoating.

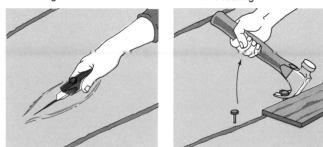

nails, and by buckling of the roofing at the seams. To repair leaky seams, sweep out the seams to remove accumulated dust and dirt, cut all buckles that terminate at the seams, and insert a strip of roofing in the same manner as for larger breaks.

Roll roofing may be applied over old wood shingles or other roofing materials, providing that the surface of the old covering is in reasonably good condition and that it has been made smooth in the same manner as for mineral-surfaced asphalt shingles. Otherwise, the worn roofing should be removed and the roof deck prepared in the same manner as for the application of asphalt shingles. Follow the directions supplied by the manufacturer.

Although smooth-surfaced roll roofings were fairly common at one time, their use for surfacing is not recommended today. Asphalt shingles are the preferred treatment, and mineral-covered roll roofing is a less expensive second choice. Smooth-surfaced asphalt does not weather as well because the coatings are not protected from the action of sunlight by mineral granules. If you already have such a roof, however,

you should know how to maintain it. Also, these roofings can be used for outbuildings and temporary structures at a a lower cost than the others. Maintenance instructions, plus application materials, usually come with each package of roll roofing.

To achieve the best service, this roofing material should be recoated at regular intervals with bituminous roof coating. Seams that have opened should be recemented and any small holes in the covering filled with asphalt cement. Loose nails should be pulled, the resulting holes sealed with asphalt cement, and new nails driven.

Coating materials are usually composed of an asphaltic base and mineral fiber, thinned to heavy brushing consistency with a volatile solvent. Fatty acid pitch-base coatings are also available. Follow the directions of the manufacturer.

Smooth-surfaced roll roofing may be applied over other roofing, provided that the surface of the old covering is not too badly deteriorated. When this type of roofing has to be removed, it is suggested in most cases that mineral-coated roofing be applied for longer, less maintenance-prone wear.

TILE ROOFINGS

The most commonly used roofing tile consists of molded hard-burned shale or mixtures of shale and clay, but metal tile is also available. Good clay tile is hard, fairly dense, and durable and may be obtained in a variety of shapes and textures. Most roofing tile of clay is unglazed, although glazed tile is sometimes used in homes.

Clay tile roofings that have been properly manufactured and applied require very little maintenance. If a tile is broken, it should be removed with a nail ripper and replaced with a new tile of the same color as the original set in roofing cement.

Clay tile can be applied over an old roof

covering provided that the covering is in reasonably good condition. The roof framing should be examined to determine whether or not the additional weight of the tile can be carried safely and, if not, additional framing or bracing should be added. A competent contractor is best consulted at this stage. Where the old roofing is left in place, all defective portions should be repaired and the surface made as smooth and solid as possible. If the old roof covering is too worn or damaged to provide a proper laying surface for the new tile, it should be removed and the sheathing or roof decking made smooth and solid.

WOOD SHINGLE AND
ASBESTOS-CEMENT SHINGLE ROOFINGS

Factors that influence the service life of wood-shingle roofs are pitch and exposure of the roof, durability of the wood in the shingles (red cedar is best), preservative treatment of the shingles, and kind of nails used in fastening.

Wood shingles are usually manufactured in lengths of 16, 18, and 24 inches and in random widths varying from 2½ to 14 inches. On roofs of average pitch, shingles should be laid with about one-fourth of their length exposed. On steeper pitches, the exposure should not exceed one-third the length of the shingle.

On new roofs, wood shingles are frequently laid on open sheathing or slats to permit ventilating the underside. An open deck not only costs less but permits the shingles to dry quickly. The slats are usually 1 x 4-inch boards, spaced to accommodate the nailing of the shingles.

Hot-dipped zinc-coated nails of the proper size and shape are generally recommended for fastening wood shingles, although blued-steel nails may also be used. Longer nails are required for reroofing over old covering than for new construction.

Wood shingles that are cracked do not

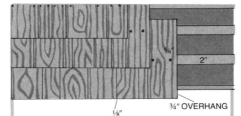

1. Place copper beneath cracked shingle.

2. Cut off first row of old shingles.

3. Nail 1 x 4 in the space.

4. Space new shingles 1/8-inch apart and nail them down.

2″

¾″ OVERHANG

⅛″

5. Use chalk line to keep shingles straight.

Slats for wood shingles.

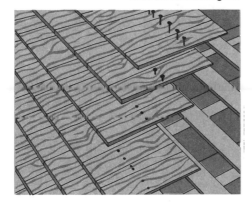

necessarily cause leaks unless the courses are not lined up properly, in which case they may admit moisture to the nail heads in the course below and cause nail failure. To stop the leak, a piece of tin or copper may be placed under the cracked shingle.

Wood shingles may be applied to old roofs as well as new. If the old roofing is in reasonably good condition, it need not be removed. Before applying the new shingles, all warped or deteriorated shingles should be tightly nailed or replaced. To finish the edges of the roofing, the exposed portion of the first row of old shingles along the eaves should be cut off with a sharp roofer's hatchet or saw, and a 1 x 4 wood strip nailed in the space with the outer edge flush with the eave line. Treat the edges along the gable ends in a similar manner. New shingles should be spaced approximately ⅛ inch apart to allow for expansion in wet weather. They should project between ½ and ¾ inch beyond the edge of the eaves. Each shingle should be fastened with at least two nails placed about ⅝ inch from the edges and about 2 inches under the overlap of the course above; the nails must penetrate the slats to which the original shingles are nailed. The lines of the shingles may be kept parallel to the eaves and ridges by checking the course with a chalk line.

If it becomes necessary to remove the old roofing, the deck should be prepared in the same manner as for a new roof. New shingles should be doubled at the eaves and should project from ½ to ¾ inch beyond the eaves. Courses should be properly aligned and shingles spaced and nailed as above.

●

Asbestos-cement shingles are manufactured from portland cement (see p. 219) and asbestos fiber formed in molds under high pressure. The finished product is hard, fairly tough, and durable. Asbestos-cement shingles are available in a variety of colors and textures and may be obtained in rectangular, square, and hexagonal shapes, in single or multiple units.

Asbestos-cement shingles usually require little maintenance. Occasionally, however, a shingle may become broken and need replacement. The broken shingle should be removed by cutting or drawing out the old nails with a ripper (as with slate or tile roofing). A new shingle, similar to the old one, is then inserted. The new shingle should be fastened by nailing through the vertical joint between the shingles in the overlying course approximately 2 inches below the butt-end of the shingle in the second course above. A piece of sheet copper about 3 x 8 inches should be inserted over the nail head and should extend about 2 inches under the course above. The metal should be bent slightly before insertion to hold it firmly in place.

Asbestos-cement shingles may be applied over an old roof covering if the roof is in reasonably good condition. The framing should be inspected and, if necessary, reinforced to carry the additional weight of the new shingles safely. If the new roofing is to be laid over old wood shingles, loose shingles should be securely nailed. Warped, split, or decayed shingles should be replaced.

If the old roofing is in poor condition, it may be more economical to remove it entirely than to make the repairs necessary to provide a sound, smooth surface for the new roofing. If the old roofing is removed, loose sheathing boards should be securely nailed and defective material replaced. If the sheathing is in very bad shape, perhaps it would pay to recover the entire surface with exterior plywood.

ROOF DRAINAGE

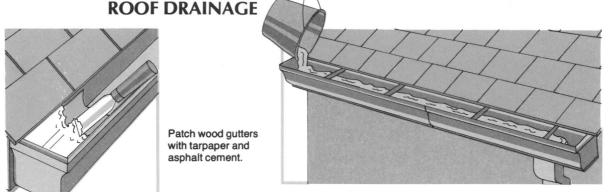

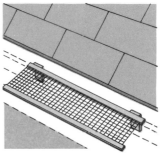

Patch wood gutters with tarpaper and asphalt cement.

Check gutter pitch with a pail of water.

Every house, regardless of what type of roofing material is employed, should be equipped with some method of carrying off and effectively dispensing with the large volumes of rainwater that can otherwise create a number of structural problems. Without such a system, water can seep into the earth around the building and cause wet basements, wood decay, peeling paint, and even termite damage. A typical rainfall drainage system includes gutters, downspouts, and leaders to bring the water to the ground and a storm sewer or drywell to absorb the water.

Most gutters today are made from galvanized steel, copper, or aluminum, although wood gutters can still be found on many older structures. In recent years, fiberglass drainage systems have been introduced, and their beneficial features (relatively light weight, ease of installation, etc.) are making them more and more attractive to home builders and renovators.

Metal gutters should be painted to avoid the corrosive, oxidizing actions of the weather. Galvanized gutters may otherwise rust once the thin zinc coating wears away, and unpainted copper gutters will stain adjoining surfaces. A thin coating of roofing cement on the inside of galvanized steel gutters will help prevent rusting.

Wood gutters should be treated with wood preservatives and then coated with exterior paint. Lining the inside of these

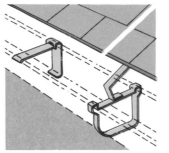

Gutter hanger.

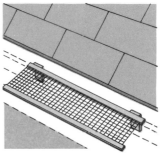

Gutter guard.

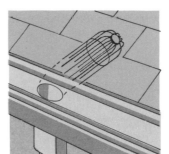

Downspout strainer.

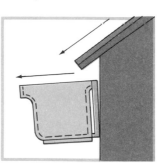

Gutters should slant outward.

Electric heating cable for areas where ice and snow accumulation is a problem.

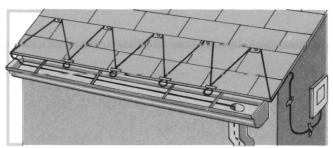

gutters with roofing cement will further prevent decay. Small holes in wood gutters can be patched with pieces of tarpaper and asphalt cement.

Because water seeks its own level, a slight downward pitch to the drainage end of the gutter is necessary. If there is not enough pitch the water will not flow effectively to the downspout. A sagging gutter will alter the pitch and, hence, reduce the flow rate. This can cause the gutter to overflow and will hasten rusting and other corrosive actions.

One way to check gutter pitch is to pour a pail of water in the end of the gutter opposite the downspout or leader end. Make note of the areas where water accumulates — it is these areas that need modification. You may need gutter hangers (available at most hardware stores for a small price) to increase the pitch or elevate a sagging length of gutter.

Leaves and other debris can impair the efficiency of a gutter. Periodic cleaning, especially after a storm, will prevent debris from accumulating. To save yourself the time involved with these cleaning operations, you may wish to install wire gutter guards. These work in much the same way that a screen door prevents insects from coming indoors, although here the idea is to prevent leaves from entering the gutters. Downspouts should be equipped with similar screens to strain out the debris and thus prevent clogging.

In the winter months, especially in areas where heavy snowfalls are common, ice and snow may pile up in the gutters instead of harmlessly sliding off the roof. The weight of accumulated snow is often enough to pull gutters loose. To avoid problems of this sort, the outside edges of the gutters should be hung lower than the edge of the roof eaves. This allows ice to slide off without taking the gutter along. If this does not prevent the buildup, it would be wise to install electric heating cables in areas where accumulation is a problem.

DOWNSPOUTS

With a good strainer properly installed, downspouts rarely become clogged. Nonetheless, it is a good idea to flush them out once a year with a garden hose, thus forcing out small particles that could accumulate and become a clogging problem.

Many household drainage systems end with the downspout, and the water merely flows into the soil beneath it. This keeps the soil constantly damp and provides an ideal breeding ground for insects, including termites. Wood decay is accelerated by the dampness, and structural damage can occur to concrete foundations. To avoid these often costly problems, the downspout discharge should be carried a safe distance (at least 8 to 10 feet) away from the house.

This can be accomplished by digging a shallow trench of the required length (with a downgrade, of course, away from the downspout). Line the trench with clay tile, covering joints with tarpaper before backfilling. If the soil that the tile empties into is absorbent, no other efforts are required. If not, some alternate means of disposal must be found.

Never connect the drainage system to a septic tank or cesspool that handles your household sewage. Many municipalities allow rainwater runoff to flow into community sewer lines—others forbid this practice because a heavy rainfall may overflow raw sewage at the treatment plant.

If your community does not allow rain drainage into a sewer, a drywell can be constructed to handle the runoff problem. To make a simple drywell, dig a hole big enough to accommodate a large wooden barrel. Remove the top and bottom of the barrel and then place it in the hole. Fill the barrel with rocks up to approximately 5 inches from the top; cover with screening. Fill the remaining space with soil. Lead drainage tiles into the drywell.

For larger houses, or in areas where

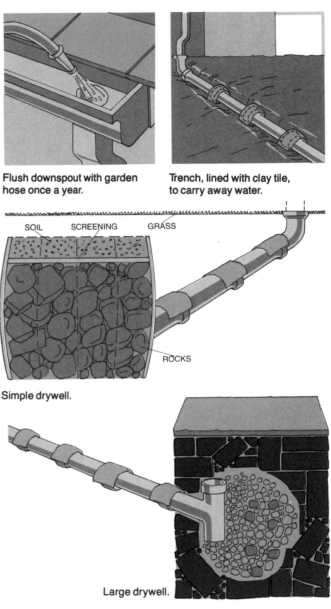

Flush downspout with garden hose once a year.

Trench, lined with clay tile, to carry away water.

SOIL SCREENING GRASS

ROCKS

Simple drywell.

Large drywell.

heavy rainfalls are the norm, bigger drywells may be necessary. These can be built in the same fashion as cesspools—large holes lined with masonry blocks laid without mortar. The tops of the wells should be covered with reinforced concrete set below the ground level.

Home Repairs Made Easy

PORCH REPAIRS

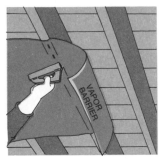

Staple vapor barrier beneath joists.

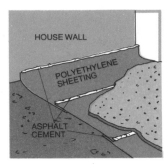

Cover ground beneath porch with sheeting.

Sagging Porch

If a porch has a major problem, it is usually manifested by sagging. This means that one or more of the structural members has deteriorated, usually because of excess moisture. The underside of a porch is much like the crawl space of a home, except that

it is not as completely enclosed and the usual moisture-preventive steps have not been taken. Use the same preventive methods on porch crawl spaces as for those under the house itself (see p. 185).

Staple a vapor barrier to the underside of the porch floor joists, after first making any necessary repairs to structural members (see below). Cover the ground beneath the porch with polyethylene sheeting or heavy felt paper, overlapping the seams and the house wall 3 or 4 inches and sealing all seams and the wall joint with asphalt cement. Then spread a 2-inch-thick layer of sand over the area.

You'll have to get in under the porch to take these measures, of course, which may mean removing latticework, or perhaps some of the masonry that forms the foundation of many porches. If you're lucky, it will be only latticework, because you may cause more problems than you solve by blasting through masonry.

Once inside, you may find some company. Rats, mice, cats, and other animals love the cozy space under a porch. So take a flashlight — and maybe a baseball bat. Check all the wood beams and joists. Some may be obviously decayed, others less obviously so. Dig a penknife into all of the structural members to see if they are in good shape or not.

Most sag problems can be cured by running new joists next to the old ones, but first you have to get the porch up to the right level. Unlike the structural members

Raise the porch flooring with a brace.

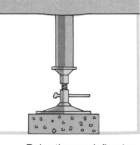

Raise the porch flooring with a jack.

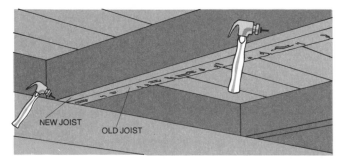

Nail new joists next to the old ones.

Nail floor boards to joists from above.

of the main part of the house, there isn't usually much weight bearing on the joists, so try to raise the flooring with a piece of 4 x 4 or 2 x 4, braced against a solid surface below. If that doesn't work, rented adjustable jacks should do the job.

Once the floor is level again, nail new joists next to the old, driving nails into both the old joists and the beams on each end. Afterwards, nail the floorboards down into the new joists from above.

If the main beams or supports of the porch are also in poor condition, you can try buttressing them as with the joists. This may not be possible, in which case you don't have much choice except to remove the porch entirely. You can build a new one if you're "into" porches, but economically it's not too wise.

Replacing Damaged Floorboards

There is no reason why porch flooring shouldn't last as long as the other wood in a home. If kept painted with a good porch-and-deck paint, and if moisture doesn't collect underneath, the boards should endure. But if this painting is neglected, and moisture problems in the crawl space are also ignored, rotted floorboards are likely.

Most porch flooring is of the tongue-and-groove variety. When replacing damaged sections, it is important not to mar the surrounding boards. The section must be cut away over the nearest joists. To replace just a board or two, mark off the section of board to be removed at an exact right angle to the joists. A framing square will help here. With an electric drill or brace and bit, make large, interconnected holes inside the lines on both ends of the damaged section. With a large wood chisel, break out the damaged portion by striking along the grain.

Remove the pieces, being particularly

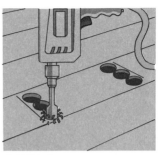
1. Mark board over joists.

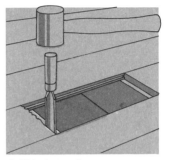
3. Chisel along grain.

5. Mark new board.

7. Fit new board into place.

2. Drill holes.

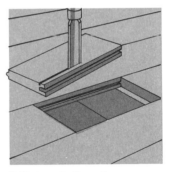
4. Chisel at ends.

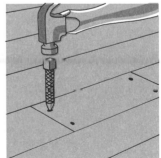
6. Remove bottom of grooved edge.

8. Nail securely.

careful not to damage the tongue or groove of the boards on either side. Chisel out the remainder of the board on the outside of the drilled holes, making sure that you cut exactly on the line. Pull out any remaining nails and clean out all debris.

Now put a new board along the removed section, and mark carefully where the damaged section was, again at an exact right angle using the framing square. Saw along the lines and chisel off the *bottom* of the grooved edge so that the board will slip into the open space. (Leave the top portion of the grooved edge.) Slip the board into place and nail through the top with aluminum or galvanized flooring or finishing nails. Use two nails on each end, set them, and cover with wood filler.

Porch Steps

If porch treads are simply worn down, the easiest way to repair them is to pry them up with a wrecking bar, turn them over, and nail them in place bottomside up.

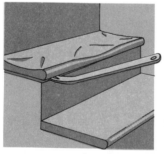

To repair porch steps:

1. Pry up worn tread (left).

2. Turn it over and nail it into place (below left).

3. Round edges of new tread with rasp and sandpaper (below).

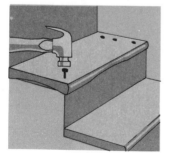
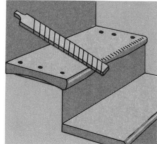

Outside steps are not ordinarily rabbeted or dadoed. Use aluminum or galvanized finishing nails, set the nails, and fill the holes with wood putty.

When new treads or risers are needed, take an old one to the lumberyard and try to find a match. If you can't match exactly, buy lumber of a greater width and rip to fit. (Today's dimensional lumber is slightly thinner than that of times past, but this need be of no concern, as the structural strength is essentially the same, or greater.) Rounded edges can be duplicated with a rasp and sandpaper. Apply wood preservative to new wood before nailing in place.

Porch Railings

Porch railings also suffer from the elements and neglect. Replacement is routine, by removing the rotted rail or baluster and replacing with a new one—if you can find a matching piece. It may be impossible to find a matching baluster for many old-fashioned railings, and a new one may have to be fabricated. You can do this yourself if you have a lathe. Otherwise, take the old one to a millworking shop and have a new one turned. The joints on exterior work are usually simple, and you should be able to knock out the deteriorated pieces with a hammer and replace them without complicated joinery by nailing through the rail into the baluster, or toenailing the baluster to the rail.

Nail through the rail into the new baluster.

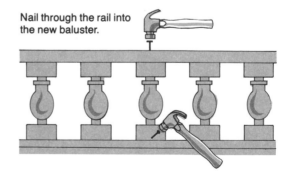

WORKING WITH CONCRETE AND BLACKTOP

Although driveways and sidewalks can be made of a variety of materials such as brick, stone, or gravel, most are composed of concrete or blacktop (asphalt). There is no such thing as a "cement" driveway. Cement is merely a small (though very important) ingredient in a concrete mix.

Concrete is made up mostly of "aggregate" (crushed stone or other inorganic matter) and sand, mixed with cement and water. In a very real sense, cement is the "glue" that holds the mixture together. When mixed with water, it is called by the accurate and descriptive phrase "cement paste."

The cement used in concrete is portland cement, a soft, fine, grayish-green powder made from pulverized limestone and other ingredients. The term portland was applied because the concrete made from it resembled Portland stone, a widely used building material of the 19th century.

The usual concrete mix for driveways and sidewalks is roughly 10 percent portland cement, 17½ percent water, and 72½ percent sand and medium-size aggregate. Concrete mixes can vary from a lean, stiff mix of 15 percent water, 7 percent portland cement, and 78 percent sand and large, coarse aggregate to a rich, wet mix of 20 percent water, 14 percent portland cement, and 66 percent sand and small, fine aggregate. The aggregates are broken down into fine, medium, and coarse. Sand is actually a very fine aggregate, as is crushed gravel. Coarse aggregate is usually crushed stone, but it can also be gravel or blast-furnace slag.

There are quite a few important steps involved in laying long-lasting concrete, and if any of them are omitted or skimped on, the result can be flaking, scaling, or some other form of deterioration. Concrete that has been carefully mixed, placed, and cured should last several lifetimes. But even when perfectly constructed, it has several natural enemies—trees, children with hammers, and frosts, to name just a few.

MINOR CONCRETE REPAIRS

The art of concrete repair has advanced greatly in the past decade or so. New repair mixes containing a vinyl or epoxy ingredient have made minor repairs quick and easy. Except for large cracks, special patching mixes are recommended rather than the standard concrete formula. Standard concrete does not adhere well to old concrete.

Patching compounds can be "feathered" to smooth edges, which makes them ideal for repairs that need a fine edge. They can also be applied on top of old concrete without elaborate preparation. Vinyl or epoxy compounds can be used to fill in small concrete sections that have settled because of poor soil preparation or frost. These formulas are also fine for filling small cracks and holes. Chipped step corners also can be fixed with this type of patch without using forms. Applications should follow the manufacturer's directions.

Feather edge of patch.   Repair step corner.

 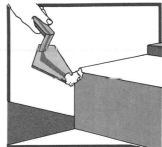

REPAIRING LARGE CRACKS AND
BADLY FLAKING CONCRETE SURFACES

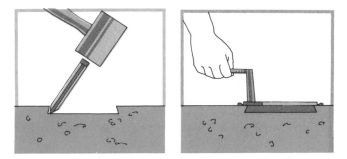

Undercut crack.   Trowel in concrete.

Most large holes and cracks could also be filled with these modern cement patches, but the compounds are too expensive to be used on a large scale. When a lot of crack-filling is to be done, it is just as easy and and considerably cheaper to use regular concrete, first undercutting the crack to a V-shape with a chisel. (Your dentist does the same when he puts a filling in a tooth.) This provides "tooth" for the concrete patch. A standard concrete mix is then pressed into the crack with a trowe or similar instrument. Most building supply houses sell small bags or pails of premixed concrete for this purpose. Or you can mix your own, as described on p.225 for major repair work.

●

When the surface of concrete is badly flaked or pitted, it is probable that a poor job was done in the first place. It may be possible to save the old concrete without replacing it, but the repair could be only temporary, and eventually you might have to tear up the whole job. Before resorting to that drastic step, there are several things you can try.

If only a small section is involved, scrape off all the flaking material with a wire brush. Be sure to get rid of any old concrete that has started to crack or deteriorate. Chip it out with a cold chisel and a mash

hammer. Then cover the surface with vinyl or epoxy patching mix.

If the deteriorated area is a large one, this method may prove too expensive, particularly since it isn't guaranteed to last. One way to avoid a complete replacement is to use the old concrete as a base and pour a new surface on top of that. You must allow at least 2 inches of thickness for the new concrete. If there isn't room to pour another 2 inches of the old, you will have to dig out 2 inches of the old concrete, in which case it is probably easier to dig up the whole thing. Most private sidewalks can be raised 2 inches without disturbing the landscape, but a driveway is another matter. Raising it that high may cause rainwater to drain into your garage, or be just enough to catch your bumper or muffler as you enter or leave. Sidewalks along the public right-of-way may be prescribed by building codes. Study the implications of a 2-inch rise in the surface before you decide to pursue that method.

Before pouring new concrete on top of the old, wire-brush the old surface and rough it up with a sledgehammer and/or an application of 20 percent muriatic acid and 80 percent water. Be sure to wear gloves and boots when working with muriatic acid, and protect your eyes. Then, 2-inch forms are built, as described on p. 223.

Wire-brush flaking area.   Chip away old concrete.

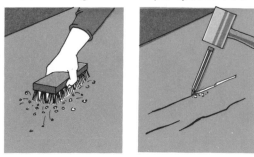

REPAIRING HEAVED SIDEWALK SECTIONS

Temporary repair around heaved section.

Break up old section with a sledgehammer.

A heaved-up concrete section may be caused by severe weather contrasts or by undermining tree roots. In either case, the cure for the sorry condition involves breaking up the old slab (as far as the adjacent expansion joint) and putting in a new one. If weather conditions prevent it, or if you simply don't have the time or stomach to tackle the complete repair, it will at least help to avoid accidents if you create a slope around the heaved portion of walk. Use the patching material discussed above to smooth around the offending section as best you can. But vow to do a complete repair job in the not-too-distant future.

For the permanent repair, break up the old section using a sledgehammer or—if you can rent or borrow one—a jackhammer. Concrete was meant to last, so don't expect an easy time of it.

Once the old concrete is removed, you can determine whether or not a tree root was the cause of the problem. If so, take an axe and cut off the offending root. Any tree that is strong enough to heave concrete is strong enough to withstand the loss of one root.

Break up old section with a jackhammer.

Cut off tree roots.

Install wire mesh.

If no roots are found, you can assume that Jack Frost did the dirty deed. In that case, it is wise to install wire reinforcing mesh before pouring the new section as described on p. 227.

Steps in Pouring Concrete

Whether you're pouring a small new section of sidewalk or a whole new driveway, the basic techniques are the same—it's merely a matter of greater or lesser effort. Just make sure that the effort is well expended and that the job is done right. Doing it right involves the following steps:

1. Preparation of the subgrade (unless you are pouring new concrete on top of old)
2. Formwork
3. Mixing
4. Placement
5. Finishing
6. Curing

Each of these steps must be done carefully and correctly. If any one of them is done improperly, the entire job will probably be ruined, and you'll be right back where you started.

IRON TAMPER

SUBGRADE PREPARATION

Concrete work can be compared to baking a cake. Getting the proper ingredients together in the right proportions is most important, but you also have to find the right pan and prepare it. The "pan" in this case is the formwork. And instead of greasing the pan, you have to prepare the ground.

Second to poor mixing, the most frequent error in concrete work is poor soil preparation. Slabs will settle, crack, and fall apart in poorly prepared or compacted soil. If that was your problem before, take a good look at the subgrade. It should be free of all organic matter such as sod, grass, roots, and soft or mucky ground. If some spots are very hard and others very soft, the concrete will surely crack from settling in the softer areas. Hard spots should be broken up, soft ones filled in and compacted.

On the other hand, do not simply remove whatever soil is under your slab and replace it with fill.

If settling and cracking were not problems before, the subgrade is probably all right; as long as it is reasonably uniform and free of vegetable matter, it is better left alone. All it should need is tamping of the top portion that was disturbed by removing the old section. Undisturbed soil is better than soil that has been dug out, replaced, and poorly compacted.

If the soil is soft and highly organic, it should be dug out and replaced with fill. Remove about 4 to 6 inches of the subgrade to a depth of 8 to 10 inches below the surfaces of the adjacent sections. Be careful not to undercut the sound concrete.

Gravel, crushed stone, or blast-furnace slag can be used for fill, but sand is usually preferred for small sections because it can be leveled and compacted more easily. Rake the material, then check with a level and straightedge; it should be as level as possible. For a compactor, you can probably rent an iron tamper, or you can make your own with a 2 x 2 or 2 x 4 handle nailed to a base of ¾-inch plywood or 2 x 6 lumber. For small areas, a 2 x 4 alone will probably suffice. What you use is not as important as using it well. Make sure that you compact the soil completely. Then check it with the level, take down any high spots and fill low spots, and tamp again.

SELFMADE TAMPER

Home Repairs Made Easy

SETTING FORMS FOR POURING CONCRETE

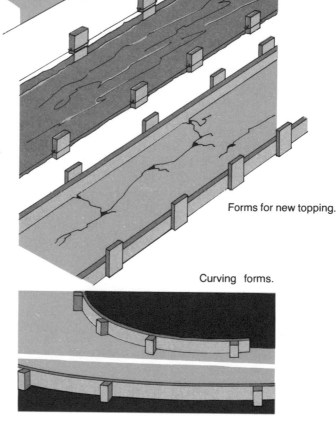

STAKE

ADJACENT
SECTION

FORMS

Form for a
small repair.

Drive in stakes around the
edges of concrete to be
replaced.

Tie strings on stakes.

OLD CONCRETE

Forms for new topping.

Curving forms.

Concrete walks and driveways are normally 4 inches thick, although you may find thinner slabs in garden walks or other walks that bear little traffic. If your driveway has any appreciable truck traffic, such as an oil delivery truck, you may want to consider a 5-inch slab. The best guideline here is to make the new section as thick as the old one unless you suspect that thinness was the cause of the original problem. You can always pour a thicker slab, but never a thinner one.

The most common form material is 2 x 4 lumber. Because a nominal "2 x 4" is actually 1½ x 3½ inches, there will be a ½-inch gap at the bottom of the form, but this is no cause for concern. The important thing is that the top of the form be exactly even with the surface of the concrete to be poured. For a small area, simply place a 2 x 4 flush with the top of the adjacent sections and butted against the outside edges. Drive sharpened 1 x 3s, 2 x 2s, or metal rods as stakes into the ground around the outside edges of the forms. Use the existing concrete itself as a form where it butts up against the new section.

When replacing large pieces or an entire walk or drive, the formwork is somewhat more complicated. Assuming that the old grade was acceptable, drive in several stakes around the edges before you demolish the old work, and mark them to show the top of the walk or drive. After the old concrete has been taken out, run a string line between these marks to serve as a guide for the new forms. If there is a straight run from one section to the next, simply drive in stakes at both ends and tie the line between. Adjust the forms to that

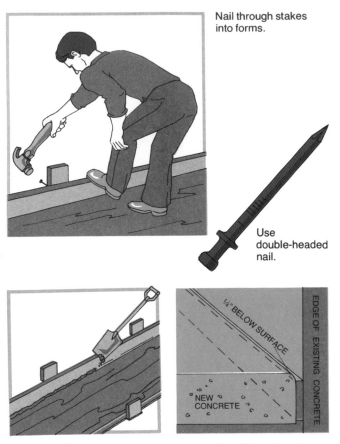

Nail through stakes into forms.

Use double-headed nail.

Backfill under form to keep concrete from escaping.

Install isolation joints to separate floors from walls.

level. Line stakes should be set every 8 feet and the string pulled as taut as possible.

If the old grade wasn't correct, pour concrete to a new one. The ideal slope is ¼ inch per foot. It all depends on the terrain, though, and you can't have that type of slope on a hilly driveway. Just make sure that you don't pitch a driveway toward the garage, or a walkway toward a patio or the house. Concrete acts as a conduit for rainwater, and improper sloping is an open invitation to drainage problems.

Use 2 x 4s for forms even though you may be pouring a 2-inch topping over old concrete. The forms must be butted firmly against the sides of the old material. Gentle curves may be formed with ¼-inch exterior plywood or one-inch lumber. Plywood, with the outside grain running vertically, or tempered hardboard are best for sharp curves.

Drive in stakes at each end of short runs and every 4 feet on long runs. Regular spacing is all right for gentle curves, but drive stakes every 1 to 2 feet for short-radius curves. For very sharp curves, you may need 2 x 4 stakes. Drive stakes tight against the outside of the forms and nail through the stakes into the forms — hold the forms with your foot while nailing. If you have difficulty doing this, set temporary stakes on the inside of the forms to hold them during nailing, and remove them when everything is nailed together and before pouring concrete. Use double-headed nails; they are easier to pull out after the forms are removed.

When the stakes are all in place, backfill under the forms to keep the concrete from escaping underneath. Install isolation joints, made of ¼- or ½-inch premolded fiber (available at building supply houses), at intersections such as driveway-to-walk or walk-to-house. The joint material should be ¼ inch below the surface of the surrounding concrete.

THE PROPER CONCRETE MIX

Since it is vital to get the right proportions in your concrete mix, take the worry out by using premixed bags on smaller jobs. Premix saves time and trouble as well as anxiety over the right proportions. For large jobs you can order "readymix" from a concrete service to be delivered by cement-mixer truck.

It is less expensive, of course, to mix your own concrete. Sometimes you may find that a concrete truck cannot get to the site, and you will have to mix your own anyway. And, unless you have several willing helpers, you will not be able to handle the large loads that readymix suppliers deliver. For one or two workers, it is easier to mix smaller loads and place them in stages.

Portland cement is purchased in bags from local building and mason supply houses. Bags weigh 94 pounds in the United States and are one cubic foot in volume. In Canada, bags weigh 80 pounds each and hold ⅞ cubic foot.

For the average concrete application, the following proportions are ideal:

94 pounds of cement (one U.S. bag)
215 pounds of sand
295 pounds of coarse aggregate
5 gallons of water

A regular bathroom scale is accurate enough for weighing the materials. Use a 3- to 5-gallon galvanized bucket to hold the material, but be sure to weigh the pail first and deduct its weight from the weight of the material. ("Zeroing" the scale with an empty bucket may be easier on your arithmetic.) Don't put more material in the bucket than you can readily handle—it's heavy. Put the sand and aggregate into three or four buckets of equal weight. Once you get the right weight established, mark a line on the bucket for each ingredient and return the scale to the bathroom.

A simpler, although less accurate, way to measure is by volume. To achieve the ideal mix mentioned above, use 1 part portland cement to 2¼ parts sand and 3 parts aggregate. Add 5 gallons of water for each bag of cement. Both of these one-bag formulas should yield approximately ⅙ cubic yard of concrete, enough for a typical section of sidewalk.

When buying aggregates, make sure that they are clean and free of organic matter. Don't bring in stones or sand from the beach. Order fresh, clean, dry sand and gravel or crushed stone from a dealer who specializes in such materials. The coarse aggregate should be "well graded," with a range of sizes from small to large but not too many of any one size. The maximum aggregate size for a 4-inch slab should be one inch in diameter.

In most areas of the United States and all of Canada, concrete should contain an "air-entraining" agent. This can be premixed into the cement (preferably) or be added to the water. Air-entrainment causes tiny bubbles to form inside the concrete. Hardened concrete always contains some minute particles of water, and freezing temperatures cause this water to expand. This is one of the most frequent causes of concrete scaling. The microscopic bubbles created by air-entrainment act as relief valves for the expanding concrete, and also help resist the effects of salt deicers.

HOW MUCH CONCRETE DO YOU NEED?

To estimate your concrete needs, multiply length times width in feet to get the area, then multiply again by the thickness of the slab. The usual 4-inch slab is $\frac{1}{3}$ foot thick, so take $\frac{1}{3}$ of the area. If, for example, you are pouring a sidewalk section 4 by 4 feet, 4 inches thick, you have:

4 x 4 = 16 square feet of surface
16 x $\frac{1}{3}$ = 5.3 cubic feet
Because there are 27 cubic feet in a cubic yard, divide your total by 27:
5.3 cubic feet ÷ 27 = .2 cubic yard

You should always figure on a little extra for waste and spillage, so ¼ cubic yard is just about right in this example. If using premix, determine the coverage on the bag (usually $\frac{1}{3}$ cubic yard for 45 pounds, $\frac{2}{3}$ for 90) and buy accordingly. If you are mixing your own, figure on about 1 $\frac{1}{3}$ bags of portland cement, plus 1 $\frac{1}{3}$ times the other ingredients used in either of the one-bag formulas previously given. (If you want to order readymix, you'll have to have a lot more concrete work to do. Most dealers require a minimum of one cubic yard per delivery.)

You may find it easier to remember that for 4-inch slabs there are 1.23 yards of concrete for every 100 square feet. For small areas, figure .12 yards for every 10 square feet. Two-inch slabs are half of that.

MIXING THE CONCRETE

Small batches of concrete can be mixed by hand on a piece of plywood. You can mix on top of existing concrete if you clean up well afterward, or in a mortar box (you may be able to rent one). For a job of any considerable size, rent a portable mixer.

Premix is dumped in a pile, then a hollow is made in the center and the label-recommended amount of water added. When mixing concrete from scratch, spread the sand out evenly on the mixing surface, then add the cement. Mix both thoroughly by turning over with a square-end shovel until they have a uniform color without streaking. Spread this mix out evenly, then add the coarse aggregate. Again turn over thoroughly. Form a hollow as with the premix.

After water has been added, use the shovel to fold all the materials over toward the center, and continue mixing until all water, cement, sand, and aggregate have been thoroughly combined.

PLACING THE CONCRETE MIX

When the concrete has been thoroughly mixed, or when the readymix arrives, everything should be in readiness for placing. Although job requirements may differ, most employ the following tools: concrete hoe or square-end shovel, straightedge or strike board (a straight 2 x 4 works well), float, edger, groover, trowel, broom, and garden hose. You may also need a wheelbarrow and/or chute to get the mix where you want it to go. Some sort of materials to aid the curing process should also be on hand (see p. 230). Use the hose to wet down the area before pouring concrete.

Never try to wheel concrete up a steep grade. A small grade here and there can be managed, particularly if you can get a good start. But trying to push a wheelbarrow uphill from a standing start is a heavier job than most of us can handle. If you expect difficulty in getting readymix concrete to the site, explain the problem to the dealer. He may be able to suggest a solution. If not, your only choice is machine-mixing close to the site.

Place the concrete in the forms to full depth, spading along the sides to complete filling. Try to lead the concrete as close as possible to its final position without too much dragging and shoveling. Start in one corner and continue pouring until you reach the other side. Use the shovel or concrete hoe to get as uniform coverage as possible.

When you have poured enough concrete to fill the forms, the next operations—striking off and rough-floating—should follow immediately. A prime requisite for successful finishing is that rough-floating must be completed before bleeding water starts to appear on the surface of the concrete.

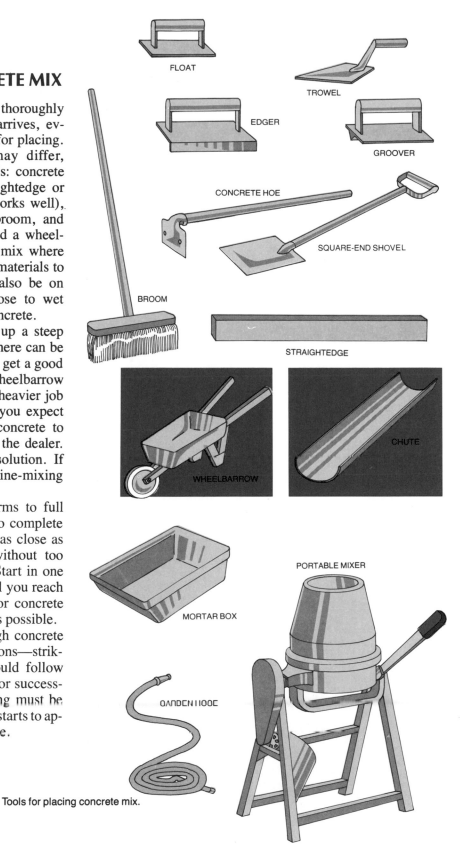

Tools for placing concrete mix.

Strike off the surface with a straightedge.

Work float forward, tilting it slightly away from you.

Flatten float if you pull it back.

STRIKING OFF, FLOATING, EDGING, AND CUTTING CONTROL JOINTS IN CONCRETE

Bull float.

After placing, strike off the surface with a 2 x 4 straightedge, working it in a sawlike motion across the top of the form boards. The strike-off or "screeding" action smooths the surface while cutting off excess concrete to the proper elevation. Go over the concrete twice in this manner to take out any bumps or fill in low spots. Tilt the straightedge slightly in the direction of travel to obtain a better cutting effect.

Work trowel inside form to cut the concrete away from the form (left).

Moving edger forward (below left).

Pulling edger back (below).

Immediately after striking off, the surface is rough-floated to smooth it and remove irregularities. Use a wood hand float for most patchwork, but try to rent a large bull float if you are doing a big job. The float is tilted slightly away from you as you push it forward, then flattened as it is pulled back.

If you use air-entrained concrete, the finishing process can begin almost immediately after rough-floating. Even without air-entrainment, you do not have to wait long on a hot, dry, windy day. If the weather is cool and humid, however, you may be forced to wait several hours. The key to proper timing is whether or not there is water sheen on the surface. Begin when the sheen has disappeared, which happens sooner on days when quicker evaporation can be expected.

Ordinarily, the surface should be ready for finishing by the time you have finished cutting the concrete away from the forms. This is accomplished by working a pointed trowel along inside of the forms to a depth of about one inch.

The first finishing step is edging, which should take place as soon as the surface is stiff enough to hold the shape of the edging tool. Edging produces a neat, rounded corner to prevent chipping and other damage, which could be a problem once the forms are removed. The edger is run between the forms and the concrete, with the body of the tool held almost flat on the concrete surface. When moving the edger either forward or back, the leading edge should be tilted slightly upward. Be careful not to let the edger sink too deeply into the concrete, since deep indentations may be difficult to remove with subsequent finishing.

A control joint is a groove cut into the concrete to keep cracks from extending throughout an entire concrete surface. In walks and drives, control joints should be spaced at intervals equal to the width of the slab. They are desirable whenever a slab of concrete extends more than 10 feet in any direction.

Most patchwork should not require new control joints. If you're replacing only a section of concrete, control joints as such will not be needed. You will recall, though, the recommendation that any bad section be replaced up to the adjacent new joints to replace the ones that were lost when you removed that section. And you will, of course, need new control joints if you are replacing more than one section.

Use the groover and straightedge to make control joints. The cutting edge should be deep enough to cut into the slab about one-fourth of its thickness. In most cases, that means the cut should be about an inch deep. When replacing old control joints, place the groover bit into the wet

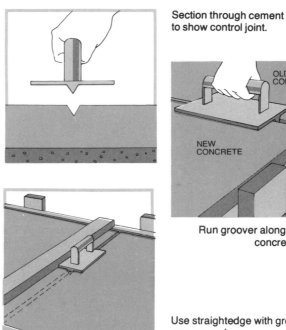

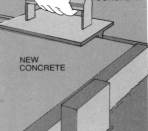

Section through cement to show control joint.

OLD CONCRETE

NEW CONCRETE

Run groover along existing concrete edge.

Use straightedge with groover on new work.

concrete where it meets the existing work. One side of the tool body should be run along the existing concrete while the other side runs on the new work, cutting a groove as precisely as possible between the two. Be careful not to press down too hard on the wet side so that the line goes crooked. Even pressure on the hardened side should keep the tool level.

When making control joints in completely new work, use a piece of 2 x 4 or similar board as a guide. When grooving across a sidewalk or driveway, the board should rest on, and be at right angles to, the forms. Push the groover into the concrete and move forward while applying pressure to the back of the tool. After the joint is cut, turn the tool around and pull back over the groove to provide a smooth finish.

FINISHING AND CURING CONCRETE

After edging and grooving are completed, final floating takes place. This procedure embeds large aggregate near the surface, compacts the concrete, and removes inperfections left in the surface by previous operations. Using the wood float, work over the entire surface. Hold the float flat on the surface and use a slight sawing motion in a sweeping arc to fill in holes and smooth ridges and lumps.

Before doing anything more, compare the appearance of the finish-floated surface with that of the surrounding concrete. In many cases, this is the final step. The new surface should look slightly rough and have a nonskid texture. If it matches the old, the finishing job is done.

When the existing concrete has a glassy-smooth surface, it has no doubt been steel-troweled, and you will have to do the same to make the new surface match. Use a rectangular, steel-bladed trowel; at least two passes over the surface are necessary. If it isn't smooth enough after two, make a third. The trowel should make a ringing sound as the blade passes over the hardened surface. Don't be too concerned if the new patch doesn't exactly match the old. Even an experienced mason is hard put to accomplish that.

If there are irregularly spaced scratch marks across the old surface, it was probably "broomed." To match this, go over the floated surface with a stiff-bristled "garage" broom. If the lines on the old work are wavy, swing the broom in a similar pattern. If they are straight, work the broom over the surface in a straight line. Again, don't expect a perfect match. It just isn't possible.

A swirled surface is accomplished with a hand float or trowel. Try both to see which comes closer to matching the original. With either tool work in a fanlike, semicircular motion, applying pressure as you swing your arm in an arc over the surface. Don't move your wrist, just your arm.

●

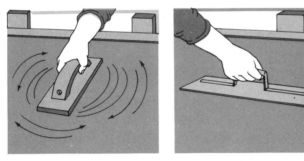

Floating.　　　　　Steel-troweling.

Brooming.　　　　　Swirling.

The chemical reaction that takes place between cement and water is called hydration, a curing process that must continue for several days to a week after placing to attain maximum durability. If too much water is lost by evaporation, the chemical reaction ceases. The same is true when temperatures get below 50 degrees F. Hydration slows almost to a standstill as the temperature approaches the freezing mark.

Curing is a vital step in concrete work. It is essential to keep water in the concrete the right length of time. As soon as the finishing process is complete and the surface is hard enough so that it will not be damaged, curing should begin. In warm weather, the curing process must continue for five days. For every 10 degrees less than 70, add an extra day (six days at 60 degrees, seven at 50 degrees). At no time should the temperature of the concrete fall below 50 degrees. If there is a chance that this will happen, you shouldn't be laying concrete at all.

The recommended curing method for the do-it-yourselfer is to keep the concrete surface damp by covering it with wet burlap. Rinse out the burlap before use, particularly if it is new, and spread over the slab. The burlap should be checked several times a day to see that it does not dry out. Periodic sprinkling, at least daily, will keep the burlap moist.

Another method of keeping the surface wet during curing is by running a sprinkler or soaking hose continuously over the surface. Never let the surface get dry, because only partial curing will ruin the job. For small jobs, you might try "ponding"—building sand or earth dikes around the edges of the slab and filling with water. The

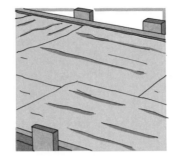

Cover concrete with wet burlap for curing.

Keep burlap moist, sprinkling it periodically.

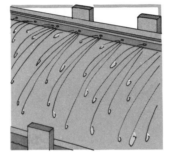

Run water continuously over concrete from soaking hose.

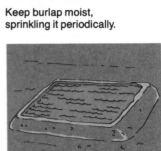

"Ponding" to keep concrete moist for small jobs.

water must be deep enough to cover the entire surface of the concrete and prevent formation of dry spots.

BLACKTOP REPAIR

The reasons for blacktop breaking up or deteriorating are similar to those for the same conditions in concrete. An additional problem with blacktop, however, is that it is easier for water, oil, etc., to get through and attack from underneath. A good sealer applied every year or two gives added protection against such damage.

Like concrete, blacktop must not be applied when the temperature is likely to fall below 50 degrees F. No matter how badly your driveway may need patching during the winter, it will just have to wait until the birds return—and probably later.

When blacktop starts to crack and break up, the deteriorated sections should be removed. Dig out the area underneath and fill in with the old broken-up blacktop. Blacktop patch is available at reasonable cost from most building supply dealers.

Tamp down the subgrade thoroughly, and fill with gravel or other solid material if the depth is more than 2 inches. Pour in the new blacktop patch and smooth over the top with a shovel. The secret of blacktop repair is that it should be tamped down thoroughly. In this case, a metal tamper is a necessity. (You should be able to rent one.) Keep tamping until the patch is smooth and level, then run over it a few times with your car's tires. Do this as gently as possible—don't skid or "burn out" or do anything else to disturb it. Your car is merely acting as a roller.

Let the patch dry and harden for a few days. It should be as good as new. Blacktop adheres well to old blacktop. You can even apply new blacktop on top of old.

1. Dig out old blacktop.

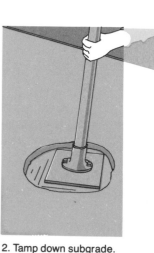

2. Tamp down subgrade.

3. Smooth patch.

4. Tamp patch.

Apply sealer to blacktop.

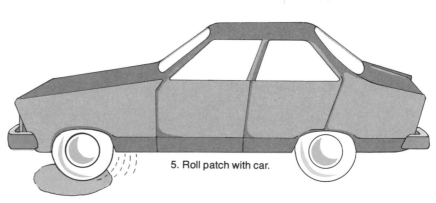

5. Roll patch with car.

PATIO REPAIRS

Patios can be built of a variety of materials. The principal ones are concrete, brick, stone, and patio block, the latter being a type of flat cinder block. Although all these materials are long-lasting when used correctly, they are subject to the same types of stresses as are driveways and sidewalks. There is also the frequent problem of poor original construction.

Concrete Patio Repairs

Since a concrete patio is simply a concrete slab, just like a driveway or sidewalk, repair techniques are the same as those detailed on pp. 219-231. Use vinyl latex or epoxy patching mixes for small holes and cracks or wherever feathered edges are needed. For large cracks and holes, undercut the damaged portion and fill with standard concrete mix. Replace badly damaged sections by digging out the old work and forming, as directed on pp. 223-224.

When the entire surface needs repair, patios are much better suited to the addition of a 2-inch topping course than walks or driveways, since the additional height usually causes no problems. There should be no difficulty with people tripping over raised areas, as there might be on a sidewalk, and you don't have to worry about damaged mufflers or drainage problems, as you would for a driveway. Attached patios are ordinarily sloped away from the house and toward the lawn, where rainwater will do more good than harm.

Raising the patio height may even be beneficial. Many patios are situated below the first-floor level of the house, and often the step down is too high to begin with. But raising the patio could pose problems if the house is laid on a slab and the patio is almost at first-floor level already.

If you are considering topping the patio,

Patio with exposed-aggregate finish for topping.

an excellent and attractive way to do this is with exposed-aggregate concrete. (Exposed aggregate is often referred to as terrazzo, but true terrazzo utilizes a different installation technique and contains decorative and more expensive aggregates such as quartz, granite, or marble chips.) In an exposed-aggregate finish, the aggregates in the mix are kept near the surface, and the cement paste that usually covers them is washed and brushed away. Although regular aggregates can be used, the surface is much more colorful and handsome if rounded, beach-type stones are used. An "ex-ag" surface is highly durable and slip-resistant as well as attractive.

When building a new exposed-aggregate concrete slab, many contractors do the job in two stages—a base course topped with the ex-ag course. Topping an existing patio with a layer of exposed-aggregate concrete follows the same principle.

To lay a 2-inch topping course, order or mix concrete with a low "slump" (a measure of workability.). There should be a high proportion of coarse-to-fine aggregates so that the larger ones stay near the surface. With only 2 inches of concrete to lay, it is easier to keep the larger aggregates near the top than if you were starting from scratch.

Kneel on board to test
hardness of concrete.

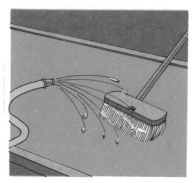

Wet and brush the surface
(try to get a helper).

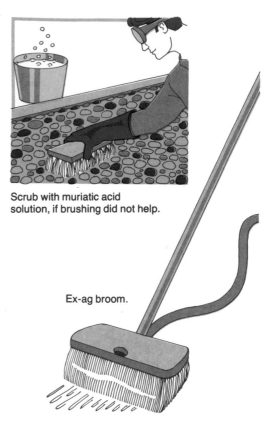

Scrub with muriatic acid
solution, if brushing did not help.

Ex-ag broom.

The usual concrete construction techniques can be followed, except that rough-floating is done gently to keep the larger stones from being pressed down too far. When the water sheen disappears, and the concrete can bear a man's weight on a piece of one-inch lumber without indentation, it's time to expose the aggregate. Begin washing and brooming as described below, but if the stones become dislodged or overexposed, wait another 15 to 30 minutes, then try again.

Two persons are better than one for this operation. One worker washes down the surface with a fine spray from a garden hose while the other brushes the surface

lightly with a stiff-bristled broom, preferably nylon. If you can't find a helper, alternately wash and broom. The combination of washing and brooming should remove all

1. Level topping mix
off below forms.

2. Spread aggregate stone
evenly over the surface.

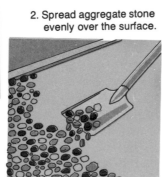

3. Tap the aggregate down
into the concrete.

4. Go over the entire
surface with the float.

the cement paste and film from the surface of the aggregate.

Be prepared for some hard brushing, because any cement paste remaining on the surface will leave it looking dull and lifeless. A special ex-ag broom, which is attached to the hose and sprays water at the same time, is ideal for this job if you can borrow or rent one. If, in spite of your efforts, the surface looks rather grimy, give it another rubdown with a 20 percent muriatic acid solution. Follow the usual precautions when working with the acid—wear protective clothing and protect your eyes.

"Seeding" is another method by which the do-it-yourselfer can achieve an exposed-aggregate finish. The topping mix is spread in the usual manner, but is leveled off ⅜ inch to ½ inch below the top of the forms. This allows room for the aggregate to be spread over the top of the concrete. The base coat is struck off and floated as usual. The aggregate stone is then spread evenly over the surface with a shovel and filled in by hand where necessary until the entire surface is covered completely with aggregate. If the first few stones start to sink to the bottom, wait another 30 minutes or so until the mix is a little stiffer.

When there is an even stone cover, tap the aggregate down into the still pliable concrete with a 2 x 4 or a wood float. Then go over the entire surface with the float, working the stones well into the mix until they are completely covered by cement paste. The surface will then look just about as it did before you started seeding.

Wait about another hour, until the seeded slab can bear the weight of a man on a piece of lumber. Washing and brooming can then proceed as above.

Brick Patio Repairs

Brick patios are normally built by one of two methods. The easiest both to lay and repair is the brick-in-sand patio, in which a bed of sand is put down and leveled. Sometimes cement is mixed with the base sand for a more stable bed. Then the bricks are simply set on top, with more sand being swept in later to fill the joints. Brick patios may also be put down over a mortar bed, with mortar joints between the bricks.

Although a brick-in-sand patio is more likely to heave and settle than the other type, especially over the winter months, it is simpler to repair. Any bricks that come up or sink down below the level of the others are removed. You may need an old screwdriver or other tool to dislodge the first, but the adjacent ones can be lifted out easily by hand.

If the bricks in question have settled, lay in some extra sand (any sand will do for this—even beach sand) and tamp it down well. Watering helps to settle the sand and compact it. When the bed is satisfactory, reinstall the bricks the same way they were laid before. In this type of patio, the bricks are butted as tightly as possible against one another. When all have been replaced, spread more sand over the top and work it down between the cracks with a stiff-bristled broom. Spray the patio with a hose, then sweep in more sand. It may take three or more similar applications before the brick is again locked into position so that no more sand can be worked in.

Since mortared brick patios should be set on top of a concrete base slab, heaving and settling of the brick itself should be relatively rare. If a few bricks do exhibit such problems, remove them by chipping out the mortar with a brick chisel or cold chisel. You probably won't be able to remove all the mortar, but you should get enough so that you can pry up the bricks with a chisel or wrecking bar.

If the problem is settling, chip out any crumbly mortar underneath and replace with new. Lay in enough new mortar to bring the surface level with the rest. Stan-

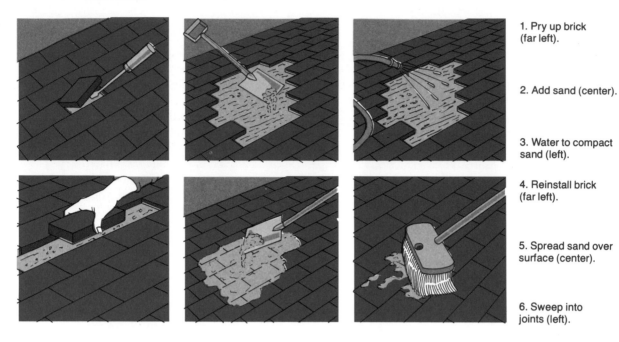

1. Pry up brick (far left).

2. Add sand (center).

3. Water to compact sand (left).

4. Reinstall brick (far left).

5. Spread sand over surface (center).

6. Sweep into joints (left).

dard or common brick is nominally 2¾ inches in depth, counting mortar, with the actual brick size 2¼ inches. But not all brick is alike, so measure what you have. For mortar, it is easiest to purchase premixed mortar from a masonry or building supply dealer. If you mix your own, use the same proportions used for laying a new bed (see below).

When the brick is heaved, it is more difficult to repair. The brick and mortar must be removed and the concrete base chipped off to bring it down to the surrounding level. Then proceed as above. If tree roots have caused the heaving, remove all the concrete

in the affected section, chop off the root as far back as possible, then pour new concrete. After curing, replace the brick as above.

When the patio is badly heaved or settled, it is probable that the concrete was poorly laid originally. In that case, all the brick will have to be removed, the concrete broken up or topped, and a whole new patio installed. Lay the slab as directed on pp. 219-231. After thorough curing, make a mortar of 1 part masonry cement (premixed with lime) and 4½ parts of sand. Add water, a little at a time, until the mix has the consistency of soft mud. Spread a ½-inch

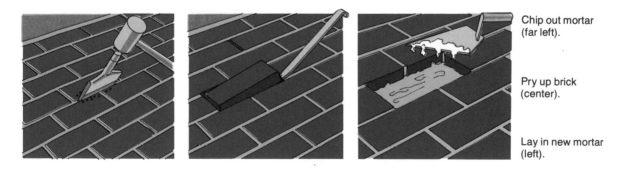

Chip out mortar (far left).

Pry up brick (center).

Lay in new mortar (left).

1. Spread mortar (far left).

2. "Butter" brick (center).

3. Lay brick into mortar bed (left).

bed over a small section at a time. After removing as much old mortar as possible from the old brick (or using new brick), "butter" the brick on both edges and one end with ½ inch of mortar and lay into the mortar bed. Continue working in this manner a section at a time until the repair is completed.

Fortunately, most repair jobs to mortared brick involve only repointing or tuck-pointing crumbling mortar. Since you won't want to repeat the job in the too-near future, all weak or loose joints should be repointed along with the ones that are obviously crumbled.

The crumbled mortar should be chiseled out to a depth of about an inch, even though the deterioration is only at the surface. The greater depth will give the mortar a better hold. Wear safety glasses or goggles when doing this type of work to prevent eye injuries from flying mortar chips.

The mortar mix used for tuck-pointing should be stiffer than normal mixes. One part masonry cement is mixed with 2¼ to 3 parts of clean sand, with less water than for normal use. The mix is about right when it slides from the trowel in a sideways position, but clings when the trowel is turned upside down. Special repointing mortar can be bought at most building supply dealers.

After dampening all the areas to be repointed, force the mortar into the joint with a trowel. Do the short joints first, then the long ones.

4. Force mortar into joint.

Flagstone Patio Repairs

The problems encountered with flagstone are very similar to those with brick patios. Most stone patios are laid in mortar, but plain sand is often used. Use the same repair procedures for stone as you would use for brick laid in the same way.

One difficulty may be in removing large stones. They are quite heavy, and you may need either a helper or some device to remove stones. One way to remove them without help is by placing a piece of pipe or a wood dowel or steel rod next to the stone to be removed, and lifting the stone just enough to rest a corner on the rod. A pry bar can help you accomplish this. The stone can then be shoved onto the rod and rolled over out of the way so that you can work beneath.

If stone has been broken badly, it may need replacement. With random shaped and colored stone, you should be able to find a replacement easily enough. The stone doesn't have to match its mates in either size or shape, although it should vaguely re-

Lift at least a corner of the stone onto the rod (right).

Roll the stone out of the way (far right).

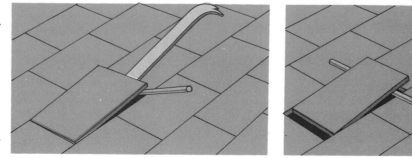

Cutting stone with a cold chisel.

semble the others. Try to select a piece that is shaped similarly to the one being replaced. It can be somewhat smaller, but not bigger. Fill in the surrounding spaces with mortar.

You'll have a tougher time finding a replacement when your patio is the more formal type, with matched rectangular stones. Color is usually not a problem, because few are exactly alike anyway, but you will have to find a piece that matches the damaged one in size. If you can't find one, have the stone dealer cut one to your specifications.

Try to avoid having to cut stone to fit. It *can* be cut with a cold chisel and a heavy mash hammer, but that is at best an inexact science. If you must do it, score a line first on all sides with a chisel, then keep banging at it on one side and then the other until it breaks. Unfortunately, it often breaks in the wrong place, so buy a couple of pieces.

Since stone comes in various thicknesses, be sure to get one that is the same as the one it is replacing—or as close as possible. If you have to choose between a slightly thicker or thinner one, choose the thinner and fill the gap with new mortar.

Patio Block

Patio block is made in standard sizes. Damaged blocks are fairly simple to replace. Procedures are the same as for brick. You shouldn't have to do any cutting; but if you do, it's easy to cut with a brick chisel and a heavy hammer.

POOL CARE

The swimming pool used to be the super symbol of Hollywood success, but today you can find swimming pools in the most humble urban and suburban backyards. New methods and new materials, along with new affluence, account for this pool proliferation. Crowded public beaches accessible only by crowded highways are the determining factors that cause many families to provide their own facilities for "getting in the swim."

To insure season-long swimming fun, a certain amount of time has to be devoted to the "non-fun" aspects of swimming pools —the care and maintenance of the pool. Basically, it is a simple job if done properly and at the required intervals. When these routine tasks are neglected, trouble begins.

One of the most important aspects of pool care is maintaining a proper chemical balance of the water. A glass of water coming out of the tap looks and (usually) tastes clean and clear. Put the same water in a 20 x 40-foot pool and it may look entirely different (taste is quite another matter).

That's why you shouldn't use your pool the first day you fill it up, regardless of how tempting it is and how hot the weather. The first thing you should do is turn on the filter and let it run for a day. The filter will remove the minerals and other solids that are present in most water. Any turbidity in the water should be removed, and the water should look sparkling clear after the first day.

From the very first day you fill your pool, its purity must be guarded by a chemical disinfectant. Some purifying agent, whether it be chlorine, bromine, or iodine, must be maintained in the pool water; and enough of it must remain in the water to kill disease-carrying bacteria that are brought into the water by bathers.

Chlorine is the most widely used disinfectant. Ideally it should be used at one part per million (ppm), and must have at least 0.6 ppm of "free residual chlorine." The actual ratio is really very small, since 100 percent activity is gained by only one drop of chlorine for every one million drops of water.

In addition to keeping the proper chemi-

Pool "Feeding"

To keep you and your family "in the swim" throughout the season, these simple rules are suggested by the National Swimming Pool Institute:

Don't be a know-it-all. Read carefully the directions for all chemicals you intend to add.

Don't overdose. Measure exact amounts. Pool chemicals—like medicine—should be used only in specified amounts. Too much can cause irritating side-effects.

Don't guess. Take time to learn to use a test kit. Be sure to replace reagents (test fluids) each season to assure accuracy.

Establish a routine for testing and treatment. A few minutes every day— or every other day—can make the job easy and assure you a pool in tiptop shape.

Don't work too hard. If you find that taking care of your pool is too much work, check yourself—you are doing something wrong.

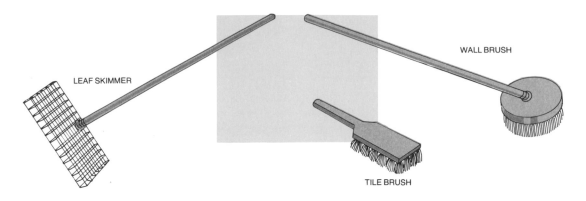

LEAF SKIMMER

WALL BRUSH

TILE BRUSH

cal balance, a few other things should be done to keep your pool clean and fresh.

Manually skimming the pool's surface is one. You'll need a standard "leaf skimmer," a netlike pool-cleaning tool designed especially to rid the pool's surface of leaves, bugs, debris, and other floating contaminants. Most leaf skimmers are equipped with long handles to enable you to reach the pool's center while standing on the deck.

You should also brush down walls and tile regularly. You'll need a stiff-bristled tile brush to clean near the waterline and a wall brush to clean the walls below.

Vacuuming the pool bottom is yet another chore. You'll need a special pool vacuum for this. There are many models and types. Consult your dealer as to the types best suited to your pool.

Don't forget to clean the built-in skimmer's basket and the hair-line strainer in the pump. No special equipment is needed for this. Remove the skimmer basket and the hair-line strainer from the pump. Dispose of the debris that has collected in them and replace them. This should be done as frequently as possible; daily is preferred, or even more often during the spring and fall when there is a heavy fall-out of flower petals or leaves from trees and bushes. Failure to keep the strainer clean will result in reduced circulation of the water through the pump and filter.

Clean the filter regularly. A dirty filter will result in decreased recirculation and consequent dirty water. Consult the directions of the filter manufacturer for the correct procedure for your particular filter. Most likely you should "backwash," or reverse the flow of water.

Hose the deck clean. A garden hose is all you need. This should be done during every pool-cleaning.

Remove and clean skimmer basket.

POOL REPAIR

A properly designed and installed swimming pool should last many years before repairs are required, provided that normal maintenance routine is faithfully followed. Major cracks or breaks in a concrete or Gunite pool are best repaired by a professional. Minor cracks and holes can easily be filled by the do-it-yourselfer.

The pool must be drained at least below the level of the damaged area. Chip away all loose concrete from the crack and wirebrush the area clean. Butyl rubber is the most easily applied material for such repairs —look for it at your hardware store in both paste and liquid form. Work the paste into the crack or hole with a putty knife, smoothing it with the surface. A waterproof liquid rubber is then applied over the entire surface with a brush, roller, or spray gun. The liquid immediately forms a seamless membrane that protects the patch. It should be allowed to set for 12 to 18 hours (check label directions) and will bond perfectly to the concrete.

For larger holes and crevices, a special epoxy (again, see your hardware dealer or a swimming pool supplier) can be mixed with cement to form an impregnable, waterproof "epoxycrete." This is then troweled onto the damaged area, forming a smooth barrier to protect the surface.

As a preventive measure, you can apply an all-weather sealer to the pool walls. This will prevent cracking, powdering, chipping, or staining of the concrete caused by freezing or most chemicals. It is applied with a roller, mop, or brush at any temperature above 40 degrees. It dries to a glossy finish.

Accidental rips or cuts in a vinyl pool liner can be repaired with a special kit available at most hardware stores and pool supply dealers. Follow the manufacturer's directions.

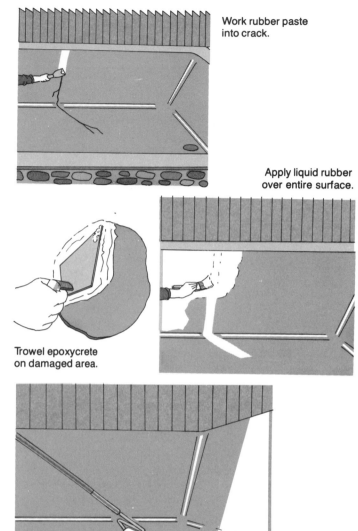

Work rubber paste into crack.

Apply liquid rubber over entire surface.

Trowel epoxycrete on damaged area.

Apply all-weather sealer.

Plug all openings with
rubber plugs.

Stuff semi-inflated
tube into skimmer.

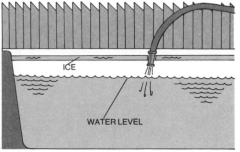

Check water level below ice
and refill if it has receded.

PAINTING AND WINTERIZING THE POOL

Many concrete pool owners leave their pools unpainted, but paint does make a pool more attractive. The trouble with painting is that it's like the first drink for an alcoholic. You'll have to keep up the paint job once it's applied, and repainting will be necessary every few years.

There are two main points regarding pool painting. First, use alkali-resistant paints for concrete or Gunite. Second, make sure that the surface is prepared properly.

Remove the water and repair all cracked or damaged areas to present a smooth surface throughout (same techniques as described on pp. 219-221. If the paint is just dull or rubbed off, a thorough scrubbing is all that is necessary. If there is peeling or flaking, it may be necessary to remove the old paint completely. If so, sandblasting is the best way. You can rent the equipment, but it is probably best to have professional sandblasters do the job.

●

In most parts of North America, there are at least a few months of the year when the weather is too cold for swimming. It is most important to leave the water in a pool.

The water inside the pool serves to brace the walls against pressures created by frozen or shifting earth on the outside walls.

Before shutting your pool down for the winter clean it thoroughly. Lower the water to below the inlet suction fitting. Remove the lights, and drain all lines at lowest points. Insert rubber plugs tightly in all openings so that no water may enter.

Fill the pool again to within two inches of the bottom of the skimmer opening. Make certain that the main drain valve is closed off. Add an extra-heavy dose of chlorine. Spread the pool cover if you are using one.

Place all removed parts in a dry, warm place and properly oil, grease, or paint where necessary. Plug all lines so that vermin or mice cannot enter the system. Remove the diving board and store it on its edge. Disconnect all electrical energy. Stuff a semi-inflated bicycle tube into the skimmer to absorb pressures created by freezing and thawing.

Check the pool from time to time. If water has receded below the ice on top, refill with a garden hose until the water meets the ice. Suspended ice can cause pool damage.

EMERGENCIES!

Not every household emergency poses a hazard to life, limb, and property, but when the house is plunged into darkness or the toilet bowl is overflowing and water is cascading down the stairs, it seems serious enough—and it is. You should always plan for the worst, and then hope that your planning is for naught. But if you should be called upon to administer "first aid" to a household malady, either while waiting for a repairman to wend his way to your home or as a stopgap until you can make permanent repairs yourself, is is best to "Be Prepared."

One of the basic preparations is to have an emergency toolbox ready to be whisked to the scene of the problem.

You should include a claw hammer and an assortment of nails, a screwdriver, pliers, and a knife. A staple gun with a good supply of staples should also be there. At least one flashlight is a must—and make sure the batteries are in good working condition. A couple of kerosene lanterns can be most helpful. A supply of candles should also be kept nearby, along with something to hold them, even if it's your collection of old Chianti bottles.

Keep a loaded calking gun nearby. A can of asphalt cement should also be in your arsenal. A couple of large sheets of poly-ethylene (available at any hardware store) can prove invaluable. Wire and rope and several lengths of 1 x 2 or 1 x 3 lumber are other items that may come in handy, as will a roll of masking tape. Rock salt and electric heating cable provide two different methods of attacking ice buildup

Like a well run ship, the well run home should be ready to deal with emergencies. All family members should be acquainted with certain procedures and fixtures, such as shut-off valves and circuit breakers. When (if) something does go wrong, you can't expect to head for the family library and look for this book to tell you what to do. This is one chapter you should study in advance and be ready to put into practice as soon as it's needed. Quick action in an emergency can prevent costly damage to materials, furnishings, and equipment—and, in some situations, to the family members themselves.

Plumbing Emergencies

Here are the most common emergencies that may occur and the action to take. The name, address, and phone number of a plumber who offers 24-hour service should be posted in a conspicuous place near your telephone.

Burst pipe or tank—Immediately cut off the flow of water by closing the shutoff valve nearest to the break. Then arrange for repair.

Toilet overflow—Do not use toilet until it is back in working order. Check for and remove stoppage in bowl outlet, or in drain line from closet to sewer or septic tank. If stoppage is due to root entry into pipe, repair of pipe at that point is recommended.

Rumbling noise in hot-water tank—This is probably a sign of overheating, which could lead to the development of explosive pressure. (Another indication of overheating is hot water backing up in the cold-water supply pipe.) Cut off the burner immediately. Be sure that the pressure-relief valve is operative. Then check (with a ther-

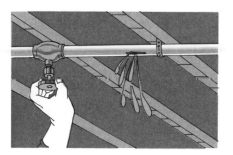

Close shutoff valve nearest leak.

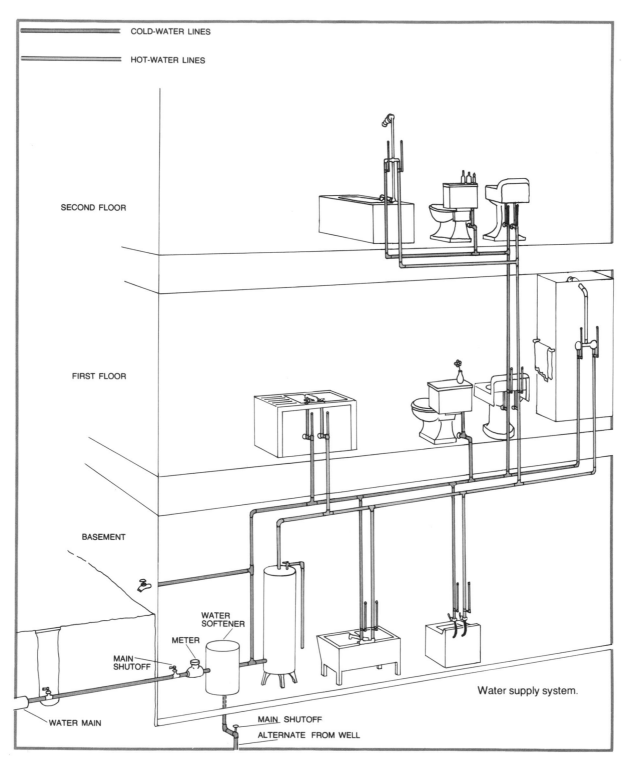

COLD-WATER LINES

HOT-WATER LINES

SECOND FLOOR

FIRST FLOOR

BASEMENT

WATER
SOFTENER

METER

MAIN
SHUTOFF

WATER MAIN

MAIN SHUTOFF

ALTERNATE FROM WELL

Water supply system.

Home Repairs Made Easy • Emergencies

mometer) the temperature of the water at the nearest outlet. If above that for which the gauge is set, check the thermostat that controls the burner cutoff. If you cannot correct the trouble, call a plumber.

Cold house—If the heating system fails (or if you close the house and turn off the heat) when there is a chance of sub-freezing weather, completely drain the plumbing system. A drain valve is usually provided for this purpose at the low point of the supply piping. A pump, storage tank, hot-water tank, toilet tank, water-treatment apparatus, and other water-system appliances or accessories should also be drained. Put antifreeze in all fixture and drain traps.

Hot-water and steam heating systems should also be drained when the house temperature may drop below freezing.

Roof Leaks

When your roof springs a leak during a storm, it would be the height of idiocy to attempt a repair from the outside. Just do what you can from underneath, as outlined on p. 206. After the storm, it may be possible to make a temporary repair from above if the leak is close enough to the edge of the roof that you can reach it from a ladder. Do not attempt to go on the roof whenever it is wet or covered with snow or ice. Use the plastic sheeting for temporary repair. Slip the plastic under the course of shingles above the leaking area, which you can mark by inserting a piece of wire through the leak from underneath. Staple the sheeting to the roof, then calk around the edges. If the wind is blowing and threatens to lift up the patch, nail 1 x 2 strips around the exposed edges. When you later make a permanent repair the nail holes will have to be filled, but it's certainly better than having water pour through the leak.

Leakage may be caused when water from thawing snow on the roof can't run off because the gutters are frozen. The water backs up under the roof shingles and finds its way inside the house, usually causing extensive damage. You can prevent this type of damage by making sure that gutters and downspouts are kept clear so that water can flow off freely. An electric heating cable may be run along the lower edge of the roof above the gutters (see p. 213); it should be turned on during a storm before snow can accumulate.

Gas Odor

When you detect the odor of gas, get everybody out of the house—fast! Don't tarry, but if there is time, turn the furnace thermostat all the way down so that the burner doesn't come on, possibly setting off an explosion. Needless to say, don't strike a match or light up a smoke to calm your nerves. Keep everyone at a distance and call the local gas company immediately, preferably from a neighbor's phone. If this is not possible, and the gas odor is not too strong, hold a handkerchief over your nose and reenter the house to call the utili-

Temporary roof repair: Staple sheeting over leak (right).

Calk around edges (below left).

Nail board around edges (below right).

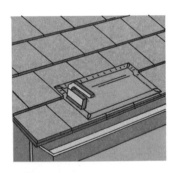

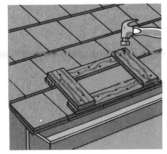

ty—or just dial the operator and explain your problem. Then get back outside, and don't go into the house again until the servicemen have come and repaired the leak. Above all, don't take chances!

Broken Windows

When a falling tree branch smashes through a window, you probably don't want to take the time to reglaze it, and in fact it may be impossible to do so with Jack Frost nipping at your fingers. This is one place where your polyethylene sheeting will do the job—if not as well as the glass, at least enough to keep out the wind and the snow. Staple the sheeting around the window frame, doubling it at the edges for additional strength. To seal the edges, use masking tape.

If you weren't foresighted enough to lay in a supply of polyethylene, you can, of course, use other materials to cover the opening. A piece of corrugated cardboard cut to the proper dimensions and stapled or taped in place will do the job—at least until it becomes saturated with water, when you can replace it with another piece of cardboard. Even a blanket tacked over the opening is better than nothing at all, although it will shut out the light, and you may never even know when the storm has subsided.

Rope ladder for upper stories is helpful.

Fire!

Fire is the dread nightmare of most homeowners and apartment dwellers, and it deserves to be. But prompt and proper action upon the discovery of a household fire can minimize the danger, at least to the inhabitants. Unfortunately, all too often a homeowner will attempt to battle a "small" blaze himself, only to lose precious minutes and have it develop into a total holocaust.

Train all members of your family to shout "Fire!" as loudly as possible at the first sign of flames or smell of smoke. They should, of course, be warned against deliberate false alarms (crying "Wolf!"), but an accidental false alarm is better than no alarm at all. Everyone in the house should be aroused and flee. Never linger to save possessions—they are not worth a life!

Next (not before) call the fire department. As mentioned above, it is best to do this from a neighbor's house. In most cases, you need simply dial the operator. Be sure to clearly state your full address.

If the fire is confined to a small area and you have a safe and sure exit available, you can reenter the house and use an extinguisher or water to fight the blaze until the firemen arrive. But be certain you know what you are doing. Don't, to use an obvious example, throw water on a grease fire—it will only spread the flames. If there is any

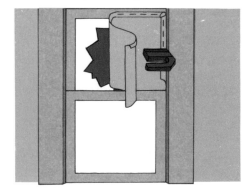

Staple sheeting over broken window.

question of your own safety, do not try to fight the fire yourself. Homes are replaceable (and usually insured). People may be insured, but they are not replaceable.

Once again, the key to avoiding disaster is prevention. Make sure that every member of the family knows what to do in case of fire. Every room should have an alternate escape route; rooms on upper floors should have windows that are easily opened. If there are not lower roofs onto which occupants can jump, provide rope ladders or similar means of descent, and make sure that children are well acquainted with their use.

You will probably never have to put these precautions into practice. But if you do, lives will be saved.

Icy Sidewalks

It is elementary to keep sidewalks free of ice. An icy sidewalk is an invitation to injuries and lawsuits. Chemical melters such as rock salt will do the job, although they may cause some damage to concrete as well as corrosion to cars that are driven over them. These consequences are certainly small compared to the alternatives. You might also consider keeping a large supply of clean sand, and use it to skidproof walks and driveways. It is easy to sweep away when there is no longer a need for it.

Furnace Failure

When you find yourself without heat, first check the main switch. It may have been accidentally turned off (not an uncom-

mon occurrence when it is located along a basement stairway where it may be brushed against by a person carrying a load of laundry or whatever into the basement). Also check for a blown fuse or tripped circuit breaker.

Take a look at the thermostat to see whether it has been turned down. Often, the obvious will be the cause of the problem. Remove the thermostat cover and inspect the workings for dirt or dust that may be clogging the mechanism.

Next check the fuel supply. If you have oil heat, look at the gauge atop the storage tank. If it is near the "Empty" mark, you can suspect that this is the cause of your chilly discomfort. Call for a refill. With gas heat, make sure that an intake valve has not inadvertently been shut off.

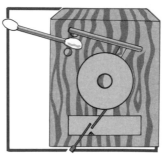

Check thermostat for dust.

Check gas valve.

SEASONAL CHECKLIST
FOR ROUTINE MAINTENANCE

Do-it-yourself home care knows no seasons. Most homeowners make a year-round project of keeping their places in tiptop shape — after all, it's a matter of pride of possession. But some jobs are seasonal, or at least are better done at one time than another. Intended only as a general guide, this seasonal checklist will help you schedule regular maintenance around the house. Of course, much of the actual scheduling depends on the climate of the area in which you live, but the list will help to remind you when it's time to do what.

January

- Give yourself a few days to let the shock of the holidays wear off, then make a New Year's resolution to keep things in top shape for the next twelve months. You can start by repairing all those annoying squeaks and squeals in the floors and stairs that betrayed you every time you came tiptoeing in late at night after one of those many holiday office parties.

- And it's a good time to check out the plumbing, especially those leaky faucets that have advanced from drip-drips to roaring deluges. Some washers should do the trick. Drains that go glug-glug and pipes that go bang-bang should also be silenced, as well as the toilet tank that doesn't know enough to shut up (or off).

- As long as you are on a quiet kick, pick up a kit of household oil, stick lubricants, and the like and take a quick trip about the house, treating hinges, appliance doors, chairs, furniture casters, drawers, and whatever else might squeak (or stick). By now you ought to have the quietest and slickest house in the neighborhood.

- But don't let all that quiet put you to sleep—there is one more job to do. Make it a regular practice to open the faucet at the bottom of the hot-water heater and drain off any rusty water. This will help to insure long life for that hard-working appliance.

February

- Winter weather starting to get on your nerves? Perk up with a touch-up campaign, repairing and refinishing chips and nicks in furniture, cabinets, and porcelain fixtures.

- It's a good time, too, to patch any plaster cracks that have made their appearance during the cold months.

- With winter waning, this might be the time to refinish hardwood floors that are showing signs of heavy wear worsened by wet-weather traffic.

March

- Whether the month comes in like a lion or a lamb, you know that spring can't be too far off. How about repairing and repainting the outdoor furniture so that it will be ready when those nice days finally arrive.

- Before you know it, screen time will be here. Now is your chance to make any necessary repairs—before the bugs come around.

- When the spring thaw comes, make a close check for leaks, particularly around doors and windows. Remember that April showers are on the way, and be prepared.

April

- Those April showers will being May flowers—and a lush new growth of lawn. Get that lawnmower in shape, making needed mechanical repairs, sharpening the blade, and lubricating according to the manufacturer's instructions.

- Once again it's time to drain off any rusty water that has accumulated in the hot-water heater.

May
- Air conditioner in shape? You'll be needing it any day now, so make needed repairs and follow the manufacturer's directions for preseason maintenance (check owner's manual).
- While you are in an electrical frame of mind, how about repairing lamps, small appliances, nonworking fixtures, and faulty switches that have accumulated over the winter.

June
- Bug time, but don't let them bug you. The first line of defense is screening to keep them out, so make sure that a screen is repaired immediately after your neighbor's daughter blasts a home-run ball through it. Also make sure that you have the proper pesticides on hand to fight off those little beasties that make it through the outer defense line.
- Summer water shortages are becoming increasingly common in many areas, so guard against water wastage by making sure that dripping faucets and running toilets are promptly repaired.

July
- Muggy weather can cause excessive condensation inside the house, which in turn can cause drawers, doors, and windows to stick and, in extreme cases, damage to floors, walls, and ceilings. Take corrective action as necessary.
- Don't let the hot weather make you forget that it's time to drain off the water heater again.

August
- If you have been a diligent weekend handyman all year long, you have earned a vacation this month, so head for the mountains or the shore, or just relax in your backyard with a cool drink

and ponder the pitiful plight of your neighbor who has put off all his home-care projects until now.

September
- Old Man Winter may still seem to be far off, especially on those "dog days," but he is heading your way, so get ready for him. Make sure your house is weathertight, calking around doors and windows where necessary and installing weatherstripping if it is needed. Repair any damaged storm sash.
- Don't wait for a cold snap to get your heating system in shape. Have it cleaned (or do it yourself, but this can be a messy job). Replace filters, check boilers and humidifiers, etc. Make sure the smoke pipe between furnace and chimney is solid and not leaking or corroded. If in doubt, replace it.

October
- Don't let the World Series distract you—now you *have* to get ready for winter. Between innings, check your basement walls for cracks that could cause trouble under cold-weather pressures. At halftime of the College Game-of-the-Week, make a prewinter calk walk around the house, filling cracks and joints between various components and dissimilar materials. It will give you peace of mind come SuperBowl time.
- Time, too, to retire outdoor furniture and accessories; make sure they are properly protected during the nasty months—especially if you store them in a damp or exposed area.
- It's time again to—guess what? That's it, drain the hot-water heater. It's paying attention to regular tasks like this that means long, trouble-free life for your home and its equipment.

November
- With the chill winds starting to blow, make sure that weatherstripping around doors and windows is snugly in place.

- Turn off the water supply to outside faucets and drain these lines to avoid freezing problems.
- Holiday season is on the way, so this is a good time to fix up and paint up. Repair plaster cracks and rejuvenate rooms with a new coat of paint or a bright modern wallpaper print. This might also be the time to put down that new vinyl floor in the kitchen, or to tile the bathroom walls.

December
- It's a good idea to be prepared for wintertime emergencies, so get together a kit and be ready for the worst, while hoping for the best. Include such items as plastic sheet (in case a storm breaks a window or pokes a hole in the roof), staple gun, shovel, hammer and nails, lanterns or flashlights, calking gun, etc.
- Before you put that string of lights on the Christmas tree, check carefully to make sure that the wires are in good condition—not frayed or exposed at the sockets. And while you are at it, check out lamp and appliance cords throughout the house and make any necessary repairs.
- You've done a good year's work, so now you deserve to relax with a cup of eggnog before starting the New Year. Cheers!

The wintertime emergency arsenal.

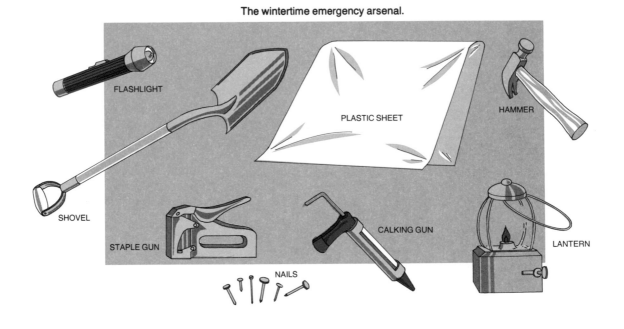

FLASHLIGHT

PLASTIC SHEET

HAMMER

SHOVEL

STAPLE GUN

NAILS

CALKING GUN

LANTERN

Index